PENGUIN BOOKS

TONGUES OF FIRE

Karen Armstrong was brought up in Worcestershire and in Birmingham. In 1962 she entered a Roman Catholic order of nuns, and in 1967 went to Oxford University to read English Language and Literature, with a view to teaching in one of the convent schools of the order. In 1969, however, she left the religious life but stayed at Oxford, where she graduated in 1970 and continued to read for a thesis on Tennyson's poetic style for which she was awarded a B.Litt in 1975. From 1973 to 1976 she was Tutorial Research Fellow at Bedford College, London University, where she taught nineteenth- and twentieth-century literature, and from 1979 to 1982 she taught at James Allen's Girls' School, Dulwich, where she was head of the English Department. She is now a freelance writer and broadcaster, living in London.

Karen Armstrong has written two autobiographical works, *Through the Narrow Gate* and *Beginning the World*. She is also the author of *The First Christian*, a study of St Paul, and she wrote and presented the documentary series *The First Christian* for Channel 4. Other recent broadcasts include *Varieties of Religious Experience*, also for Channel 4, which was a series of ten interviews exploring the nature of the religious experience across the world religions.

KAREN ARMSTRONG

TONGUES OF FIRE

AN ANTHOLOGY OF RELIGIOUS AND POETIC EXPERIENCE

PENGUIN BOOKS
IN ASSOCIATION WITH
CHANNEL 4 TELEVISION COMPANY LIMITED

Penguin Books Ltd, Harmondsworth, Middlesex, England
Viking Penguin Inc., 40 West 23rd Street, New York, New York 10010 U.S.A.
Penguin Books Australia Ltd, Ringwood, Victoria, Australia
Penguin Books Canada Ltd, 2801 John Street, Markham, Ontario, Canada L3R 1B4
Penguin Books (N.Z.) Ltd, 182–190 Wairau Road, Auckland 10, New Zealand

First published by Viking 1985
Published in Penguin Books 1987

Made and printed in Great Britain by
Richard Clay Ltd, Bungay, Suffolk

This anthology is dedicated to the six poets who took part in the television series *Tongues of Fire*:

Seamus Heaney, Peter Levi, Czeslaw Milosz, Craig Raine, D. M. Thomas and Derek Walcott, in gratitude for all they have taught me.

EDITOR'S ACKNOWLEDGEMENTS

This anthology is dedicated in gratitude to the poets who took part in the television series *Tongues of Fire*, but I owe special thanks to Craig Raine, not only for his work as Consultant to the series, but for coming along each night to the filming and giving me much-needed moral support. I must thank Adam Clapham, Bruce Palling and Diane Freeman of Griffin Productions for their help and hard work during the production; also Nicholas Fraser and Michael Jones of Panoptic Productions, and John Ranelagh of Channel 4 Television for their encouragement and most helpful suggestions. Very many thanks also to Lisa Gartside of Griffin Productions and Nick Wetton of Penguin Books for their hard work in getting the necessary permission to print poems in the anthology. Many thanks to the Poetry Society for their help throughout.

CONTENTS

2. COMFORT AND JOY — 87

3. VOCATION — 109

4. SEX AND RELIGION 151

5. WISE PASSIVENESS 181

8. VISION AND IMAGINATION 265

9. DESOLATION AND ECSTASY 295

INTRODUCTION
TONGUES OF FIRE

The author of the Acts of the Apostles (traditionally believed to be St Luke) gives this account of the birth of the Church, when the Holy Spirit descended upon Jesus' Apostles and they began, miraculously, to speak in strange 'tongues':

> **When Pentecost day came round, they had all met in one room, when suddenly they heard what sounded like a powerful wind from heaven, the noise of which filled the entire house in which they were sitting; and something appeared to them that seemed like tongues of fire; these separated and came to rest on the head of each of them. They were all filled with the Holy Spirit, and began to speak foreign languages as the Spirit gave them the gift of speech.**
>
> **Now there were devout men living in Jerusalem from every nation under heaven, and at this sound they all assembled, each one bewildered to hear these men speaking his own language. 'Surely,' they said, 'all these men are Galileans? How does it happen that each of us hears them in his own native language?' . . . Everyone was amazed and unable to explain it. Some, however, laughed it off. 'They have been drinking too much new wine' they said. (Acts 2:1–7; 12–13)**

Most people today, confronted with this kind of religious experience, feel much the same kind of scepticism and distaste as these people in Jerusalem. They may not accuse the mystic or the ecstatic of being drunk, but they may well think that he is hysterical or mentally ill. It's a far cry from a tasteful evensong at the parish church. However, even a cursory reading of the New Testament shows that early Christianity was essentially an experience of violent religious fervour. There was speaking in tongues, ecstatic trance, spontaneous prophecy when the prophet claimed to be possessed by the Spirit of Jesus. An early Christian, if he were transported to a typical church service today, would probably be bewildered by its rationality, moderation and disciplined control. Indeed, a few verses later in Acts, when St Peter is preaching his first sermon in 'tongues' to the multinational congregation, he asserts that the new era of Christianity is characterized precisely by these kind of religious phenomena, quoting the Old Testament prophet Joel in support of his claim:

> **In the days to come – it is the Lord who speaks –**
> **I will pour out my spirit on all mankind.**
> **Their sons and daughters shall prophesy,**
> **your young men shall see visions,**
> **your old men shall dream dreams**

Even on my slaves, men and women,
in those days, I will pour out my spirit
(Acts 2:17–18)

For the Christian, Peter is adamant, this religious experience is the rule, not the exception. It is not reserved for a select few; even despised castes – slaves and women – will experience it. Today, born-again Christian, Pentecostal and charismatic sects have mushroomed in all Christian sects and denominations, convinced that this – and this alone – is true Christianity. Are they right?

There was nothing particularly unusual about Pentecost. This type of ecstatic behaviour is found in every religion and every culture. In Islam the dervishes whirl themselves into ecstasy, the Hindu guru walks barefoot over a bed of nails, Christian saints levitate and develop the stigmata. In all religions a meditation is practised by adepts that leads to the visions and trance-like dream states described by St Peter. The doctrinal interpretation of these phenomena obviously differs from one religion to another. A Christian mystic will say he has achieved union with God, while a Buddhist, who doesn't believe in God, will say he has attained Nirvana, or a higher state of Enlightenment. Yet the experiences themselves seem to be much the same. If the Christian author of the fourteenth-century mystical text *The Cloud of Unknowing* had had a chance to speak to a Sufi, one of the mystics of Islam, he would have found that they had a lot in common, even though their contemporaries – Christians and Moslems – were butchering one another in the Crusades in the name of God. When the religious experience of mankind is examined critically, it almost seems that there is one, universal religion of mysticism, while the more dogmatic forms of religion seem irrelevant to the findings of the mystics and even dangerous.

One of the characteristics of deep religious experience in all religions is that it is ineffable – it cannot be put into words. The religious man is transported to a state where words and logical reasoning no longer apply. He has passed beyond the world of concepts on which language depends. So it is surprising that so many mystics in all religions (except Judaism, which is an interesting exception) feel impelled to express their experience in writing. Very often they choose to express themselves in poetry, because poetry forces language out of the everyday mode to explore aspects of life that defy a purely rational interpretation. Indeed, once the connection between poetry and mysticism has been made, it becomes clear that the poet and the mystic often have very similar experiences. They tend to view their 'vocation' in much the same way – in fact, poets often see themselves as 'prophets' and 'visionaries', even when they have no religious beliefs at all. The word 'inspiration' is used by both poets and mystics in a way that takes us back to the account of Pentecost. 'Inspiration' means simply being possessed by a spirit, and frequently poets feel themselves possessed by something outside themselves, just as the Apostles were 'filled with the Holy Spirit'. It is interesting, too, that this 'Spirit' manifested itself in terms of inspired language. This 'something' that appeared 'seemed like tongues of fire'.

In this anthology I want to explore the nature of this religious experience in poems by mystics and religious men of different faiths. Side by side with these religious poems there will be poems that are not specifically religious, but which show how closely the experience of the poet mirrors experiences that we usually label religious. Somebody with religious faith may see that in the poet, God 'works in a mysterious way' – that the poet is touched by God, even though he doesn't realize it. Other people may come to the conclusion that when the mystic is 'meditating' and the poet is 'creating', they are both engaged in the same kind of purely natural activity, and that there is no question of supernatural agency in the mystical experience, any more than there is in the poetic.

I am not a poet. I cannot imagine myself ever hauling a poem up, bit by bit, from my subconscious. It is an activity that I deeply admire, but which is alien to the way I think and function. Similarly, although I was 'religious' for many years and spent a good seven years professionally intent on meditation, I never had a 'mystical' experience, nor indeed any purely religious experience at all that I had not manufactured for myself by listening to a rousing, emotional sermon, for example, or by the music and aesthetics of the Mass. What 'religious experiences' I had I knew were natural and not supernatural, and were largely self-induced. I cannot begin to imagine having a vision or experiencing the joys of contemplation described by the saints. It is, like poetic creation, something alien to me, just as alien as the Apostles' behaviour seemed to the crowds in Jerusalem at Pentecost. There are many people throughout the world who have never had a vision, never had any experience of the 'divine' or the 'ineffable', but they would still say stoutly – and correctly – that they are 'religious' people. They go to church, mosque, temple or synagogue, hold firmly to the creeds of their religion and live according to its ethical teaching. They derive great comfort from their religion. Most of them would say that their religion is the 'true' religion, and that other faiths are at worst false or evil, or at best mistaken or less complete than their own. They look up to their mystics and visionaries, but humbly consider themselves to be on a lower religious plane. Most religious people are like this; despite St Peter's claim that ecstasy and vision are now the order of the day, most people have not enjoyed these experiences.

Now that travel from one part of the globe to another is so easy, it is more and more difficult to accept the, as it were, 'nationalistic' views of religion. It used to be the case that if you were born in Europe, you were automatically a Christian, if in China or Japan a Buddhist, if in India a Hindu or a Sikh. Your religion was 'right' and the other religions, so dimly and imperfectly seen because of the problems of distance and communication, were 'false'. Religions were entirely different from one another, it was thought. Now that we know and understand other religions better, it is the similarity that strikes us rather than the difference. Today, scholars like Ninian Smart and Cantwell Smith tend to divide religions differently. There are, they suggest, only two religions. Firstly, there is the 'Mystical' religion, which, as we shall see, is so remarkably similar in all cultures. Secondly, there is the more dogmatic religion where people belong to the great institutional religions that they view in a dogmatic and sectarian way – Christianity as right and Buddhism as wrong. People who adopt this 'Sectarian' religion are like I was when I belonged to the Roman Catholic Church, assented to the Creed, was charitable to the Protestants but felt they were in error, received the sacraments and lived, thus, an intensely spiritual life, praying and meditating without experiencing anything supernatural. These two religions – the Mystical and the Sectarian – coexist in all the great religions. The contemplative nun engaged in mystical prayer exists in the Church alongside the regular Church-goer; the Sufi mystic prays and meditates alongside the 'ordinary' Moslem who worships devoutly at the mosque; the Buddhist crowds who attend temple worship have often no intention of embarking themselves on the systematic course of meditation and good living of the monk in quest of Enlightenment. The Christian nun, the Sufi and the Buddhist monk would all agree that they have a great deal in common. There is today, for example, a vital interchange of ideas between Zen and Christian contemplatives. Theirs is one religion, and cultural and doctrinal differences are essentially superficial to the religious life they lead. On the other hand, your average Christian and Moslem would hotly deny that they had anything in common at all.

St Luke, when he wrote about Pentecost, had in mind a famous Old Testament story. He deliberately wrote his account of the descent of the Spirit as a parallel and a contrast to the story of the Tower of Babel.

> **Throughout the earth men spoke the same language, with the same vocabulary. Now as they moved eastwards they found a plain in the land of Shinar where they settled. They said to one another, 'Come, let us make bricks and bake them in the fire.' – For stone they used bricks and for mortar they used bitumen. – 'Come,' they said, 'let us build ourselves a town and a tower with its top reaching heaven. Let us make a name for ourselves, so that we may not be scattered about the whole earth.'**

> **Now Yahweh came down to see the town and the tower that the sons of men had built. 'So they are all a single people with a single language!' said Yahweh. 'This is but the start of their undertakings! There will be nothing too hard for them to do. Come, let us go down and confuse their language on the spot, so that they can no longer understand one another.' Yahweh scattered them thence over the whole face of the earth, and they stopped building the town. It was named Babel, therefore, because there Yahweh confused the language of the whole earth. It was from there that Yahweh scattered them over the whole face of the earth. (Genesis 11:1–9)**

It is hard to feel much devotion to this peevish and insecure God, who seems to fear, as he so often does in Genesis, man's ever growing knowledge and the development of human culture and civilization. The story dates from a very primitive Hebrew theology. However, St Luke sees the story differently. Man in his unredeemed sinfulness had tried to scale the heavens by his own natural powers, and God had punished this hubris by scattering man and sowing linguistic discord. Once people can no longer talk to one another, misunderstanding and hostility must thrive. At Pentecost man did not have to build a tower to reach heaven: God sent his Spirit down to earth. The linguistic confusion of Babel is healed. In Jerusalem all the different nationalities could understand the Apostles, who were inspired by tongues of fire:

> **'Surely,' they said, 'All these men speaking are Galileans? How does it happen that each of us hears them in his own native language? Parthians, Medes and Elamites; people from Mesopotamia, Judaea and Cappadocia, Pontus and Asia, Phrygia and Pamphylia, Egypt and the parts of Libya round Cyrene; as well as visitors from Rome – Jews and proselytes alike – Cretans and Arabs; we hear them preaching in our own language about the marvels of God.' (Acts 2:7–11)**

Luke is here preaching St Paul's theology: that in Christ there are no more distinctions between men. The Christian experience has abolished barriers of race, class and sex: 'In Christ there is neither Jew nor gentile, slave nor free, male nor female' (Galatians 3:28). This new unity is symbolized by the new unity of language, just as the pride and sinfulness of man had produced a confusion of tongues and hostility between the myriad nations.

Two thousand years later one has to smile ironically at Luke's hopeful heralding of a new age, particularly as Christianity has done much to aggravate the discord of warring peoples. It has a particularly intolerant stance towards aliens and rebels: Christians have crucified and murdered Jews and Moslems;

Protestants and Catholics have murdered one another; both have murdered their heretics. Yet I should like to use the two stories of the Tower of Babel and Pentecost to make a further comparison. In the Pentecost story we have an example of Mystical religion based not so much on dogma and organization as on direct contact with God, which results in ecstatic inspiration. The result is harmony and understanding among men. However, the second form that man's religious bent takes, that of Sectarian religion, is too often like the Babel story. It tends to build man-made structures of theology in an attempt to reach God. The strongholds of faith thus constructed with great human skill and insight provide comfort for all who dwell therein. But sometimes it forgets that God is greater than man's ideas of Him; it thinks that its human structures are impregnable, and this must bring about an insecurity as the structures tend to crumble over the years. The insecurity breeds intolerance, and it leads practically to worshipping a human creation; it is idolatry to be dogmatic. The great organized religions, with their inspiring theologies and rituals, have therefore an in-built weakness. It is also unfortunate that many of the charismatic and Pentecostal groups springing up in the Churches today return to primitive forms of religious experience – speaking in tongues, prophecy and healing – but are extraordinarily dogmatic and intolerant. Often they are fundamentalist and literal in their interpretation of Scripture, a characteristic that has tended, in the history of the Church, to bedevil the more insecure theologians. Colin Urquhart, for example, a leading born-again Christian and a priest of the Church of England (which prides itself on its tolerance), has recently written that all forms of Eastern meditation and Oriental religions are inspired by the Devil. A devotion to direct religious experience does not necessarily make a sect belong to the Mystical religion. If it relies heavily on a doctrinal position and is fundamentalist and intolerant, there may well be a good deal of hysteria in the religious phenomena it encourages. It is interesting here to note that perhaps the most tolerant of the world's great religions is Buddhism. The various schools of Buddhism often differ from one another profoundly, yet they all get on together remarkably well. There has been none of the persecution, inquisition and execution of heretics that has cast a blight over so much religious history. The reason for this must partly be due to the fact that while there are gods in the Buddhist world, they are less important than the Buddha, the Enlightened man: Buddhism ranks religious experience and the mystical path to Enlightenment higher than theology (the study of the gods). And while there are many myths taught about the Buddha, the Buddhist is quite clear that these are fictional myths – rather a different approach from that of the Judaeo-Christian tradition that insists that its myths are history – and that way lies fundamentalism and shrill hysterical intolerance.

Just as poets have so often inveighed against the 'meddling intellect' that destroys reality by dissecting and analysing it away, so the great spiritual writers in all religions have made it clear that the intellect must be laid aside if the mystic is to attain that sense of unity with the ultimate Reality. This does not mean that they advocate a mindless fundamentalism. The great poets may often have denounced the 'intellect', but they have usually shown spectacular intelligence in their poetry, just as the great mystical writers have usually been men of intelligence and learning. After St Thomas Aquinas had dictated the last sentence of his massive theological work, the *Summa Theologica*, he laid his head in his hands in apparent despair. When the scribe asked him what was wrong, he said that all he had written was only straw, compared with what he had seen.

When most of us pray, we are often really only talking to ourselves. We tend to tell God what he should be doing about the world, as though God shared our political views, our ethical standards and was a creature of about the same intellectual standing as ourselves. When we make him 'speak' to us, what we are really doing is endorsing our own opinions. It is hard to avoid creating a God in our own image and likeness – an ideal of 'God' as we with our limited intelligence, emotional weaknesses and prejudices think he ought to be. Terrible things have been done in the name of such 'Gods' throughout history, and while we, with a different historical perspective, deplore – for example – the great witch hunts of the sixteenth and seventeenth centuries, the theologians and priests involved were men of sophistication and intelligence who sincerely believed that it was the will of God that they torture and burn thousands of women. There is no reason to suppose that our 'Gods' may not be similarly limited in quite different ways, for they are merely projections of self. It is not enough for a mystic who wants God as He is in Himself – a Self that could be a terrible shock to the system:

> **For my thoughts are not your thoughts, my ways not your ways – it is Yahweh who speaks. Yes, the heavens are as high above the earth as my ways are above your ways, my thoughts above your thoughts. (Isaiah 55:8–9)**

A mystic differs from the 'ordinary' believer because he wants to be absorbed by his God or by Reality. Most of us don't want to be absorbed or disappear at all; we don't really – if we are honest – want to lose our ego. We are hanging on to it like mad, and often using our prayers to prop it up, endorse its needs and assuage its fears of the things that threaten it. But the mystic sets out on a journey of systematic meditation and asceticism to lose himself and get free of the claims of his clamorous ego. He wants to encounter

God in 'the dark night of the soul' that St John of the Cross spoke of The author of *The Cloud of Unknowing* defines this darkness:

> **When you first begin, you find only darkness, and, as it were, a cloud of unknowing. You don't know what this means except that in your will you feel a simple steadfast intention, reaching out towards God. Do what you will, this darkness and this cloud remain between you and God, and stop you both from seeing him in the clear light of rational understanding, and from experiencing his loving sweetness in your affection. Reconcile yourself to wait in this darkness as long as is necessary, but still go on longing after him whom you love. For if you are to feel him or to see him in this life, it must always be in this cloud, in this darkness. (*Cloud*, III)**

This darkness is simply a 'lack of knowing' (*Cloud*, IV); a darkness that is frightening and without comfort must be the ambience of the mystic, or he will remain trapped in himself, embedded in the confines of his limited knowledge and personality. The mystic will not even allow himself to draw comfort from the pious thoughts about God or religion that comfort the ordinary believer. When he is intent on the business of meditation, no hymn singing, no ritual can help him:

> **. . . it profits little or nothing to think even of God's kindness or worth, or of our Lady, or of the saints or angels, or of the joys of heaven, if you think thereby by such meditation to strengthen your purpose. (*Cloud*, V)**

The work of meditation demands a courage and a discipline that few can endure, a death to all the mystic knows and a leap into the unknown, which must always be frightening. It offers no security of the familiar but a forgetting of all we are, all we know and all that we have achieved.

> **But now you will ask me, 'How am I to think of God himself, and what is he? and I cannot answer you except to say 'I do not know!' For with this question you have brought me into the same darkness, the same cloud of unknowing where I want you to be! For though we through the grace of God can know fully about all other matters, and think about them – yes, even the very works of God himself – yet of God himself can no man think. Therefore I will leave on one side everything I can think, and choose for my love that thing which I cannot think! Why? Because he may well be loved, but not thought. By love he can be**

> **caught and held, but by thinking never. Therefore, though it may be good sometimes to think particularly about God's kindness and worth, and though it may be enlightening too and a part of contemplation, yet in the work [of mysticism] now before us it must be put down and covered with a cloud of forgetting. And you are to step over it resolutely and eagerly, with a devout and kindling love, and try to penetrate that darkness above you. Strike that thick cloud of unknowing with a sharp dart of longing love, and on no account whatever think of giving up. (*Cloud*, VI)**

Everything that can be thought about has to be left 'on one side'. Indeed, these pious and comforting thoughts about God's 'kindness and worth' must vigorously be 'put down', 'trampled' on (*Cloud*, VII) as though they were an evil temptation. For the mystic, even the Christian mystic who claims that God has revealed himself wholly in Christ (and the author of the *Cloud* writes most movingly of Jesus), God is always an enigma. If questions arise about the nature of this God, the contemplative is to reply that he does 'not even know the first thing about him' (*Cloud*, VII). Essentially, to be a mystic is to be an agnostic. When the immediate answer to the question 'What is God' is 'I do not know', it is clear that there is no dogmatic insistence on religious 'beliefs'. Agnosticism is the religion of the mystic in a profound way.

It is this agnosticism that distinguishes the mystic from the Sectarian believer, who knows at once what is the answer to the question 'What is God?' and is eager to give it to you. Indeed, he will argue fiercely with somebody who disagrees with him. At the age of eight I learned a Catechism answer to the question: 'God is the supreme Spirit, Who alone exists of Himself and is infinite in all perfections.' It didn't mean very much to me then, and, I am bound to say, it means very little to me now. It is rather a pompous and arid definition. However, the very attempt to define 'God' in a sentence with however many built-in safeguards reflects a certain religious arrogance. Once there are answers to unknowable questions, fierce dogmatism must ensue, if only because of the insecurity that must derive from the impossibilities of the position.

This freedom from the shackles of limited rationality is essential to all mysticism. Thus the Buddha:

> **. . . the monk with the ceasing of reasoning and investigation, in a state of internal serenity, with his mind fixed on one point, attains and abides in the second *jhana* of joy and pleasure arising from concentration, and free from reasoning and investigation. (*Early Buddhist Scriptures*, p. 63)**

Any desire for the consolations of form is seen as a means of clinging on to the ego, of grasping at reality selfishly to prop up the self that must be laid aside. 'Form is not yours, O Monks. Give it up,' the Buddha exhorts sternly. 'Sensation, perception, the formations and consciousness are not yours. Give them up!' (*Dhammapada*, v. 62) The forms of religion, the forms of art, are means that man uses to explain the universe to himself, and such activity means that the monk will only embed himself in his own perceptions instead of passing beyond these, as the mystic should, to be wholly absorbed by the Reality of Nirvana and its Enlightenment. Jewish mystics, similarly, have always distinguished between the two aspects of God: the God of Revelation and God as He exists in Himself. All men, according to their capacities, may 'know' God as He chooses to reveal Himself – in the Scriptures, in the Law of Moses and in Nature. But God as He is in Himself, the *En Sof*, may never be known by mere man. When Moses asked God to reveal His name to him from the burning bush, God refused to tell him, using a Hebrew idiom of deliberate vagueness: 'I am who I am.' To know the name of somebody was to gain power over him in the Semitic world of that time; the name revealed a thing's inner essence. To invoke a god by his name meant that you understood his nature and so could control him. God's reply to Moses can be translated: 'Never you mind who I am.' When Moses begged God to show him His face, God replied: 'No man can see my face and live.' A Jewish mystic never would presume to know God, the *En Sof*, or even to attain to union with him, and indeed Judaism is for this very reason more a religion of practice than a religion of theology. Islam, in its mysticism, is in a sense the most agnostic of all faiths, surprising as this may seem to the Westerner who sees the Ayatollah Khomeini's fundamentalism as typical of the Moslem faith. The great thirteenth-century mystic Ibnu 'l-'Arabí expresses the Islamic position well:

> **Do not attach yourself to any particular creed exclusively, so that you may disbelieve all the rest; otherwise you will lose much good, nay, you will fail to realize the real truth of the matter. God, the omnipresent and omnipotent, is not limited by any one creed, for, He says, 'Wheresoever ye turn, there is the face of Allah' (Koran 2:109). Everyone praises what he believes; his god is his own creature, and in praising it he praises himself. Consequently he blames the beliefs of others, which he would not do if he were just, but his dislike is based on ignorance. If he knew Junaid's saying, 'The water takes its colour from the vessel containing it', he would not interfere with other men's beliefs, but would perceive God in every form of belief. He has opinion, not knowledge: therefore God said, 'I am in My servant's**

> **opinion of Me', i.e. 'I do not manifest Myself to him save in the form of his belief.' God is absolute or restricted, as he pleases; and the God of religious belief is subject to limitations, for He is the God who is contained in the heart of His servant. But the absolute God is not contained in any thing, for He is the being of all things and the being of Himself. (*Eastern Poetry and Prose*, p. 148)**

It is a marvellous summary of all we have been saying so far. The mystics of all religions realize that a man's 'god' is his own creature and in praising it he praises himself. Sufism was deeply affected by both Buddhism and Christianity, and we can see this very clearly here. Triumphing over other peoples' religious beliefs is precisely what the Buddhists would call an 'unskilful' state; unskilful because it can only hinder a man's path to Enlightenment to be so confined in egotism. In the distinction between the God of Revelation and the Absolute God, we have the same preoccupation that we have seen in both Christian and Jewish mysticism.

The renunciation involved in this 'forgetting', this agnosticism that shuns the comforts of absolute belief, is a kind of death. It is certainly a death of the ego with its opinions and prejudices. This is why mystics speak of their life as a dying. Sufism, wrote a great mystic, 'is this, that God should make thee die to thyself and should make thee live in him'. A Sufi calls this process of death to self *faná*'; it is a tranced extinction of the self in God, clearly reminiscent of St Paul's 'I have been crucified with Christ, and I live now not with my own life but with the life of Christ who lives in me' (Galatians 2:19–20). The whole of the Buddhist way of Enlightenment is to renounce the ego and be eventually absorbed in the bliss of Nirvana. The great Buddhist teacher Sariputra defined Nirvana as 'the extinction of passion, of aversion, of confusion'. It is a state that is quite unimaginable to the unenlightened man. The Buddha described it thus:

> **There is, monks, that stage where there is neither earth nor water nor fire nor wind nor the stage of infinity of space nor the stage of the infinity of consciousness nor the stage of neither consciousness nor non-consciousness; neither this world nor the other world nor sun and moon. There, monks, I say there is neither coming nor going nor staying nor passing away nor arising. Without support or going on or basis is it. This is indeed the end of pain.**
>
> **There is, monks, an unborn, an unbecome, an unmade, uncompounded; if, monks, there were not here this unborn, unbecome, unmade, uncompounded, there would not here be an**

> **escape from the born, the become, the made, the compounded. But because there is an unborn, an unbecome, an unmade, an uncompounded, therefore, there is an escape from the born, the become, the made, the compounded. (*Udāna*, VIII, 1, 3)**

In order to get to this state, everything that is known has to be left behind because to take any conceptions with you means that you will never attain to what is *in*conceivable. It is a way of death that Christian mystics have often called the Way of Negation. Instead of saying what God *is*, you have to dwell on what God is *not*; otherwise you are still creating a god for yourself out of limited and therefore distorting concepts. John of the Cross speaks in words that are very similar to the Buddha's:

> **. . . the soul must journey by knowing God through what He is not, rather than through what He is, it must journey, insofar as possible, by way of the denial and rejection of natural and supernatural apprehensions. This is our task now with the memory. We must draw it away from its natural props and capacities and raise it above itself (above all distinct knowledge and apprehensible possession) to supreme hope in the incomprehensible God. (*The Ascent of Mount Carmel*, 2:ii)**

God is 'incomprehensible', which means that he cannot be grasped by the intellect and contained within it, as we possess and grasp concepts like the ones the Buddha mentioned: sun, moon, infinity, consciousness. So to get to Him you have to die to everything you have ever known or thought. The result of this is not extinction, however, but an absorption in God; the soul becomes 'divine':

> **God now possesses the faculties as their complete lord, because of their transformation in Him and consequently it is He Who divinely moves and commands them according to his spirit and will. As a result the operations are not different from those of God; but those the soul performs are of God and are divine operations. Since he who is united with God is one spirit with Him, as St Paul says (I Cor. 6:17) the operations of the soul united with God are of the divine spirit and are divine. (*The Ascent of Mount Carmel*, 2:viii)**

Here John of the Cross was unconsciously echoing the Sufi teacher Bukhari, who makes Allah say of his beloved servant who has achieved *faná'*, the swooning away of the ego into God,

> **. . . when I love him, I am the Hearing wherewith he heareth, and the Sight wherewith he seeth and the Hand whereby he graspeth and the Foot whereon he walketh.**

It might be argued that the Buddhist ideal differs from those that see the end of the mystic quest as a union with a personal God. A Buddhist believes that faith in God is unskilful; it can actually damage the spiritual life, because such a God is simply a projection of man's insecurities and of his ego. When the Enlightened man, the Buddha, reaches Nirvana, this is a purely human fulfilment – a natural not a supernatural one. Yet when the self is absorbed in Nirvana, the state as described by Buddhists is expressed in imagery that is very familiar to the Judaeo-Christian tradition. Nirvana is

> **the harbour of refuge, the cool cave, the island amidst the floods, the place of bliss, emancipation, liberation, safety, the supreme, the transcendental, the uncreated, the tranquil, the home of ease, the calm, the end of suffering, the medicine for all evil, the unshaken, the ambrosia, the immaterial, the imperishable, the abiding the further shore, the unending, the bliss of effort, the supreme joy, the ineffable, the detachment, the holy city. (*Early Buddhist Scriptures*, p. 172)**

The point is surely that after the mystic has broken through to a Reality that is inconceivable from our present standpoint, purely rational concepts or labels like 'God' or 'Nirvana' cease to have meaning. Only the experience itself can explain what has happened.

Yet this kind of 'vision' is not confined to mystics. We find that genuinely creative thinkers tend to speak much the same language. Thus in *The New Men*, C. P. Snow has this to say about the 'inspiration' of a scientist:

> **Martin had been visited by an experience which might not come to him again. So far as I could distinguish, there were two kinds of scientific experience, and a scientist was lucky if he was blessed by a visitation of either just once in his working life. The kind which most of them, certainly Martin, would have judged the higher was not like the one he had just known: instead, the higher kind was more like (it was in my view the same as) the experience that the mystics had described so often, the sense of communion with all-being. Martin's was quite different, not so free from self, more active: as though, instead of being one with the world, he held the world in the palm of his hand. (pp. 50–51)**

Words like 'blessed', 'visitation', 'free from self', belong to the world of religion, and the layman would not expect to find them on the lips of scientists.

Again, Arnold Toynbee says of the historian that there are 'moments in his mental life – moments as memorable as they are rare – in which temporal and spatial barriers fall and psychic distance is annihilated'. Toynbee says that Gibbon had an experience of 'communion' that seemed to him a kind of presence. He

> **found himself in communion not with this or that episode of History but with all that had been or was to come. In that instant he was directly aware of the passage of History gently flowing through him in a mighty current, and of his own life welling like a wave in the flow of a vast tide . . . An instant later the communion ceased.**

It is not really surprising that creative thinkers and mystics all seem to have the same type of experience. Both are reaching out towards as yet uncreated reality, reality that has not yet been conceived in the mind of man. Indeed, Toynbee goes on to suggest that the religious element is simply an extension of the creative:

> **. . . the historian's inspiration is preparing him for an experience that has been described as the Beatific Vision by souls to whom it has been vouchsafed. (*A Study of History*, X, 128–139)**

Rational activity will help the inventive thinker only up to a point. As long as he struggles rationally, he is, necessarily, imprisoned in ideas and forms of thought that have already been established. He cannot break through to anything new. He has, like the mystic, to draw his mind 'away from natural props and capacities' and reach for something, as it were, 'above himself', just as John of the Cross did. Like the mystic he must 'journey, insofar as possible, by way of the denial and rejection of natural and supernatural apprehensions', strike against the cloud of unknowing that is his present ignorance in the hope of piercing it.

When he does get these ideas, they have the effect of something 'given' from outside himself. Toynbee speaks of presence, vision and of inspiration – perhaps the same kind of phenomenon as the 'possession' experienced at Pentecost. Darwin writes that 'ideas and beliefs are certainly not voluntary acts. They come to us we hardly know *how* or *whence*.' Often they present the answer to a problem in a flash, after a long struggle, quite often triggered off by something irrelevant and apparently trivial. There is a sense of awakening or discovery, and often this inspiration occurs when the thinker is relaxing or doing something that has nothing to do with the problem. The obvious example of this is Archimedes, of course, who discovered the answer to his geometrical problem in the bath, whence he leapt with the cry '*Eureka!*'. He had 'found' something that had long eluded him in his study. We have all had this experience in a minor way – ideas will suddenly come to us, especially when our minds are relaxed and receptive and no longer actively fighting with concepts and problems. When we urge people to 'sleep on' a problem, we are recommending just this kind of relaxation, from which we hope that a new outlook or solution can emerge.

Very often religious conversions follow this pattern. If we look at the experience of Wesley or of St Augustine, we see a pattern that recurs again and again in the lives of holy men. They both struggled and wrestled with the problem of God for a long time, indeed they agonized over it. Then suddenly, in a flash, the answer came so strongly that it seemed, like Darwin's ideas, to come from outside themselves. In Augustine's case he heard a 'voice' urging him to 'take and read' his New Testament. Of course, Archimedes had already formulated his famous principle subconsciously. He had already collected and stored away all its ingredients in his mind, and suddenly they came together with such force that it was as though he had 'found' something that existed already. It's surely possible also to interpret Augustine's experience in much the same way. He too had already made his great decision to be converted subconsciously, and in a flash all its elements fused together.

It often happens that this inspiration strikes us when we are relaxing, when our minds are in a receptive rather than in a rationally excited state. In such a receptive mood we are more open to the layers of the subconscious. William James in *The Varieties of Religious Experience* says that all his researches left him with one unshakeable conviction:

> **It is that our normal waking consciousness, rational consciousness as we call it, is but one special type of consciousness, whilst all about it, parted from it by the filmiest of screens, there lie potential forms of consciousness entirely different. We may go through life without suspecting their existence; but apply the requisite stimulus, and at a touch they are there in all their completeness, definite types of mentality which probably somewhere have their fields of application and adaptation. No account of the universe in its totality can be final which leaves these other forms of consciousness quite disregarded. (p. 338)**

Until fairly recently most of us would have dismissed this idea as a piece of whimsy, but now people are beginning to take these alternative states of consciousness much more seriously. It is not just that Freud and Jung have given us quite a different idea of how the mind works; scientists also have recently taken an interest in establishing the physical changes wrought in the brain by activities like meditation. It has been discovered that when people meditate – whether they are Zen monks in Japan or Christian Carthusians in the United States – there are electrical changes in the brain that can be measured on an EEG. It seems that in all cultures, meditation induces that kind of receptivity and relaxation (characterized by the brain rhythm that scientists call *alpha*, as opposed to *beta* which is found in our everyday rational state) that brings the conscious and the unconscious mind together. Zen has been described as the Prayer of the Unconscious. The monk withdraws into his subconscious and experiences calm, trance and peace by various well-tried and universally discovered and applied techniques. These techniques can produce ecstasy that can be defined as the achievement of a new vantage point from which to view the world. Literally, 'ecstasy' means that the soul leaves the body, but one could say, perhaps more accurately, that man is trying to liberate himself from the ego. Most of us are too concerned with practical living and what James calls the 'rational consciousness' to be aware of this dimension. A lot of us are just not capable of this type of activity, which should be viewed as a talent like playing the piano brilliantly. Scientists have now discovered that the meditation techniques evolved in all the great religions by mystics lead to a massive suppression of the critical rational consciousness. But not everybody is capable, they have also discovered, of producing these alpha rhythms. Some people have a natural genius for producing them, others improve their skill by the techniques of meditation, others are never able to acquire them at all.

In all religions the people engaged constantly in this meditation have adopted a similar style of living that will help them to foster this particular state of mind more successfully. It is clear that to be endlessly occupied in the getting and spending of the world will only encourage an aggressive rationality that could become habitual, so the meditator very often withdraws from the world in some way into some kind of solitude. They all experience a compulsion to practise this meditation. It is impossible to force yourself by will power into this receptive state of mind. To try to do this is a contradiction in terms, because such will power is very much beta activity and very ego-full. This compulsion they very often interpret as a 'vocation' or calling. Because this constant and intense exposure to the subconscious has obvious psychological dangers – 'God' knows what one may encounter in there! – the monk always works at his meditation with a teacher, a guru or spiritual director. Often to reinforce this support and control, they live in community and live lives of a simplicity and a monotony that again clearly help to silence the critical faculty and enhance a creative, receptive state of mind – they are not endlessly having to meet new challenges or exercise any rational ingenuity. Such meditation is seen as a full-time job, involving all aspects of life and personality.

In other words, it is being discovered that people like St John of the Cross and Teresa of Avila are not *necessarily* oddballs. They were people making use of faculties natural to man, people with a special talent for a kind of activity that for most of us is impossible. The exotic mystical states, it is now widely believed, do not prove that there is any kind of divine intervention. It is not a supernatural activity but a perfectly natural one. The Buddhists, with their ideal of a mysticism of purely human enlightenment, have always seen this. This is not to deny that a lot of these 'saints' or meditators were extremely disturbed. The Zen Buddhists say that anybody who is psychologically sick and comes to meditation to be cured of his neuroses can only get sicker. Meditation should carry a government health warning: it can seriously damage your health. Not only do you have to have an in-built ability, but you have to have a very stable personality to be able to cope with the strains involved in this perpetual diving into the subconscious. Saints like Catherine of Siena or Margaret Mary Alacoque do not seem to me to have had the necessary stability. An account of their frequent ecstasies and visions that were not achieved as part of a controlled process, but happened 'out of the blue' (Margaret Mary was always falling downstairs and Catherine once nearly got burnt alive when she fell into the fire in ecstasy while cooking a meal) makes them seem purely hysterical symptoms. The frequent fasts of both women brought on anorexia nervosa, and their social behaviour, apart from being eccentric (to put it mildly), was also extremely ego-full. On the other hand, somebody like Teresa of Avila, who started off pretty hysterically, was a much more stable person. Her writings, as well as her life's work of founding a religious order under very difficult circumstances, show that she was a very practical woman, with shrewd good sense and a delightful sense of humour. She was also an extremely intelligent person. Just because rationality must be laid aside does not mean that mindless stupidity is the order of the mystical day. Teresa is constantly bemoaning the dangers women fall into in the spiritual life because they are not educated. They are thus (she was, of course, writing in sixteenth-century Spain) prey to all sorts of delusions and illusions. To guide oneself through all the dangers of the mystical life demands a high intelligence and good sense. To encourage a non-rational state of mind actually demands considerable mental power, and poor Margaret Mary, one feels, was a very stupid woman as well as being an unstable one.

The lives of the saints should be read as a warning by people who embark on a path of mystical experience. The meditation centres that mushroomed in the West during the 1960s can be rather suspect, and lead to all sorts of dubious and neurotic results if the 'gurus' don't know what they are doing or if one of their motives is commercial gain. Again, I confess myself to be unimpressed and very worried indeed about a lot of this charismatic revival in the Christian Churches. The services I have attended seem to me to be characterized more by mass hysteria than by genuine 'inspiration'. The speaking in tongues seems far from the New Testament ideal. The whole point of the Apostles' 'tongues' was that everybody could understand them. St Paul too is insistent that people should understand these 'tongues'. He says that people should not speak in tongues more than one at a time during the services (at many of the modern services I have been to the whole congregation does it together to music), because if an unbeliever (like me) happened to walk in, he would think that the Christians were all mad. Further, if somebody does speak in tongues, Paul insists that there is a translator there for the benefit of the congregation. Modern congregations seem to delight in incomprehensible gibberish. The fundamentalist stance of many of these new sects is also suspect, because it often leads to an aggressive intolerance of other people's beliefs which, besides being opposed to the dictates of Christian charity, is also deeply opposed to the true agnosticism of mystical experience. The fundamentalist teachings often show a similar delight in unintelligence that we noted with the cult of tongues. There is nothing holy about stupidity. The type of agnosticism that the mystic preaches demands, in fact, a good deal of intellectual maturity. The search for immediate religious experience today is understandable. People seem tired of the formalism and anachronism of a lot of organized religion, but not every experience is a good one. Alongside other 'religious' phenomena like the stigmata they can be not divine but all too human, not supernatural but hysterical and neurotic.

To show that the true mystic is deeply intelligent, one need only recall Einstein, who said:

> **The most beautiful emotion we can experience is the mystical. It is the sower of all true art and science. He to whom this emotion is a stranger . . . is as good as dead. To know that what is impenetrable to us really exists, manifesting itself to us as the highest wisdom and the most radiant beauty, which our dull faculties can comprehend only in their most primitive forms – this knowledge, this feeling, is at the centre of all true religiousness. In this sense, and in this sense only, I belong to the ranks of devoutly religious men.**

To see religious activity as purely natural, as natural in its way as that of the artist and scientist – indeed, essentially as the same activity as that of art and science – obviously poses a lot of questions about supernatural interpretations of religious experience. It is also clear that of all creative people, the poet resembles the mystic very closely. He is more directly involved with the un-rational, or rather with alternative 'visions' of reality, than the historian or the scientist. Like the mystic he has a 'gift' that other people have not. Like the mystic he seeks for some kind of solitude. In his description of his craft he too uses words like 'grace' and 'inspiration'. He speaks of his poems being 'given' to him, as it were, coming from outside himself 'in a flash' or else erupting sometimes violently from the subconscious. Craig Raine has spoken of the importance of 'listening' to a poem as it emerges, as though it had an independent life of its own, just as the mystic insists on the essentially receptive nature of prayer. Often poets speak of the process of inspiration as a kind of possession. They also see the poetic imagination as creative. 'The imagination,' said Keats, 'is like Adam's dream. He awoke and found it truth.' Emerging from the tranced receptivity of his dream of creation, the poet discovers that he has found a new independent reality – as Adam dreamt of Eve and woke up to find her really beside him. Art, like religion, can provide a consolation akin to religious consolation in that its artifice imposes form on the chaotic reality of everyday life: like religion, art evolves myths and visions of reality to console and comfort. All religion, says William James, starts with the perception that something is wrong with the universe, whether that is expressed by the Buddha's 'Existence is suffering' or the Christian doctrine of Original Sin. Religion then seeks to find a solution, just as the poet does by trying to fuse together discords into a harmonious vision. The ambiguities that the poet discovers in the language are a form of agnosticism, for the truly great poem eludes a clear, simple statement of what it is supposed to be about.

It could be said that it is in their goals that poetry and religion differ from one another most. The poet's aim is expression; he has to embody his vision in words. For the mystic 'the end is silence', because the Reality he encounters is far beyond words. But perhaps the difference is not so extreme as it seems at first. Like the mystic the poet constantly feels the tension between words and the reality he sees; he is often striving to say the unsayable and to say it as well as he can. But the likeness is closer than that. The mystic does not remain on a solitary mountain top in an endless trance. All religious traditions are insistent that once the mystic has experienced God or a higher state of consciousness, he has a duty to return to the everyday world of rationality. Somehow he has to incarnate his vision in humdrum reality. Francis of Assisi and Ignatius Loyola after their mystical experiences founded religious orders, and were deeply involved in the world of religion and politics. The Sufi may be absorbed in Allah, but insists that after *faná'*, the extinction of the self in God, there succeeds the state of *baqá'* – of a newly realized self. The Sufi does not live in a monastery; he generally leads an ordinary family life, having to integrate his vision with the everyday world. The Buddhist, however high a state of consciousness he has achieved, must return to the world to practise Compassion for all living things. He has, they say, to 'return to the market place'. In all traditions the major test of the validity of a religious experience is whether or not the mystic is able to live normally and healthily in the world. I believe that Margaret Mary and Catherine of Siena fail that test. Zen might well be defined as the prayer of the unconscious, but others would qualify this: it is the prayer of the unconscious made conscious. Like the poet the mystic also has to incarnate his vision and integrate it in reality.

It may, then, he helpful to see the poetic and the religious experiences side by side, and this is what this anthology sets out to do. It is not exhaustive. My selection of poems is a personal one, but it might provide a starting point for other ideas. I am not saying that poetry and religion are identical – there are differences – but the two are linked. When Luke described the first Christian religious experience of Pentecost, its immediate outcome was a new form of language, and it is a new form of language that the poet seeks. The Spirit of God, Luke says, seemed involved with language, expressing itself in tongues of fire.

1.
'EXISTENCE IS SUFFERING'

(The Buddha)

Nobody would ever embark on the arduous path of religion were it not clear that something is wrong with the world. Religion offers to save men from pain and suffering. It is to find some kind of solution to the problem of evil in the world, to the appalling facts of sickness and death that we have never learned to accept, that we embark on the religious life. In fact, so strong is our conviction that pain and death should not be, that most religions have evolved a myth of a golden age when evil did not exist. Then man sinned and let it loose upon the world. For whether you call it 'sin' or 'ego', it is clear that a lot of the pain we suffer is due to man's selfishness, to his insatiably greedy ego that needs to be propped, comforted and protected. Not only do we damage other people to satisfy this self, but frequently we damage ourselves also. It is liberation from the self that is the prime goal of the mystical path. Only when we have left this grasping self behind, the religions say, can we begin to save ourselves and save the world.

The first poems in this section show us a world full of suffering that is arbitrary and inescapable. There is a fear of the lack of meaning in this suffering, an absence of any significance and a terrifying void. For some poets, like Thomas Hardy or Craig Raine, the only honest response to this emptiness is a rejection of religion and its comforts. For the atheist there is only the emptiness; there is no God 'out there'.

Not everybody is capable of this bleak refusal of comfort. There is a religious faith that is simply a means of escape from this sad and unsatisfactory world. The misery of life makes John Clare, for example, 'long for scenes where man has never trod'. He wants another world without the sufferings that are found here, and this different world he associates with God. Experiencing this universal misery, man needs to say to something, 'Lord have mercy on us!', and so a God is created out of our need. This response is born of hopelessness. God is not a burning reality but simply an alternative. Poets like Tennyson and Nashe are dreaming of God as an alternative world where there is no more suffering. It is a religion that has a large element of wish fulfilment.

However, Geoffrey Hill offers quite a different solution in 'Genesis': it's no good trying to abstract God from suffering and seeing him as a 'bloodless' alternative. Suffering and violence are at the very core of life, and therefore of religion. They cannot be separated. When Coleridge's Ancient Mariner shoots the Albatross, he gives no reason for his action. He just does it, arbitrarily, senselessly, as though such pointless violence were at the heart of his nature. But, just as spontaneous as his act of violence is the act of love that makes him bless the water-snakes 'unaware' and so redeem himself. Man is a complex of love and violence. There is nothing very special about the Mariner either before or during his ordeal. He is commonplace man, and after his suffering finds a comfort in the practice of ordinary religion. He is no mystic; he has not the character to endure the solitude, but finds his greatest consolation is to walk 'together' to the church 'in a goodly company'.

There are sufferings that pose questions that are too difficult to be eased away by such simple consolations. William Blake in 'London' and the Jewish poet Abba Kovner in his poem about the Holocaust are wrestling with the problem of human evil. How can such evil be explained by or absorbed into a religious context? Human evil can make the idea of a beneficent God look like a futile myth, and the religious man has to struggle very hard to make sense of such suffering in a conventional religious atmosphere.

Yet even if we adopt a religious faith wholeheartedly, it is a sad fact of life that it does not exempt us from suffering. Indeed, sometimes we create for ourselves a suffering that is essentially religious in origin. We feel intense guilt and shame because of our sins and our failures in the religious life. Czeslaw Milosz writes about guilt in his poem dedicated to Raja Rao, the friend who had tried unsuccessfully to convert him to Hinduism. For Milosz, guilt is a displacement of the self, an exile from the best self that is as sharply felt as the poet's own political exile. In *Paradise Lost* Adam in his first guilt and shame feels himself displaced and no longer at home in the world of Paradise. He is no longer, as Milosz puts it, 'what he should have been'.

Like Milosz, many Christians find it impossible to be liberated from the self, even by Christ. John Donne spends far more time in the fourth Holy Sonnet bemoaning his 'blacke soule' than in celebrating 'Christ's blood', which he mentions in the concluding couplet almost as an afterthought. This obsessive Christian guilt is not assuaged by Christ's sacrifice – rather, it is enhanced by it. He has done so much for me, and I so little for Him, is the constant cry. This sort of guilt a Buddhist sees not as holy and commendable, but as an 'unskilful state'. It can only be damaging to the spiritual life because it is pure egotism. It makes the self far too important. In fact, Donne casts himself into a rather noble and heroic role in 'Holy Sonnet XI', being spat on by the Jews in Christ's stead; and in 'Holy Sonnet VII' he sees God stopping the whole gigantic operation of the Last Judgement simply to give him, Donne, a little more time to repent! All Joseph Addison can think of when he imagines himself confronting the majesty of God after death is 'How shall I appear?' Christina Rossetti may well ask 'Who shall deliver me?', for true to form she only refers briefly to God in the last stanza and seems far more interested in embedding herself in her pathological self-hatred. Gerard Manley Hopkins cannot even do that in 'I wake and feel the fell of dark'. His poem finishes not with God but with hell, which is, he realizes, nothing but the eternal endurance of the self. Guilt like this is neurotic and essentially unreligious. Fortunately, a blessed touch of redeeming humour towards the self is shown by both Hopkins and Donne in 'My own heart let me more have pity on' and 'A Hymne to God the Father', which deflates this blown-up portrayal of the sinful self.

Other religions are able to handle the question of sin more peacefully than Christians often do. Solomon Ibn Gabirol, the eleventh-century Jewish poet, is far more convinced of God's love and healing than his own sin in 'Before I was Born'. Christians tend to see the Law of Moses as prohibitive, nit-picking and a massive, guilt-inducing burden, but this is a false picture that is given to us by the polemics of the New Testament. When we read of Gabirol putting on sackcloth and ashes in 'Separation from the Torah', a Christian may well expect him to start lashing himself into a frenzy of guilt. But no, he's just grief-stricken because he is too ill to go out and hear the Law (the Torah) read. It's the disappointment of a man unable to meet his lover; the Torah, not his own performance, is the important thing. George Herbert in 'Love' has much the same attitude. In all these poems the poets ask how their sinfulness can hurt the pure God who created them, and they rely far more on God's healing than on their own efforts. In the *Bhagavad-Gita* Krishna tells Prince Arjuna that the spiritual life and mystical path are extremely difficult. There are bound to be failures, and if the mystic feels despair, he must simply 'bring Me thy failure', instead of driving himself crazy with a remorse that is really only a display of pride and ego-full behaviour.

Suffering and sin are inevitable. They should therefore be used creatively in the spiritual life. Some Christians see that sin can be a source of joy; as the ancient prayer the '*Exultet*' has it: 'O happy fault of Adam which merited such a redeemer!' Solomon Ibn Gabirol and the thirteenth-century Jewish poet Todros Ben Judah Abulafia both see suffering as redemptive.

Poets too can use suffering creatively. Keats in 'Sleep and Poetry' sees an understanding of suffering as essential for a great poet. Wordsworth in *The Prelude* sees not only suffering but guilt as essential. It is creative; instead of wallowing in it, like a Christian, he sees it as helping him to build up 'the calm existence' that he enjoys when he is 'worthy' of himself. Instead of letting the guilt fester, he projects it outside himself in imagery and blends incongruous and apparently discordant aspects of reality together in a new harmonious vision. In being creative his guilt has redeemed both himself and his poetry. Poetry does not offer an escape from guilt and suffering. Anne Sexton cannot accept the religion of wish fulfilment: 'Need is not quite belief,' she says. She was born 'doing reference work in sin' and this, she concludes, is what poems are doing.

CZESLAW MILOSZ
Proof

And yet you experienced the flames of Hell.
You can even say what they are like: real,
Ending in sharp hooks so that they tear up flesh
Piece by piece, to the bone. You walked in the street
And it was going on: the lashing and bleeding.
You remember, therefore you have no doubt: there is a Hell for certain.

THOMAS HARDY
During Wind and Rain

They sing their dearest songs –
He, she, all of them – yea,
Treble and tenor and bass,
    And one to play;
With the candles mooning each face . . .
    Ah, no; the years O!
How the sick leaves reel down in throngs!

They clear the creeping moss –
Elders and juniors – aye,
Making the pathways neat
    And the garden gay;
And they build a shady seat . . .
    Ah, no; the years, the years;
See, the white storm-birds wing across!

They are blithely breakfasting all –
Men and maidens – yea,
Under the summer tree,
    With a glimpse of the bay,
While pet fowl come to the knee . . .

Ah, no; the years O!
And the rotten rose is ript from the wall.

They change to a high new house,
He, she, all of them – aye,
Clocks and carpets and chairs
On the lawn all day,
And brightest things that are theirs . . .
Ah, no; the years, the years;
Down their carved names the rain-drop ploughs.

EDWARD THOMAS

Out in the dark over the snow
The fallow fawns invisible go
With the fallow doe;
And the winds blow
Fast as the stars are slow.

Stealthily the dark haunts round
And, when a lamp goes, without sound
At a swifter bound
Than the swiftest hound,
Arrives, and all else is drowned;

And I and star and wind and deer
Are in the dark together, – near,
Yet far, – and fear
Drums on my ear
In that sage company drear.

How weak and little is the light,
All the universe of sight,
Love and delight,
Before the might,
If you love it not, of night.

DYLAN THOMAS

Do Not Go Gentle into That Good Night

Do not go gentle into that good night,
Old age should burn and rave at close of day;
Rage, rage against the dying of the light.

Though wise men at their end know dark is right,
Because their words had forked no lightning they
Do not go gentle into that good night.

Good men, the last wave by, crying how bright
Their frail deeds might have danced in a green bay
Rage, rage against the dying of the light.

Wild men who caught and sang the sun in flight,
And learn, too late, they grieved it on its way,
Do not go gentle into that good night.

Grave men, near death, who see with blinding sight
Blind eyes could blaze like meteors and be gay,
Rage, rage against the dying of the light.

And you, my father, there on the sad height,
Curse, bless, me now with your fierce tears, I pray.
Do not go gentle into that good night.
Rage, rage against the dying of the light.

EMILY DICKINSON

I heard a Fly buzz – when I died –
The Stillness in the Room
Was like the Stillness in the Air –
Between the Heaves of Storm –

The Eyes around – had wrung them dry –
And Breaths were gathering firm
For that last Onset – when the King
Be witnessed – in the Room –

I willed my Keepsakes – Signed away
What portion of me be
Assignable – and then it was
There interposed a Fly –

With Blue – uncertain stumbling Buzz –
Between the light – and me –
And then the Windows failed – and then
I could not see to see –

EMILY BRONTË

'No coward soul is mine'

(Last Lines: 2 January 1846)

No coward soul is mine,
No trembler in the world's storm-troubled sphere;
I see Heaven's glories shine,
And Faith shines equal, arming me from fear.

O God within my breast,
Almighty, ever-present Deity!
Life – that in me has rest,
As I, undying Life, have power in thee!

Vain are the thousand creeds
That move men's hearts, unutterably vain;
Worthless as withered weeds,
Or idlest froth amid the boundless main,

To waken doubt in one
Holding so fast by thine infinity;
So surely anchored on
The steadfast rock of immortality.

With wide-embracing love
Thy spirit animates eternal years,
Pervades and broods above,
Changes, sustains, dissolves, creates, and rears.

Though earth and man were gone,
And suns and universes ceased to be,
And thou were left alone,
Every existence would exist in thee.

There is not room for Death,
Nor atom that his might could render void:
Thou – Thou art Being and Breath,
And what Thou art may never be destroyed.

MATTHEW ARNOLD
Dover Beach

The sea is calm to-night.
The tide is full, the moon lies fair
Upon the straits; – on the French coast the light
Gleams and is gone; the cliffs of England stand,
Glimmering and vast, out in the tranquil bay.
Come to the window, sweet is the night-air!
Only, from the long line of spray
Where the sea meets the moon-blanch'd land,
Listen! you hear the grating roar
Of pebbles which the waves draw back, and fling,
At their return, up the high strand,
Begin, and cease, and then again begin,
With tremulous cadence slow, and bring
The eternal note of sadness in.

Sophocles long ago
Heard it on the Ægæan, and it brought
Into his mind the turbid ebb and flow
Of human misery; we

Find also in the sound a thought,
Hearing it by this distant northern sea.

The Sea of Faith
Was once, too, at the full, and round earth's shore
Lay like the folds of a bright girdle furl'd.
But now I only hear
Its melancholy, long, withdrawing roar,
Retreating, to the breath
Of the night-wind, down the vast edges drear
And naked shingles of the world.

Ah, love, let us be true
To one another! for the world, which seems
To lie before us like a land of dreams,
So various, so beautiful, so new,
Hath really neither joy, nor love, nor light,
Nor certitude, nor peace, nor help for pain;
And we are here as on a darkling plain
Swept with confused alarms of struggle and flight,
Where ignorant armies clash by night.

THOMAS HARDY
The Darkling Thrush

I leant upon a coppice gate
    When Frost was spectre-grey
And Winter's dregs made desolate
    The weakening eye of day.
The tangled bine-stems scored the sky
    Like strings of broken lyres,
And all mankind that haunted nigh
    Had sought their household fires.

The land's sharp features seemed to be
    The Century's corpse outleant,
His crypt the cloudy canopy,
    The wind his death-lament.

The ancient pulse of germ and birth
　　Was shrunken hard and dry,
And every spirit upon earth
　　Seemed fervourless as I.

At once a voice arose among
　　The bleak twigs overhead
In a full-hearted evensong
　　Of joy illimited;
An agèd thrush, frail, gaunt, and small,
　　In blast-beruffled plume,
Had chosen thus to fling his soul
　　Upon the growing gloom.

So little cause for carolings
　　Of such ecstatic sound
Was written on terrestrial things
　　Afar or nigh around,
That I could think there trembled through
　　His happy good-night air
Some blessèd Hope, whereof he knew
　　And I was unaware.

31 December 1900

W. H. AUDEN
The More Loving One

Looking up at the stars, I know quite well
That, for all they care, I can go to hell,
But on earth indifference is the least
We have to dread from man or beast.

How should we like it were stars to burn
With a passion for us we could not return?
If equal affection cannot be,
Let the more loving one be me.

Admirer as I think I am
Of stars that do not give a damn,
I cannot, now I see them, say
I missed one terribly all day.

Were all stars to disappear or die,
I should learn to look at an empty sky
And feel its total dark sublime,
Though this might take me a little time.

CRAIG RAINE
Plain Song

There was the chiropodist,
whose wife had a tapeworm
or a fallopian cyst,
and there was my father

reading his tea leaves.
I was hidden behind the sofa
and could only see a turn-up
and one ox-blood Saxone loafer:

I'd taken all my clothes off
for the lavatory, hours before,
and now Mr Campbell had come.
My mother shut the kitchen door,

firmly, like a good Catholic,
snubbing the two Spiritualists.
I imagined the best china
in my father's massive fists:

a woman in hoops and crinoline,
the dainty rustic handle,
the Typhoo hieroglyphics,
the fate of Mrs Campbell

whom my mother felt so sorry for.
My father went into control
and I listened, out of sight,
to the jumbled rigmarole:

someone was passing over
to another world of love.
Why do I only now discover
the woman's thin voice

saying she will be missed,
my father's eyes rolled back
and Mr Campbell's unhappy mouth,
open like a bad ventriloquist?

AESCHYLUS

(translated by Peter Levi)

Zeus, whoever Zeus may be, if he
is pleased so to be called,
by this I speak to him:
I find no likeness though I weigh
all things in the scales but Zeus,
if I must truly throw
useless weight from my mind.

And now not even he who once was great
who with his fighting courage swelled,
he shall not be spoken: he once was:
and he that was born then
was thrown and he has gone.
Who gladly cries Zeus champion
will hit the centre mark of thought:

who has put men on the road to be wise
by the authentic law
to learn by suffering,
and painful memory drips

like sleep into the heart
and those unwilling have learnt to be wise;
maybe the blessing of those gods by force
throned on the dreadful steering-bench.

JOHN CLARE

I am – yet what I am none cares or knows,
    My friends forsake me like a memory lost;
I am the self-communer of my woes,
    They rise and vanish in oblivion's host,
Like shadows in love – frenzied stifled throes;
And yet I am, and live like vapours tossed

Into the nothingness of scorn and noise,
    Into the living sea of waking dreams,
Where there is neither sense of life or joys,
    But the vast shipwreck of my life's esteems;
And e'en the dearest – that I love the best –
Are strange – nay, rather stranger than the rest.

I long for scenes where man has never trod,
    A place where woman never smiled or wept;
There to abide with my creator, God,
    And sleep as I in childhood sweetly slept:
Untroubling and untroubled where I lie,
The grass below – above the vaulted sky.

THOMAS NASHE

Adieu, farewell, earth's bliss,
This world uncertain is;
Fond are life's lustful joys,
Death proves them all but toys,
None from his darts can fly.
I am sick, I must die.
    Lord have mercy on us!

Rich men, trust not in wealth,
Gold cannot buy you health;
Physic himself must fade,
All things to end are made.
The plague full swift goes by;
I am sick, I must die.
    Lord have mercy on us!

Beauty is but a flower
Which wrinkles will devour;
Brightness falls from the air,
Queens have died young and fair,
Dust hath closed Helen's eye.
I am sick, I must die.
    Lord have mercy on us!

Strength stoops unto the grave,
Worms feed on Hector brave,
Swords may not fight with fate,
Earth still holds ope her gate.
'Come! come!' the bells do cry.
I am sick, I must die.
    Lord have mercy on us!

Wit with his wantonness
Tasteth death's bitterness;
Hell's executioner
Hath no ears for to hear
What vain art can reply
I am sick, I must die.
    Lord have mercy on us!

Haste, therefore, each degree,
To welcome destiny.
Heaven is our heritage,
Earth but a player's stage;
Mount we unto the sky.
I am sick, I must die.
    Lord have mercy on us!

ALFRED, LORD TENNYSON

From *In Memoriam A. H. H.*

LV

The wish, that of the living whole
No life may fail beyond the grave,
Derives it not from what we have
The likest God within the soul?

Are God and Nature then at strife,
That Nature lends such evil dreams?
So careful of the type she seems,
So careless of the single life;

That I, considering everywhere
Her secret meaning in her deeds,
And finding that of fifty seeds,
She often brings but one to bear,

I falter where I firmly trod,
And falling with my weight of cares
Upon the great world's altar-stairs
That slope thro' darkness up to God,

I stretch lame hands of faith, and grope,
And gather dust and chaff, and call
To what I feel is Lord of all,
And faintly trust the larger hope.

LVI

'So careful of the type'? but no.
From scarped cliff and quarried stone
She cries, 'A thousand types are gone:
I care for nothing, all shall go.

'Thou makest thine appeal to me:
I bring to life, I bring to death:
The spirit does but mean the breath:
I know no more.' And he, shall he,

Man, her last work, who seem'd so fair,
Such splendid purpose in his eyes,
Who roll'd the psalm to wintry skies,
Who built him fanes of fruitless prayer,

Who trusted God was love indeed
And love Creation's final law –
Tho' Nature, red in tooth and claw
With ravine, shriek'd against his creed –

Who loved, who suffer'd countless ills,
Who battled for the True, the Just,
Be blown about the desert dust,
Or seal'd within the iron hills?

No more? A monster then, a dream,
A discord. Dragons of the prime,
That tare each other in their slime,
Were mellow music match'd with him.

O life as futile, then, as frail!
O for thy voice to soothe and bless!
What hope of answer, or redress?
Behind the veil, behind the veil.

GEOFFREY HILL

Genesis

I

Against the burly air I strode,
Where the tight ocean heaves its load,
Crying the miracles of God.

And first I brought the sea to bear
Upon the dead weight of the land;
And the waves flourished at my prayer,
The rivers spawned their sand.

And where the streams were salt and full
The tough pig-headed salmon strove,
Curbing the ebb and the tide's pull,
To reach the steady hills above.

II

The second day I stood and saw
The osprey plunge with triggered claw,
Feathering blood along the shore,
To lay the living sinew bare.

And the third day I cried: 'Beware
The soft-voiced owl, the ferret's smile,
Cold eyes, and bodies hooped in steel,
Forever bent upon the kill.'

III

And I renounced, on the fourth day,
This fierce and unregenerate clay,

Building as a huge myth for man
The watery Leviathan,

And made the glove-winged albatross
Scour the ashes of the sea
Where Capricorn and Zero cross,
A brooding immortality –
Such as the charmed phoenix has
In the unwithering tree.

IV

The phoenix burns as cold as frost;
And, like a legendary ghost,
The phantom-bird goes wild and lost,
Upon a pointless ocean tossed.

So, the fifth day, I turned again
To flesh and blood and the blood's pain.

V

On the sixth day, as I rode
In haste about the works of God,
With spurs I plucked the horse's blood.

By blood we live, the hot, the cold,
To ravage and redeem the world:
There is no bloodless myth will hold.

And by Christ's blood are men made free
Though in close shrouds their bodies lie
Under the rough pelt of the sea;

Though Earth has rolled beneath her weight
The bones that cannot bear the light.

SAMUEL TAYLOR COLERIDGE

From *The Rime of the Ancient Mariner*

PART I

An ancient Mariner meeteth three Gallants bidden to a wedding-feast, and detaineth one.

It is an ancient Mariner,
And he stoppeth one of three.
'By thy long grey beard and glittering eye,
Now wherefore stopp'st thou me?

The Bridegroom's doors are opened wide,
And I am next of kin;
The guests are met, the feast is set:
May'st hear the merry din.'

He holds him with his skinny hand,
'There was a ship,' quoth he.
'Hold off! unhand me, greybeard loon!'
Eftsoons his hand dropt he.

The Wedding-Guest is spellbound by the eye of the old sea-faring man, and constrained to hear his tale.

He holds him with his glittering eye –
The Wedding-Guest stood still,
And listens like a three years' child:
The Mariner hath his will.

The Wedding-Guest sat on a stone:
He cannot choose but hear;
And thus spake on that ancient man,
The bright-eyed Mariner.

'The ship was cheered, the harbour cleared,
Merrily did we drop
Below the kirk, below the hill.
Below the light house top.

The Mariner tells how the ship sailed southward with a good wind and fair weather, till it reached the Line.

The Sun came up upon the left,
Out of the sea came he!
And he shone bright, and on the right
Went down into the sea.

Higher and higher every day,
Till over the mast at noon –'
The Wedding-Guest here beat his breast,
For he heard the loud bassoon.

The Wedding-Guest heareth the bridal music; but the Mariner continueth his tale.

The bride hath paced into the hall,
Red as a rose is she;
Nodding their heads before her goes
The merry minstrelsy.

The Wedding-Guest he beat his breast,
Yet he cannot choose but hear;
And thus spake on that ancient man,
The bright-eyed Mariner.

The ship drawn by a storm toward the south pole.

'And now the STORM-BLAST came, and he
Was tyrannous and strong:
He struck with his o'ertaking wings,
And chased us south along.

With sloping masts and dipping prow,
As who pursued with yell and blow
Still treads the shadow of his foe,
And forward bends his head,
The ship drove fast, loud roared the blast,
And southward aye we fled

And now there came both mist and snow,
And it grew wondrous cold:
And ice, mast-high, came floating by,
As green as emerald.

The land of ice, and of fearful sounds where no living thing was to be seen.

And through the drifts the snowy clifts
Did send a dismal sheen:
Nor shapes of men nor beasts we ken –
The ice was all between.

The ice was here, the ice was there,
The ice was all around:
It cracked and growled, and roared and howled,
Like noises in a swound!

Till a great sea-bird, called the Albatross, came through the snow-fog, and was received with great joy and hospitality.

At length did cross an Albatross,
Thorough the fog it came;
As if it had been a Christian soul,
We hailed it in God's name.

It ate the food it ne'er had eat,
And round and round it flew.
The ice did split with a thunder-fit;
The helmsman steered us through!

And lo! the Albatross proveth a bird of good omen, and followeth the ship as it returned northward through fog and floating ice.

And a good south wind sprung up behind;
The Albatross did follow,
And every day, for food or play,
Came to the mariners' hollo!

In mist or cloud, on mast or shroud,
It perched for vespers nine;
Whiles all the night, through fog-smoke white,
Glimmered the white Moon-shine.'

The ancient Mariner inhospitably killeth the pious bird of good omen.

'God save thee, ancient Mariner!
From the fiends, that plague thee thus! –
Why look'st thou so?' – With my cross-bow
I shot the ALBATROSS.

PART II

The Sun now rose upon the right:
Out of the sea came he,
Still hid in mist, and on the left
Went down into the sea.

And the good south wind still blew behind,
But no sweet bird did follow,
Nor any day for food or play
Came to the mariners' hollo!

His shipmates cry out against the ancient Mariner, for killing the bird of good luck.

And I had done a hellish thing,
And it would work 'em woe:
For all averred, I had killed the bird
That made the breeze to blow.
Ah wretch! said they, the bird to slay,
That made the breeze to blow!

But when the fog cleared off, they justify the same, and thus make themselves accomplices in the crime.

Nor dim nor red, like God's own head,
The glorious Sun uprist:
Then all averred, I had killed the bird
That brought the fog and mist.
'Twas right, said they, such birds to slay,
That bring the fog and mist.

The fair breeze continues; the ship enters the Pacific Ocean, and sails northward, even till it reaches the Line.

The fair breeze blew, the white foam flew,
The furrow followed free;
We were the first that ever burst
Into that silent sea.

The ship hath been suddenly becalmed.

Down dropt the breeze, the sails dropt down,
'Twas sad as sad could be;
And we did speak only to break
The silence of the sea!

All in a hot and copper sky,
The bloody Sun, at noon,
Right up above the mast did stand,
No bigger than the Moon.

Day after day, day after day,
We stuck, nor breath nor motion;
As idle as a painted ship
Upon a painted ocean.

And the Albatross begins to be avenged.

Water, water, every where,
And all the boards did shrink;
Water, water, every where,
Nor any drop to drink.

The very deep did rot: O Christ!
That ever this should be!
Yea, slimy things did crawl with legs
Upon the slimy sea.

About, about, in reel and rout
The death-fires danced at night;
The water, like a witch's oils,
Burnt green, and blue and white.

A Spirit had followed them; one of the invisible inhabitants of this planet, neither departed souls nor angels; concerning whom the learned Jew, Josephus, and the Platonic Constantinopolitan, Michael Psellus, may be consulted. They are very numerous, and there is no climate or element without one or more.

And some in dreams assurèd were
Of the Spirit that plagued us so;
Nine fathom deep he had followed us
From the land of mist and snow.

And every tongue, through utter drought,
Was withered at the root;
We could not speak, no more than if
We had been choked with soot.

The shipmates, in their sore distress, would fain throw the whole guilt on the ancient Mariner: in sign whereof they hang the dead sea-bird round his neck.

Ah! well a-day! what evil looks
Had I from old and young!
Instead of the cross, the Albatross
About my neck was hung.

PART III

There passed a weary time. Each throat
Was parched, and glazed each eye.
A weary time! a weary time!
How glazed each weary eye,
When looking westward, I beheld
A something in the sky.

The ancient Mariner beholdeth a sign in the element afar off.

At first it seemed a little speck,
And then it seemed a mist;
It moved and moved, and took at last
A certain shape, I wist.

A speck, a mist, a shape, I wist!
And still it neared and neared:
As if it dodged a water-sprite,
It plunged and tacked and veered.

At its nearer approach, it seemeth him to be a ship; and at a dear ransom he freeth his speech from the bonds of thirst.

With throats unslaked, with black lips baked,
We could nor laugh nor wail;
Through utter drought all dumb we stood!
I bit my arm, I sucked the blood,
And cried, A sail! a sail!

A flash of joy;

With throats unslaked, with black lips baked,
Agape they heard me call:
Gramercy! they for joy did grin,
And all at once their breath drew in,
As they were drinking all.

And horror follows. For can it be a ship that comes onward without wind or tide?

See! see! (I cried) she tacks no more!
Hither to work us weal;
Without a breeze, without a tide,
She steadies with upright keel!

The western wave was all a-flame.
The day was well nigh done!
Almost upon the western wave
Rested the broad bright Sun;
When that strange shape drove suddenly
Betwixt us and the Sun.

It seemeth him but the skeleton of a ship.

And straight the Sun was flecked with bars,
(Heaven's Mother send us grace!)
As if through a dungeon-grate he peered
With broad and burning face.

Alas! (thought I, and my heart beat loud)
How fast she nears and nears!
Are those *her* sails that glance in the Sun,
Like restless gossameres?

And its ribs are seen as bars on the face of the setting Sun. The Spectre-Woman and her Death-mate, and no other on board the skeleton ship. Like vessel, like crew!

Are those *her* ribs through which the Sun
Did peer, as through a grate?
And is that Woman all her crew?
Is that a DEATH? and are there two?
Is DEATH that woman's mate?

Her lips were red, *her* looks were free,
Her locks were yellow as gold:
Her skin was as white as leprosy,
The Night-mare LIFE-IN-DEATH was she,
Who thicks man's blood with cold.

Death and Life-in-Death have diced for the ship's crew, and she (the latter) winneth the ancient Mariner.

The naked hulk alongside came,
And the twain were casting dice;
'The game is done! I've won! I've won!'
Quoth she, and whistles thrice.

No twilight within the courts of the Sun.

The Sun's rim dips; the stars rush out:
At one stride comes the dark;
With far-heard whisper, o'er the sea,
Off shot the spectre-bark.

At the rising of the Moon,

We listened and looked sideways up!
Fear at my heart, as at a cup,
My life-blood seemed to sip!
The stars were dim, and thick the night,
The steersman's face by his lamp gleamed white;
From the sails the dew did drip –
Till clomb above the eastern bar
The hornèd Moon, with one bright star
Within the nether tip.

One after another,

One after one, by the star-dogged Moon,
Too quick for groan or sigh,
Each turned his face with a ghastly pang,
And cursed me with his eye.

His shipmates drop down dead.

Four times fifty living men,
(And I heard nor sigh nor groan)
With heavy thump, a lifeless lump,
They dropped down one by one.

But Life-in-Death begins her work on the ancient Mariner.

The souls did from their bodies fly, –
They fled to bliss or woe!
And every soul, it passed me by,
Like the whizz of my cross-bow!

PART IV

The Wedding-Guest feareth that a Spirit is talking to him;

'I fear thee, ancient Mariner!
I fear thy skinny hand!
And thou art long, and lank, and brown,
As is the ribbed sea-sand.

I fear thee and thy glittering eye,
And thy skinny hand, so brown.' –

But the ancient Mariner assureth him of his bodily life, and proceedeth to relate his horrible penance.

Fear not, fear not, thou Wedding-Guest!
This body dropt not down.

Alone, alone, all, all alone,
Alone on a wide wide sea!
And never a saint took pity on
My soul in agony.

He despiseth the creatures of the calm,

The many men, so beautiful!
And they all dead did lie:
And a thousand thousand slimy things
Lived on; and so did I.

And envieth that *they* should live, and so many lie dead.

I looked upon the rotting sea,
And drew my eyes away;
I looked upon the rotting deck,
And there the dead men lay.

I looked to heaven, and tried to pray;
But or ever a prayer had gusht,
A wicked whisper came, and made
My heart as dry as dust.

I closed my lids, and kept them close,
And the balls like pulses beat;
For the sky and the sea, and the sea and the sky
Lay like a load on my weary eye,
And the dead were at my feet.

But the curse liveth for him in the eye of the dead men.

The cold sweat melted from their limbs,
Nor rot nor reek did they:
The look with which they looked on me
Had never passed away.

An orphan's curse would drag to hell
A spirit from on high;
But oh! more horrible than that
Is the curse in a dead man's eye!
Seven days, seven nights, I saw that curse,
And yet I could not die.

In his loneliness and fixedness he yearneth towards the journeying Moon, and the stars that still sojourn, yet still move onward; and every where the blue sky belongs to them, and is their appointed rest, and their native country and their own natural homes, which they enter unannounced, as lords that are certainly expected and yet there is a silent joy at their arrival.

The moving Moon went up the sky,
And no where did abide:
Softly she was going up,
And a star or two beside –

Her beams bemocked the sultry main,
Like April hoar-frost spread;
But where the ship's huge shadow lay,
The charmèd water burnt alway
A still and awful red.

By the light of the Moon he beholdeth God's creatures of the great calm.

Beyond the shadow of the ship,
I watched the water-snakes:
They moved in tracks of shining white,
And when they reared, the elfish light
Fell off in hoary flakes.

Within the shadow of the ship
I watched their rich attire:
Blue, glossy green, and velvet black,
They coiled and swam; and every track
Was a flash of golden fire.

Their beauty and their happiness.

O happy living things! no tongue
Their beauty might declare:
A spring of love gushed from my heart,

He blesseth them in his heart.

And I blessed them unaware:
Sure my kind saint took pity on me,
And I blessed them unaware.

The spell begins to break.

The self-same moment I could pray;
And from my neck so free
The Albatross fell off, and sank
Like lead into the sea.

PART V

Oh sleep! it is a gentle thing,
Beloved from pole to pole!
To Mary Queen the praise be given!
She sent the gentle sleep from Heaven,
That slid into my soul.

By grace of the holy Mother, the ancient Mariner is refreshed with rain.

The silly buckets on the deck,
That had so long remained,
I dreamt that they were filled with dew;
And when I awoke, it rained.

My lips were wet, my throat was cold,
My garments all were dank;
Sure I had drunken in my dreams,
And still my body drank.

I moved, and could not feel my limbs:
I was so light – almost
I thought that I had died in sleep,
And was a blessèd ghost.

. . .

PART VII

O Wedding-Guest! this soul hath been
Alone on a wide wide sea:
So lonely 'twas, that God himself
Scarce seemèd there to be.

O sweeter than the marriage-feast,
'Tis sweeter far to me,
To walk together to the kirk
With a goodly company! –

To walk together to the kirk,
And all together pray,
While each to his great Father bends,
Old men, and babes, and loving friends
And youths and maidens gay!

Farewell, farewell! but this I tell
To thee, thou Wedding-Guest!
He prayeth well, who loveth well
Both man and bird and beast.

He prayeth best, who loveth best
All things both great and small;
For the dear God who loveth us,
He made and loveth all.'

The Mariner, whose eye is bright,
Whose beard with age is hoar,
Is gone: and now the Wedding-Guest
Turned from the bridegroom's door.

He went like one that hath been stunned,
And is of sense forlorn:
A sadder and a wiser man,
He rose the morrow morn.

WILLIAM BLAKE

London

I wander thro' each charter'd street,
Near where the charter'd Thames does flow,
And mark in every face I meet
Marks of weakness, marks of woe.

In every cry of every Man,
In every Infant's cry of fear,
In every voice, in every ban,
The mind-forged manacles I hear.

How the Chimney-sweeper's cry
Every black'ning Church appalls;
And the hapless Soldier's sigh
Runs in blood down Palace walls.

But most thro' midnight streets I hear
How the youthful Harlot's curse
Blasts the new born Infant's tear,
And blights with plagues the Marriage hearse.

ABBA KOVNER

My Sister

(translated by T. Carmi)

My sister sits happy at her bridegroom's table.
She isn't crying.
My sister wouldn't do such a thing.
What would people say!

My sister sits happy at her bridegroom's table.
Her heart is awake.
The whole company is sipping kosher chicken broth:

The dumplings of unleavened flour
were made by her mother-in-law.
The whole company admiringly tastes the mother's marmalade.

My sister-bride sits with the bowl of honey beside her.
Such a huge crowd!
The braids of the *halah*

were twisted by father:

For forty years, praise God,
our father took out his bread from the same oven.
He never suspected that an entire people could go up in ovens,
while the world, with God's help, endures.

My sister, in her bridal veil, sits at the table alone.
From the covert of the mourners, the voice of the bridegroom draws near.
We shall set the table without you, [my sister],
the marriage-contract will be written in stone.

YEHUDA AMICHAI
On the Day of Atonement
(translated by T. Carmi)

On the Day of Atonement in 1967,
I put on my dark holiday suit and went to the Old City in Jerusalem.
I stood, for some time,
before the alcove of an Arab's shop,
not far from Damascus Gate,
a shop of buttons and zippers and spools of thread in all colours,
and snaps and buckles.
A glorious light and a great many colours
like a Holy Ark with its doors ajar.

I told him in my heart that my father, too,
had such a shop of threads and buttons.
I explained to him in my heart all about the tens of years

and the reasons and the circumstances
because of which I am now here
and my father's shop is in ashes there,
and he is buried here.

By the time I had finished,
it was the hour of 'the locking of the Gates'.*
He too pulled down the shutter and locked the gate,
and I went back home with all the worshippers.

* *Ne'ila*, the evening prayer, which concludes the Day of Atonement.

CZESLAW MILOSZ

To Raja Rao

Raja, I wish I knew
the cause of that malady.

for years I could not accept
the place I was in.
I felt I should be somewhere else.

A city, trees, human voices
lacked the quality of presence.
I would live by the hope of moving on.

Somewhere else there was a city of real presence,
of real trees and voices and friendship and love.

Link, if you wish, my peculiar case
(on the border of schizophrenia)
to the messianic hope
of my civilisation.

Ill at ease in the tyranny, ill at ease in the republic,
in the one I longed for freedom, in the other for the end of corruption.

Building in my mind a permanent *polis*
for ever deprived of aimless bustle.

I learned at last to say: this is my home,
here, before the glowing coal of ocean sunsets,
on the shore which faces the shores of your Asia,
in a great republic, moderately corrupt.

Raja, this did not cure me
of my guilt and shame.
A shame of failing to be
what I should have been.

The image of myself
grows gigantic on the wall
and against it
my miserable shadow.

That's how I came to believe
in Original Sin
which is nothing but the first
victory of the ego.

Tormented by my ego, deluded by it
I give you, as you see, a ready argument.

I hear you saying that liberation is possible
and that Socratic wisdom
is identical with your guru's.

No, Raja, I must start from what I am.
I am those monsters which visit my dreams
and reveal to me my hidden essence.

If I am sick, there is no proof whatsoever
that man is a healthy creature.

Greece had to lose, her pure consciousness
had to make our agony only more acute.

We needed God loving us in our weakness
and not in the glory of beatitude.

No help, Raja, my part is agony,
struggle, abjection, self-love and self-hate,
prayer for the Kingdom
and reading Pascal.

JOHN MILTON

From *Paradise Lost* Book IX

[Adam after the Fall]

How shall I behold the face
Henceforth of God or Angel, earst with joy
And rapture so oft beheld? those heav'nly shapes
Will dazle now this earthly, with thir blaze
Insufferably bright. O might I here
In solitude live savage, in some glade
Obscur'd, where highest Woods impenetrable
To Starr or Sun-light, spread thir umbrage broad,
And brown as Eevening: Cover me ye Pines,
Ye Cedars, with innumerable boughs
Hide me, where I may never see them more.
But let us now, as in bad plight, devise
What best may for the present serve to hide
The Parts of each from other, that seem most
To Shame obnoxious, and unseemliest seen,
Some Tree whose broad smooth Leaves together sowd,
And girded on our loins, my cover round
Those middle parts, that this new commer, Shame,
There sit not, and reproach us as unclean.

JOHN DONNE

Holy Sonnet IV

Oh my blacke Soule! now thou art summoned
By sicknesse, deaths herald, and champion;
Thou art like a pilgrim, which abroad hath done
Treason, and durst not turne to whence hee is fled,
Or like a thiefe, which till deaths doome be read,
Wisheth himselfe delivered from prison;
But damn'd and hal'd to execution,
Wisheth that still he might be imprisoned.
Yet grace, if thou repent, thou canst not lacke;
But who shall give thee that grace to beginne?
Oh make thy selfe with holy mourning blacke,
And red with blushing, as thou art with sinne;
Or wash thee in Christs blood, which hath this might
That being red, it dyes red soules to white.

Holy Sonnet VII

At the round earths imagin'd corners, blow
Your trumpets, Angells, and arise, arise
From death, you numberlesse infinities
Of soules, and to your scattred bodies goe,
All whom the flood did, and fire shall o'erthrow,
All whom warre, dearth, age, agues, tyrannies,
Despaire, law, chance, hath slaine, and you whose eyes,
Shall behold God, and never tast deaths woe.
But let them sleep, Lord, and mee mourne a space,
For, if above all these, my sinnes abound,
'Tis late to aske abundance of thy grace,
When wee are there; here on this lowly ground,
Teach mee how to repent; for that's as good
As if thou'hadst seal'd my pardon, with thy blood.

Holy Sonnet XI

Spit in my face you Jewes, and pierce my side,
Buffet, and scoffe, scourge, and crucifie mee,
For I have sinn'd, and sinn'd, and onely hee,
Who could do no iniquitie, hath dyed:
But by my death can not be satisfied
My sinnes, which passe the Jewes impiety:
They kill'd once an inglorious man, but I
Crucifie him daily, being now glorified.
Oh let mee then, his strange love still admire:
Kings pardon, but he bore our punishment.
And *Jacob* came cloth'd in vile harsh attire
But to supplant, and with gainfull intent:
God cloth'd himselfe in vile mans flesh, that so
Hee might be weake enough to suffer woe.

JOSEPH ADDISON

When rising from the bed of death,
    O'erwhelmed with guilt and fear,
    I see my Maker face to face,
        O how shall I appear?

If yet, while pardon may be found,
    And mercy may be sought,
My heart with inward horror shrinks,
    And trembles at the thought;

When thou, O Lord, shalt stand disclosed
    In majesty severe,
And sit in judgement on my soul,
    O how shall I appear?

But thou hast told the troubled mind,
    Who does her sins lament,
The timely tribute of her tears
    Shall endless woe prevent.

Then see the sorrows of my heart
Ere yet it be too late;
And hear my Saviour's dying groans,
To give those sorrows weight.

For never shall my soul despair
Her pardon to procure,
Who knows thine only Son has died
To make her pardon sure.

CHRISTINA ROSSETTI
Who Shall Deliver Me?

God strengthen me to bear myself,
That heaviest weight of all to bear,
Inalienable weight of care.

All others are outside myself;
I lock my door and bar them out,
The turmoil, tedium, gad-about.

I lock my door upon myself,
And bar them out; but who shall wall
Self from myself, most loathed of all?

If I could once lay down myself,
And start self-purged upon the race
That all must run! Death runs apace.

If I could set aside myself,
And start with lightened heart upon
The road by all men overgone!

God harden me against myself,
This coward with pathetic voice
Who craves for ease, and rest, and joys:

Myself, arch-traitor to myself;
My hollowest friend, my deadliest foe,
My clog whatever road I go.

Yet One there is can curb myself,
Can roll the strangling load from me,
Break off the yoke and set me free.

GERARD MANLEY HOPKINS

I wake and feel the fell of dark, not day.
What hours, O what black hoürs we have spent
This night! what sights you, heart, saw; ways you went!
And more must, in yet longer light's delay.
With witness I speak this. But where I say
Hours I mean years, mean life. And my lament
Is cries countless, cries like dead letters sent
To dearest him that lives alas! away.

I am gall, I am heartburn. God's most deep decree
Bitter would have me taste: my taste was me;
Bones built in me, flesh filled, blood brimmed the curse.
Selfyeast of spirit a dull dough sours. I see
The lost are like this, and their scourge to be
As I am mine, their sweating selves; but worse.

My own heart let me more have pity on; let
Me live to my sad self hereafter kind,
Charitable; not live this tormented mind
With this tormented mind tormenting yet.
I cast for comfort I can no more get
By groping round my comfortless, than blind
Eyes in their dark can day or thirst can find
Thirst's all-in-all in all a world of wet.

Soul, self; come, poor Jackself, I do advise
You, jaded, let be; call off thoughts awhile
Elsewhere; leave comfort root-room; let joy size
At God knows when to God knows what; whose smile
's not wrung, see you; unforeseen times rather – as skies
Betweenpie mountains – lights a lovely mile.

JOHN DONNE
A Hymne to God the Father

I

Wilt thou forgive that sinne where I begunne,
    Which was my sin, though it were done before?
Wilt thou forgive that sinne; through which I runne,
    And do run still: though still I do deplore?
        When thou hast done, thou hast not done,
        For, I have more.

II

Wilt thou forgive that sinne by which I have wonne
    Others to sinne? and, made my sinne their doore?
Wilt thou forgive that sinne which I did shunne
    A yeare, or two: but wallowed in, a score?
        When thou hast done, thou hast not done,
        For I have more.

III

I have a sinne of feare, that when I have spunne
    My last thred, I shall perish on the shore;
But sweare by thy selfe, that at my death thy sonne
    Shall shine as he shines now, and heretofore;
        And, having done that, Thou hast done,
        I feare no more.

SOLOMON IBN GABIROL

Separation from the Torah

(translated by David Goldstein)

You inquire gracefully of a man sick at heart,
'Why do you wear sackcloth and put ashes on your head?'
I do not mourn or grieve for someone that has died,
For every man dies. He gives no ransom instead.
But I am grief-stricken, because, being ill,
I cannot go to hear the Sefer Torah read.

Before I was Born

(translated by David Goldstein)

Before I was born your love enveloped me.
You turned nothing into substance, and created me.
Who etched out my frame? Who poured
Me into a vessel and moulded me?
Who breathed a spirit into me? Who opened
The womb of Sheol and extracted me?
Who has guided me from youth-time until now?
Taught me knowledge, and cared wondrously for me?
Truly, I am nothing but clay within your hand.
It is you, not I, who have really fashioned me.
I confess my sin to you, and do not say
That a serpent intrigued, and tempted me.
How can I conceal from you my faults, since
Before I was born your love enveloped me?

GEORGE HERBERT

Love

Love bade me welcome: yet my soul drew back,
      Guiltie of dust and sinne.
But quick-ey'd Love, observing me grow slack
      From my first entrance in,
Drew nearer to me, sweetly questioning,
      If I lack'd any thing.

A guest, I answer'd, worthy to be here:
      Love said, You shall be he.
I the unkinde, ungratefull? Ah my deare,
      I cannot look on thee.
Love took my hand, and smiling did reply,
      Who made the eyes but I?

Truth Lord, but I have marr'd them: let my shame
      Go where it doth deserve.
And know you not, sayes Love, who bore the blame?
      My deare, then I will serve.
You must sit down, sayes Love, and taste my meat:
      So I did sit and eat.

ḤAFĪẒ

(translated by R. A. Nicholson)

My soul is the veil of his love,
Mine eye is the glass of his grace.
Not for earth, not for heaven above,
Would I stoop; yet his bounties have bowed
A spirit too proud
For aught to abase.

This temple of awe, where no sin
But only the zephyr comes nigh,
Who am I to adventure within?

Even so: very foul is my skirt.
What then? will it hurt
The most Pure, the most High?

He passed by the rose in the field,
His colour and perfume she stole.
O twice happy star that revealed
The secret of day and of night –
His face to my sight,
His love to my soul!

JUDAH HA-LEVI

Heal me, my God

(translated by David Goldstein)

Heal me, my God, and I shall be healed.
Let not your anger burn, to remove me from the earth.
My potion, my medicament, depends on you
For its weakness, or its strength, its failure or its worth.
You are the one that chooses. It is not I.
For you know what is good and what is ill.
Not on my own healing do I rely.
I look only towards your power to heal.

From the *Bhagavad-Gita*

Book XII (the 'Bhaktiyōg')
(translated by Sir Edwin Arnold)

[Krishna speaks]

Yet hard
The travail is for such as bend their minds
To reach th' Unmanifest. That viewless path
Shall scarce be trod by man bearing the flesh!
But whereso any doeth all his deeds
Renouncing self for Me, full of Me, fixed

To serve only the Highest, night and day
Musing on Me – him will I swiftly lift
Forth from life's ocean of distress and death,
Whose soul clings fast to Me. Cling thou to Me!
Clasp Me with heart and mind! so shalt thou dwell
Surely with Me on high. But if thy thought
Droops from such height; if thou be'st weak to set
Body and soul upon Me constantly,
Despair not! give me lower service! seek
To reach Me, worshipping with steadfast will;
And, if thou canst not worship steadfastly,
Work for Me, toil in works pleasing to Me!
For he that laboureth right for love of Me
Shall finally attain! But, if in this
Thy faint heart fails, bring Me thy failure! find
Refuge in Me! let fruits of labour go
Renouncing hope for Me, with lowliest heart,
So shalt thou come; for, though to know is more
Than diligence, yet worship better is
Than knowing, and renouncing better still.
Near to renunciation – very near –
Dwelleth Eternal Peace!

JOHN DONNE

Hymne to God my God, in my Sicknesse

Since I am comming to that Holy roome,
    Where, with thy Quire of Saints for evermore,
I shall be made thy Musique; As I come
    I tune the Instrument here at the dore,
    And what I must doe then, thinke here before.

Whilst my Physitians by their love are growne
  Cosmographers, and I their Mapp, who lie
Flat on this bed, that by them may be showne
    That this is my South-west discoverie
    Per fretum febris, by these streights to die,

I joy, that in these straits, I see my West;
For, though theire currants yeeld returne to none,
What shall my West hurt me? As West and East
In all flatt Maps (and I am one) are one,
So death doth touch the Resurrection.

Is the Pacifique Sea my home? Or are
The Easterne riches? Is *Jerusalem*?
Anyan, and *Magellan*, and *Gibraltare*,
All streights, and none but streights, are wayes to them,
Whether where *Japhet* dwelt, or *Cham*, or *Sem*.

We thinke that *Paradise* and *Calvarie*,
Christs Crosse, and *Adams* tree, stood in one place;
Looke Lord, and finde both *Adams* met in me;
As the first *Adams* sweat surrounds my face,
May the last *Adams* blood my soule embrace.

So, in his purple wrapp'd receive mee Lord,
By these his thornes give me his other Crowne;
And as to others soules I preach'd thy word,
Be this my Text, my Sermon to mine owne,
Therefore that he may raise the Lord throws down.

SOLOMON IBN GABIROL

His Illness

(translated by David Goldstein)

Forgive me, my God, and overlook my sins,
Although one cannot fathom their number or their depth.
Remember, for my sake, your kindness, Lord,
Pay no heed to the sins of dust and earth.
Even if the decree has gone out against my life,
Annul it, my God, make it of no effect.
Consider my illness as my redemption,
And let my pain ransom me from death.

TODROS BEN JUDAH ABULAFIA

From Prison

(translated by David Goldstein)

I

If my imprisonment has no end,
I shall receive all from God as a mark of love.
If my oppressors take all my wealth,
My heart and my mind will not be enslaved.
And if they afflict me on this earth,
My soul will rejoice in the world to come.
If they kill me, I shall sing with love
As I make my way to the house of my God.
I am glad to suffer the pain he sends,
Since the reason for all comes from God.

II

Let the dew of your mercies drop upon me,
For look, my father, my leaves have fallen.
Re-establish my paths, and be with me,
For all my limbs are shaking with fear.
My enemies are many. Save me from them.
Let your love be spread over me.
See how the vultures of Fortune prey
On me, and eat my flesh all day.
Save my swallows from their depredations.
Have pity on my song-birds, on my doves.

JOHN KEATS

From 'Sleep and Poetry'

And can I ever bid these joys farewell?
Yes, I must pass them for a nobler life,
Where I may find the agonies, the strife
Of human hearts: for lo! I see afar,
O'ersailing the blue cragginess, a car
And steeds with streamy manes – the charioteer

Looks out upon the winds with glorious fear:
And now the numerous tramplings quiver lightly
Along a huge cloud's ridge; and now with sprightly
Wheel downward come they into fresher skies,
Tipt round with silver from the sun's bright eyes.
Still downward with capacious whirl they glide;
And now I see them on the green-hill's side
In breezy rest among the nodding stalks.
The charioteer with wond'rous gesture talks
To the trees and mountains; and there soon appear
Shapes of delight, of mystery, and fear,
Passing along before a dusky space
Made by some mighty oaks: as they would chase
Some ever-fleeting music on they sweep.
Lo! how they murmur, laugh, and smile, and weep:
Some with upholden hand and mouth severe;
Some with their faces muffled to the ear
Between their arms; some, clear in youthful bloom,
Go glad and smilingly athwart the gloom;
Some looking back, and some with upward gaze;
Yes, thousands in a thousand different ways
Flit onward – now a lovely wreath of girls
Dancing their sleek hair into tangled curls;
And now broad wings. Most awfully intent
The driver of those steeds is forward bent,
And seems to listen: O that I might know
All that he writes with such a hurrying glow.

WILLIAM WORDSWORTH

From *The Prelude*

Book I ('Childhood and School-time')

Ere I had told
Ten birth-days, when among the mountain-slopes
Frost, and the breath of frosty wind, had snapped
The last autumnal crocus, 'twas my joy
With store of springes o'er my shoulder hung
To range the open heights where wood-cocks run

Among the smooth green turf. Through half the night,
Scudding away from snare to snare, I plied
That anxious visitation; – moon and stars
Were shining o'er my head. I was alone,
And seemed to be a trouble to the peace
That dwelt among them. Sometimes it befell
In these night wanderings, that a strong desire
O'erpowered my better reason, and the bird
Which was the captive of another's toil
Became my prey; and when the deed was done
I heard among the solitary hills
Low breathings coming after me, and sounds
Of undistinguishable motion, steps
Almost as silent as the turf they trod.

Nor less when spring had warmed the cultured Vale,
Roved we as plunderers where the mother-bird
Had in high places built her lodge; though mean
Our object and inglorious, yet the end
Was not ignoble. Oh! when I have hung
Above the raven's nest, by knots of grass
And half-inch fissures in the slippery rock
But ill sustained, and almost (so it seemed)
Suspended by the blast that blew amain,
Shouldering the naked crag, oh, at that time
While on the perilous ridge I hung alone,
With what strange utterance did the loud dry wind
Blow through my ear! the sky seemed not a sky
Of earth – and with what motion moved the clouds!

Dust as we are, the immortal spirit grows
Like harmony in music; there is a dark
Inscrutable workmanship that reconciles
Discordant elements, makes them cling together
In one society. How strange that all
The terrors, pains, and early miseries,
Regrets, vexations, lassitudes interfused
Within my mind, should e'er have borne a part,
And that a needful part, in making up
The calm existence that is mine when I
Am worthy of myself. Praise to the end!

Thanks to the means which Nature deigned to employ;
Whether her fearless visitings, or those
That came with soft alarm, like hurtless light
Opening the peaceful clouds; or she may use
Severer interventions, ministry
More palpable, as best might suit her aim.

One summer evening (led by her) I found
A little boat tied to a willow tree
Within a rocky cave, its usual home.
Straight I unloosed her chain, and stepping in
Pushed from the shore. It was an act of stealth
And troubled pleasure, nor without the voice
Of mountain-echoes did my boat move on;
Leaving behind her still, on either side,
Small circles glittering idly in the moon,
Until they melted all into one track
Of sparkling light. But now, like one who rows,
Proud of his skill, to reach a chosen point
With an unswerving line, I fixed my view
Upon the summit of a craggy ridge,
The horizon's utmost boundary; for above
Was nothing but the stars and the grey sky.
She was an elfin pinnace; lustily
I dipped my oars into the silent lake,
And, as I rose upon the stroke, my boat
Went heaving through the water like a swan;
When, from behind that craggy steep till then
The horizon's bound, a huge peak, black and huge,
As if with voluntary power instinct
Upreared its head. I struck and struck again,
And growing still in stature the grim shape
Towered up between me and the stars, and still,
For so it seemed, with purpose of its own
And measured motion like a living thing,
Strode after me. With trembling oars I turned,
And through the silent water stole my way
Back to the covert of the willow tree;
There in her mooring-place I left my bark, –
And through the meadows homeward went, in grave
And serious mood; but after I had seen

That spectacle, for many days, my brain
Worked with a dim and undetermined sense
Of unknown modes of being; o'er my thoughts
There hung a darkness, call it solitude
Or blank desertion. No familiar shapes
Remained, no pleasant images of trees,
Of sea or sky, no colours of green fields;
But huge and mighty forms, that do not live
Like living men, moved slowly through the mind
By day, and were a trouble to my dreams.

ANNE SEXTON

With Mercy for the Greedy

(For my friend Ruth who urges me to make an appointment for the Sacrament of Confession)

Concerning your letter in which you ask
me to call a priest and in which you ask
me to wear The Cross that you enclose;
your own cross,
your dog-bitten cross,
no larger than a thumb,
small and wooden, no thorns, this rose –

I pray to its shadow,
that grey place
where it lies on your letter . . . deep, deep.
I detest my sins and I try to believe
in The Cross. I touch its tender hips, its dark jawed face,
its solid neck, its brown sleep.

True. There is
a beautiful Jesus.
HE is frozen to his bones like a chunk of beef.
How desperately he wanted to pull his arms in!
How desperately I touch his vertical and horizontal axes!
But I can't. Need is not quite belief.

All morning long
I have worn
your cross, hung with package string around my throat.
It tapped me lightly as a child's heart might,
tapping secondhand, softly waiting to be born.
Ruth, I cherish the letter you wrote.

My friend, my friend, I was born
doing reference work in sin, and born
confessing it. This is what poems are
with mercy
for the greedy
they are the tongue's wrangle
the world's potage, the rat's star.

2.
COMFORT AND JOY

The mystic leaves behind the possibilities of consolation and plunges himself into the darkness of the cloud of unknowing. He abandons the props and comforting ideas about God and his mercies in a search for God as he is in himself. There are, of course, great joys and ecstasy to be found on this mystical journey, and these will be examined later in the anthology. Most of us, however, know little about such exotic religious experiences, and this section deals with the more ordinary consolations of religion.

In the first poems of the section, we can see the comfort offered by dogma. These are the consoling thoughts about God and his mercies, which the author of *The Cloud of Unknowing* warns the mystic he must spurn as though they were an evil temptation, because, though they have their point in religious practice, they are of no use – indeed they can only impede – once the mystic has started on the mystical journey. However, for Sectarian religious people, they form the staple diet of the religious life. Abraham Ibn Ezra, the twelfth-century Jewish poet, celebrates the consolation the believer finds in the idea of an omnipotent creator: 'in his hand his soul is safe'. This sense of security runs through all joyful celebrations of dogma. God is 'our eternal home'; he's always 'the same'. If life seems bleak, the believer knows that 'God moves in a mysterious way' and that ultimately, as Dame Julian of Norwich said, 'all shall be well and all manner of thing shall be well'. In this comforting world of dogma everything has its function and place; nothing will step out of line and there can be no nasty surprises. The sufferings and vicissitudes of life have been overcome.

The Ancient Mariner after his ordeal found consolation in the religious community. He liked to walk 'together' to church 'in a goodly company'. Being part of the people of God and worshipping together increase the sense of security that faith brings with it. The worshipping Jewish congregation may, says the thirteenth-century poet Joseph Ibn Abithur, be 'earth-bound', but they are in the act of worship at one with the angels in 'the heights of heaven'. Mysteriously, by worshipping together believers are caught up into something greater than themselves. The solitude of unbelief is overcome in the solidarity of community worship. It may be a very human consolation that a religious service offers. Charles Causley, for example, in 'King's College Chapel' feels himself not rapt above himself, but in union with England's past because of the tradition, the building, the music. It is all a part of being English, and deeply, imaginatively reassuring.

However, when we turn to Christina Rossetti's 'Twice', we see a rather more worrying use of religion as compensation. It is a compensation that it is possible to see in many of the consoling religious poems about the after-life. The idea of immortality is perhaps the greatest consolation offered by most religions, but it could be said that the after-life is a profoundly unreligious idea.

Religion is about losing the self, not about assuring its eternal survival and comfort in optimum conditions. We can see this clearly in poems about the earthly and heavenly Jerusalem. The idea of the after-life has never been an important idea in Judaism, and Judah Ha-Levi's poem 'Jerusalem', which is about the earthly city, is much more selfless than those that celebrate the 'Heavenly Jerusalem'. Judah Ha-Levi will not get anything for himself in kissing the stones of the Holy City. The anonymous poem 'Hierusalem, my happy home', on the other hand, could be describing a retirement home for Christians after they have paid, in the good life, their insurance annuity premiums. The buildings, the climate, even the room service and musical entertainment are all excellent. No wonder the poet cries, 'Would God I were in thee!' It is the faith of wish fulfilment that we were examining in the last section taken to its ultimate conclusion. It is 'another country', and all unpleasant things are excluded. It is rather a relief to turn to Hopkins's 'In the Valley of the Elwy', where we return to a heaven on this earth for which God is humbly thanked. Sometimes in poems about Heaven, the poets seem avid for gain and forget to thank God for what he has already given. In nature too Hopkins seemed to find a comfort that he rarely found in religion.

Art also consoles, and it consoles in much the same way as religion. Talking of 'Books' in Book V of *The Prelude*, Wordsworth uses essentially religious vocabulary: 'ecstasy', 'vision', 'divine', 'glory'. Although, like Hopkins, Wordsworth found inspiration in nature, it is precisely the artifice of poetry ('the turnings intricate of verse') that gives it power to reveal 'In flashes' the 'light divine'. Keats and Yeats, in 'Ode on a Grecian Urn' and 'Sailing to Byzantium', also stress the eternal quality of artifice. The work of art is gloriously artificial because it is able to make beautiful very unpleasant things, like unsatisfying love affairs, desolation and old age. Just as ideas of Heaven seek 'another country', the work of art is 'out of nature'. Unlike the poets of Heaven, however, Keats and Yeats don't leave the pain of life out, but gather it 'into the artifice of eternity' by writing beautifully about it and so, in some sense, redeeming it. However, we cannot say exactly how this happens: the Grecian Urn, rather than offering us a few secure articles of faith, refuses to answer any of the poet's questions. It does 'tease us out of thought / As doth eternity', and by making us feel anew that concepts like 'eternity' must always elude thought and reason, the poem helps us to transcend them, for a moment.

Tennyson also warns against seeking too facile a comfort. It is natural for us to want to be consoled but, as Iris Murdoch has said, it can be that almost everything that consoles us is false. As the dying King Arthur prepares to sail away to the legendary heaven of Avilion, he rebukes Sir Bedivere sharply: 'Comfort thyself: what comfort is in me?' There can be no final solution, no creed that is beyond the necessity to change. In fact, 'God fulfils Himself in many ways.' Perhaps it is false to see, as Isaac Watts does, that he is 'to endless years the same'. Arthur no longer has total confidence that there is immortality, that there is Avilion. As he dies his whole mind 'is clouded with a doubt'. At the end Sir Bedivere is left desolate and alone. Similarly, in his mysterious poem 'Cuchulain Comforted', I think that Yeats warns us against too easy a comfort, even in the face of death. Cuchulain has to stop striding round clanking his armour and dreaming of battle. He has to do what everybody else does in the world of the dead, weave his shroud and accept his death. There is a ritual and communal feeling that reminds us of religious ritual with its singing and preordained rites: 'all we do / All must together do.' Cuchulain has no choice, but the Shrouds who advise him to accept his death are convicted cowards.

ABRAHAM IBN EZRA

God Supreme

(translated by David Goldstein)

God aloft in majesty,
Praised be his glory.

He created every form
Seen by us or unknown.
Thought's foundation
Was established with his name,
Who can understand him?

Those who see the good he does,
The paths through which he moves,
Can they deny his excellence?
Everything he has brought to birth
Lives to testify his worth.

A perceiver of his might,
Through his eyes, through his thought,
Through the prophets' inner sight,
Will confess him throughout his life,
For in his hand his soul is safe.

ISAAC WATTS

Our God, our help in ages past,
Our hope for years to come,
Our shelter from the stormy blast,
And our eternal home.

Under the shadow of thy throne
Thy saints have dwelt secure;
Sufficient is thine arm alone,
And our defence is sure.

Before the hills in order stood,
Or earth received her frame,
From everlasting thou art God,
To endless years the same.

Thy Word commands our flesh to dust,
'Return, ye sons of men':
All nations rose from earth at first,
And turn to earth again.

A thousand ages in thy sight
Are like an evening gone;
Short as the watch that ends the night
Before the rising sun.

The busy tribes of flesh and blood
With all their lives and cares
Are carried downwards by thy flood
And lost in following years.

Time like an ever-rolling stream
Bears all its sons away;
They fly forgotten as a dream
Dies at the opening day.

Like flowery fields the nations stand
Pleased with the morning light;
The flowers beneath the mower's hand
Lie withering ere 'tis night.

Our God, our help in ages past,
Our hope for years to come,
Be thou our guard while troubles last,
And our eternal home.

WILLIAM COWPER

Light Shining Out of Darkness

God moves in a mysterious way
His wonders to perform;
He plants his footsteps in the sea,
And rides upon the storm.

Deep in unfathomable mines
Of never-failing skill
He treasures up his bright designs,
And works his sovereign will.

Ye fearful saints fresh courage take;
The clouds ye so much dread
Are big with mercy, and shall break
In blessings on your head.

Judge not the Lord by feeble sense,
But trust him for his grace;
Behind a frowning providence
He hides a smiling face.

His purposes will ripen fast
Unfolding every hour;
The bud may have a bitter taste,
But sweet will be the flower.

Blind unbelief is sure to err,
And scan his work in vain;
God is his own interpreter
And he will make it plain.

JOSEPH ADDISON
Ode

The spacious firmament on high
With all the blue ethereal sky,
And spangled heavens, a shining frame,
Their great Original proclaim:
The unwearied sun, from day to day,
Does his Creator's power display,
And publishes to every land
The work of an almighty hand.

Soon as the evening shades prevail,
The moon takes up the wondrous tale,
And nightly to the listening earth
Repeats the story of her birth:
Whilst all the stars that round her burn,
And all the planets in their turn,
Confirm the tidings as they roll,
And spread the truth from pole to pole.

What though, in solemn silence, all
Move round the dark, terrestrial ball?
What though nor real voice nor sound
Amid their radiant orbs be found?
In reason's ear they all rejoice,
And utter forth a glorious voice,
For ever singing, as they shine,
'The hand that made us is divine'.

JOSEPH IBN ABITHUR

Sanctification

(translated by David Goldstein)

In the heights of heaven is the throne of your dwelling,
And among the earth-bound is your dominion's strength.
These praise your glorious majesty,
And these sanctify your kingdom's name.
There is none holy like the Lord, for there is none beside you.

In the heights of heaven is his throne of praise,
And the hem of his train fills his Temple.
Some on his left side and some on his right,
Above him stand the seraphim.

Among the earth-bound, acknowledged God's people,
They are standing today like poor petitioners,
Praising and thanking the Rock who redeems.
They hallow Jacob's Holy One, the God of Israel.

In the heights of heaven, the exalted angels
Emerge with fear, and return in trembling,
And greet in terror the King, the only One,
Six wings to each and every being.

Among the earth-bound, all the congregations
Approach today with their five prayers.
They sanctify God with a sound of roaring,
And you, the Holy One, dwell among praises.

In the heights of heaven God's name is complete.
Each heart springs up, all flesh bristles.
One troop cries 'Where?' to the other,
And each calls to the other, and proclaims.

Among the earth-bound are the choice of the holy ones,
Possessors of the engraved law, clinging to his name.
The Lord of Hosts arises with a strong hand,
And the Holy God is hallowed in righteousness.

In the heights of heaven are angels of the hosts,
And among the earth-bound, ponderers on the prophet's law.
These glorify with tumultuous shouting,
And these sanctify in hundreds and thousands:
Holy, holy, holy is the Lord of Hosts!

CHARLES CAUSLEY

King's College Chapel

When to the music of Byrd or Tallis,
    The ruffed boys singing in the blackened stalls,
The candles lighting the small bones on their faces,
    The Tudors stiff in marble on the walls,

There comes to evensong Elizabeth or Henry,
    Rich with brocade, pearl, golden lilies, at the altar,
The scarlet lions leaping on their bosoms,
    Pale royal hands fingering the crackling psalter,

Henry is thinking of his lute and of backgammon,
    Elizabeth follows the waving song, the mystery,
Proud in her red wig and green jewelled favours;
    They sit in their white lawn sleeves, as cool as history.

CHRISTINA ROSSETTI

Twice

I took my heart in my hand
    (O my love, O my love),
I said: Let me fall or stand,
    Let me live or die,
But this once hear me speak –
    (O my love, O my love) –
Yet a woman's words are weak;
    You should speak, not I.

You took my heart in your hand
  With a friendly smile,
With a critical eye you scann'd,
  Then set it down.
And said: 'It is still unripe,
  Better wait awhile;
Wait while the skylarks pipe,
  Till the corn grows brown.'

As you set it down it broke –
  Broke, but I did not wince;
I smiled at the speech you spoke,
  At your judgement that I heard:
But I have not often smiled
  Since then, nor question'd since,
Nor cared for cornflowers wild,
  Nor sung with the singing bird.

I take my heart in my hand,
  O my God, O my God,
My broken heart in my hand:
  Thou hast seen, judge Thou.
My hope was written on sand,
  O my God, O my God:
Now let thy judgement stand –
  Yea, judge me now.

This contemn'd of a man,
  This, marred one heedless day,
This heart take thou to scan
  Both within and without:
Refine with fire its gold,
  Purge thou its dross away –
Yea, hold it in Thy hold,
  Whence none can pluck it out.

I take my heart in my hand –
  I shall not die, but live –
Before Thy face I stand;
  I, for Thou callest such:

All that I have I bring,
    All that I am I give,
Smile Thou and I shall sing,
    But shall not question much.

JUDAH HA-LEVI

Jerusalem

(translated by David Goldstein)

Beautiful heights, joy of the world, city of a great king,
For you my soul yearns from the lands of the West.
My pity collects and is roused when I remember the past,
Your glory in exile, and your temple destroyed.
Would that I were on the wings of an eagle,
So that I could water your dust with my mingling tears.
I have sought you, although your king is away,
And snakes and scorpions oust Gilead's balm.
How I shall kiss and cherish your stones.
Your earth will be sweeter than honey to my taste.

ANONYMOUS

Hierusalem, my happy home,
    When shall I come to thee?
When shall my sorrows have an end,
    Thy joys when shall I see?

O happy harbour of the saints,
    O sweet and pleasant soil,
In thee no sorrow may be found
    No grief, no care, no toil . . .

No dampish mist is seen in thee,
    Nor cold nor darksome night;
There every soul shines as the sun,
    There God himself gives light.

There lust and lucre cannot dwell,
 There envy bears no sway;
There is no hunger, heat, nor cold,
 But pleasure every way.

Hierusalem, Hierusalem,
 God grant I once may see
Thy endless joys, and of the same
 Partaker aye to be.

Thy walls are made of precious stones,
 Thy bulwarks diamonds square;
Thy gates are of right orient pearl,
 Exceeding rich and rare.

Thy turrets and thy pinnacles
 With carbuncles do shine;
Thy very streets are paved with gold
 Surpassing clear and fine.

Thy houses are of ivory,
 Thy windows crystal clear,
Thy tiles are made of beaten gold,
 O God that I were there.

Within thy gates nothing doth come
 That is not passing clean;
No spider's web, no dirt, no dust,
 No filth may there be seen.

Ah, my sweet home, Hierusalem,
 Would God I were in thee!
Would God my woes were at an end,
 Thy joys that I might see! . . .

Thy gardens and thy gallant walks
 Continually are green;
There grows such sweet and pleasant flowers
 As nowhere else are seen . . .

Quite through the streets with silver sound
The flood of life doth flow;
Upon whose banks on every side
The wood of life doth grow.

There trees for evermore bear fruit
And evermore do spring;
There evermore the angels sit
And evermore do sing.

There David stands with harp in hand
As master of the Quire;
Ten thousand times that man were blest
That might this music hear.

Our Lady sings *Magnificat*
With tune surpassing sweet;
And all the virgins bear their parts
Sitting about her feet.

Te Deum doth Saint Ambrose sing,
Saint Austin doth the like;
Old Simeon and Zachary
Have not their songs to seek.

There Magdalen hath left her moan
And cheerfully doth sing,
With blessed saints whose harmony
In every street doth ring.

Hierusalem, my happy home,
Would God I were in thee!
Would God my woes were at an end,
Thy joys that I might see!

HENRY VAUGHAN

Peace

My soul, there is a country
    Far beyond the stars,
Where stands a wingèd sentry
    All skilful in the wars:
There, above noise and danger,
    Sweet Peace sits crown'd in smiles,
And One born in a manger
    Commands the beauteous files.
He is thy gracious Friend,
    And – O my soul awake! –
Did in pure love descend,
    To die here for thy sake.
If thou canst get but thither,
    There grows the flower of Peace,
The Rose that cannot wither,
    Thy fortress, and thy ease.
Leave then thy foolish ranges;
    For none can thee secure,
But One, who never changes,
    Thy God, thy life, thy cure.

ROBERT HERRICK

The White Island: Or the Place of the Blest

In this world (the Isle of Dreams)
While we sit by sorrow's streams,
Tears and terrors are our themes
                    Reciting:

But when once from hence we fly,
More and more approaching nigh
Unto young Eternity
                    Uniting:

In that whiter Island, where
Things are evermore sincere,
Candour here and lustre there
Delighting:

There no monstrous fancies shall
Out of hell an horror call,
To create or cause at all
Affrighting.

There in calm and cooling sleep
We our eyes shall never steep,
But eternal watch shall keep,
Attending

Pleasures such as shall pursue
Me immortalized and you,
And fresh joys, as never to
Have ending.

ISAAC WATTS

There is a land of pure delight
Where saints immortal reign;
Infinite day excludes the night,
And pleasures banish pain.

There everlasting spring abides,
And never-withering flowers:
Death like a narrow sea divides
This heavenly land from ours.

Sweet fields beyond the swelling flood
Stand dressed in living green:
So to the Jews old Canaan stood,
While Jordan rolled between.

But timorous mortals start and shrink
  To cross this narrow sea,
And linger shivering on the brink
  And fear to launch away.

O could we make our doubts remove,
  Those gloomy doubts that rise,
And see the Canaan that we love,
  With unbeclouded eyes.

Could we but climb where Moses stood,
  And view the landscape o'er,
Not Jordan's stream, nor Death's cold flood,
  Should fright us from the shore.

GERARD MANLEY HOPKINS
In the Valley of the Elwy

I remember a house where all were good
  To me, God knows, deserving no such thing:
  Comforting smell breathed at very entering,
Fetched fresh, as I suppose, off some sweet wood.
That cordial air made those kind people a hood
  All over, as a bevy of eggs the mothering wing
  Will, or mild nights the new morsels of Spring:
Why, it seemed of course; seemed of right it should.

Lovely the woods, waters, meadows, combes, vales,
All the air things wear that build this world of Wales;
  Only the inmate does not correspond:
God, lover of souls, swaying considerate scales,
Complete thy creature dear O where it fails,
  Being mighty a master, being a father and fond.

WILLIAM WORDSWORTH

From *The Prelude* Book V ('Books')

. . . he, who in his youth
A daily wanderer among woods and fields
With living Nature hath been intimate,
Not only in that raw unpractised time
Is stirred to ecstasy, as others are,
By glittering verse; but further, doth receive,
In measure only dealt out to himself,
Knowledge and increase of enduring joy
From the great Nature that exists in works
Of mighty Poets. Visionary power
Attends the motions of the viewless winds,
Embodied in the mystery of words:
There, darkness makes abode, and all the host
Of shadowy things work endless changes, – there,
As in a mansion like their proper home,
Even forms and substances are circumfused
By that transparent veil with light divine,
And, through the turnings intricate of verse,
Present themselves as objects recognised,
In flashes, and with glory not their own.

JOHN KEATS

Ode on a Grecian Urn

I

Thou still unravish'd bride of quietness,
Thou foster-child of silence and slow time,
Sylvan historian, who canst thus express
A flowery tale more sweetly than our rhyme:
What leaf-fring'd legend haunts about thy shape
Of deities or mortals, or of both,
In Tempe or the dales of Arcady?
What men or gods are these? What maidens loth?

What mad pursuit? What struggle to escape?
What pipes and timbrels? What wild ecstasy?

II

Heard melodies are sweet, but those unheard
Are sweeter; therefore, ye soft pipes, play on;
Not to the sensual ear, but, more endear'd,
Pipe to the spirit ditties of no tone:
Fair youth, beneath the trees, thou canst not leave
Thy song, nor ever can those trees be bare;
Bold Lover, never, never canst thou kiss,
Though winning near the goal – yet, do not grieve;
She cannot fade, though thou hast not thy bliss,
For ever wilt thou love, and she be fair!

III

Ah, happy, happy boughs! that cannot shed
Your leaves, nor ever bid the Spring adieu;
And happy melodist, unwearied,
For ever piping songs for ever new;
More happy love! more happy, happy love!
For ever warm and still to be enjoy'd,
For ever panting, and for ever young;
All breathing human passion far above,
That leaves a heart high-sorrowful and cloy'd,
A burning forehead, and a parching tongue.

IV

Who are these coming to the sacrifice?
To what green altar, O mysterious priest,
Lead'st thou that heifer lowing at the skies,
And all her silken flanks with garlands drest?
What little town by river or sea shore,
Or mountain-built with peaceful citadel,
Is emptied of this folk, this pious morn?
And, little town, thy streets for evermore
Will silent be; and not a soul to tell
Why thou art desolate, can e'er return.

V

O Attic shape! Fair attitude! with brede
Of marble men and maidens overwrought,
With forest branches and the trodden weed;
Thou, silent form, dost tease us out of thought
As doth eternity: Cold Pastoral!
When old age shall this generation waste,
Thou shalt remain, in midst of other woe
Than ours, a friend to man, to whom thou say'st,
'Beauty is truth, truth beauty,' – that is all
Ye know on earth, and all ye need to know.

W. B. YEATS

Sailing to Byzantium

I

That is no country for old men. The young
In one another's arms, birds in the trees
– Those dying generations – at their song,
The salmon-falls, the mackerel-crowded seas,
Fish, flesh, or fowl, commend all summer long
Whatever is begotten, born, and dies.
Caught in that sensual music all neglect
Monuments of unageing intellect.

II

An aged man is but a paltry thing,
A tattered coat upon a stick, unless
Soul clap its hands and sing, and louder sing
For every tatter in its mortal dress,
Nor is there singing school but studying
Monuments of its own magnificence;
And therefore I have sailed the seas and come
To the holy city of Byzantium.

III

O sages standing in God's holy fire
As in the gold mosaic of a wall,

Come from the holy fire, perne in a gyre,
And be the singing-masters of my soul.
Consume my heart away; sick with desire
And fastened to a dying animal
It knows not what it is; and gather me
Into the artifice of eternity.

IV

Once out of nature I shall never take
My bodily form from any natural thing,
But such a form as Grecian goldsmiths make
Of hammered gold and gold enamelling
To keep a drowsy Emperor awake;
Or set upon a golden bough to sing
To lords and ladies of Byzantium
Of what is past, or passing, or to come.

ALFRED, LORD TENNYSON

From 'Morte d'Arthur'

Then loudly cried the bold Sir Bedivere,
'Ah! my Lord Arthur, whither shall I go?
Where shall I hide my forehead and my eyes?
For now I see the true old times are dead,
When every morning brought a noble chance,
And every chance brought out a noble knight.
Such times have been not since the light that led
The holy Elders with the gift of myrrh.
But now the whole ROUND TABLE is dissolved
Which was an image of the mighty world;
And I, the last, go forth companionless,
And the days darken round me, and the years,
Among new men, strange faces, other minds.'
And slowly answered Arthur from the barge:
'The old order changeth, yielding place to new,
And God fulfils Himself in many ways,
Lest one good custom should corrupt the world.
Comfort thyself: what comfort is in me?

I have lived my life, and that which I have done
May He within Himself make pure! but thou,
If thou shouldst never see my face again,
Pray for my soul. More things are wrought by prayer
Than this world dreams of. Wherefore, let thy voice
Rise like a fountain for me night and day.
For what are men better than sheep or goats
That nourish a blind life within the brain,
If, knowing God, they lift not hands of prayer
Both for themselves and those who call them friend?
For so the whole round earth is every way
Bound by gold chains about the feet of God.
But now farewell. I am going a long way
With these thou seest – if indeed I go –
(For all my mind is clouded with a doubt)
To the island-valley of Avilion;
Where falls not hail, or rain, or any snow,
Nor ever wind blows loudly; but it lies
Deep-meadow'd, happy, fair with orchard-lawns
And bowery hollows crown'd with summer sea,
Where I will heal me of my grievous wound.'
So said he, and the barge with oar and sail
Moved from the brink, like some full-breasted swan
That, fluting a wild carol ere her death,
Ruffles her pure cold plume, and takes the flood
With swarthy webs. Long stood Sir Bedivere
Revolving many memories, till the hull
Look'd one black dot against the verge of dawn,
And on the mere the wailing died away.

W. B. YEATS
Cuchulain Comforted

A man that had six mortal wounds, a man
Violent and famous, strode among the dead;
Eyes stared out of the branches and were gone.

Then certain Shrouds that muttered head to head
Came and were gone. He leant upon a tree
As though to meditate on wounds and blood.

A Shroud that seemed to have authority
Among those bird-like things came, and let fall
A bundle of linen. Shrouds by two and three

Came creeping up because the man was still.
And thereupon that linen-carrier said:
'Your life can grow much sweeter if you will

'Obey our ancient rule and make a shroud;
Mainly because of what we only know
The rattle of those arms makes us afraid.

'We thread the needles' eyes, and all we do
All must together do.' That done, the man
Took up the nearest and began to sew.

'Now must we sing and sing the best we can,
But first you must be told our character:
Convicted cowards all, by kindred slain.

'Or driven from home and left to die in fear.'
They sang, but had not human tunes nor words,
Though all was done in common as before;

They had changed their throats and had the throats of birds.

3.
VOCATION

Some people cannot be content with ordinary levels of religious experience. Church services, private contemplation of the 'comfortable words' of religion fail to satisfy them. They want something more immediate. Also, they are not content merely to alot a portion of their lives to religion; for them religion is a full-time job. They are the Professionals. They become monks, Sufis or yōgin. But, as we have already seen, the end of the mystical path is not silence, but after the revelation there has to be a return to the world. Often the religious man feels that he has a mission to the world as a priest or a prophet. He will often say that he has a 'vocation'.

A vocation does not mean that a person literally hears a mysterious voice 'calling' him to greater religious commitment. The call often manifests itself as a need, as a compulsion. We have seen that not everybody is suited by temperament or even by the physical make-up of his brain to be a mystic. So, too, only a few people can be poets. We say poets have a 'gift', as though something has been given them from outside themselves. Unless that 'gift' is there, no amount of sustained effort will help anybody to write a good poem. Nobody forces a poet to write; it is an inner compulsion that makes him labour long and hard to create a poem out of nothingness. Similarly, without the 'mystical' gift or special aptitude for contemplation, nobody can produce that genuinely receptive mystical state. Again, nobody can force the mystic to sit down to the work of meditation. You might be able to force people into monasteries, but the medieval abuses show that once led to water, these reluctant monks and nuns could not drink. The mystical vocation also expresses itself in a compulsion; a mystic has to meditate – he can't be stopped from doing it – any more than a poet can be stopped from writing poetry.

Sometimes, though, both mystics and poets can speak of a definite moment when they knew that they were 'called' to be poets or specially dedicated religious men. The lives of the saints show, again and again, that the religious conversion (the moment when the saint 'converts', or turns his life on its head and falls into the arms of God) often follows some kind of emotional crisis or a prolonged period of stress. William James noted this in *The Varieties of Religious Experience*. 'Thou hast made us for thyself, O Lord,' was the way St Augustine referred to this period of struggle, 'and our hearts are restless until they rest in thee.' Augustine's conversion is typical and follows the regular pattern. For years he had been fighting against a growing conviction that he had to become a Christian. It was an emotional struggle, because he knew that he would have to change the whole pattern of his life. 'Lord, give me chastity,' he used to pray, 'but not yet!' The struggle became a trauma that one day came to a head.

> **I probed the hidden depths of my soul and wrung its pitiful secrets from it, and when I mustered them all before the eyes of my heart, a great storm broke within me, bringing with it a great deluge of tears. I stood up and left Alypius so that I might weep and cry to my heart's content . . . Somehow I flung myself down beneath a fig tree and gave way to the tears which now streamed from my eyes, the sacrifice that is acceptable to you. I had much to say to you, my God, not in these very words but in this strain. *Lord, will you never be content? Must we always taste your vengeance? Forget the long record of our sins.* For I felt that I was still the captive of my sins, and in my misery I kept crying 'How long shall I go on saying "tomorrow, tomorrow"? Why not now? Why not make an end of my ugly sins at this moment?'**

Having worked himself up to this pitch, he suddenly heard the 'singsong voice of a child in the next house'. The voice was singing, 'Take it and read, take it and read.' So he hurried back to Alypius and snatched a book of St Paul's epistles:

> **I seized it and opened it, and in silence I read the first passage on which my eyes fell: *Not in revelling and drunkenness, not in lust and wantonness, not in quarrels and rivalries. Rather, arm yourselves with the Lord Jesus Christ; spend no more thought on nature and nature's appetites* (Romans 13:13–14). I had no wish to read more and no need to do so. For in an instant, as I came to the end of the sentence, it was as though the light of confidence flooded into my heart and all the darkness of doubt was dispelled . . . You converted me to yourself, so that I no longer desired a wife or placed any hope in this world but stood firmly upon the rule of faith. (*Confessions*, Chapter XII)**

On the surface of it there was nothing supernatural about the occurrence at all. It was not a heavenly voice but the voice of a normal child nearby. But as soon as Augustine read the words of St Paul in this exalted frame of mind – words that he'd probably read dozens of time before – he made the break-through. We will see that poets very often experience a 'vocation' after a similar period of stress or struggle, which suggests that there is some perfectly natural process that gives new 'light' when a certain period of tension is reached. Often, James noticed, the break-through occurs when the aspirant for conversion has given up, exhausted by the struggle. It is as though the sudden relaxation from tension throws the mind, by the violent swing of mood, into a new gear. Scientists have tried to explain this very common process. Augustine, however, would not have been interested in their explanations. He knew what had happened to him – God had converted him to himself. The break-through was so sudden that it seemed 'given' to him from the outside.

Other holy men have had visions or heard supernatural voices. The prophets Ezechiel and Isaiah both had visions. The prophet Jeremiah was as reluctant a convert as Augustine, in his own way:

The word of Yahweh was addressed to me, saying,
'Before I formed you in the womb I knew you;
before you came to birth I consecrated you;
I have appointed you as prophet to the nations.'

I said, 'Ah, Lord Yahweh; look, I do not know how to speak: I am a child!'
But Yahweh replied,
'Do not say, "I am a child".
Go now to those to whom I send you
and say whatever I command you.
Do not be afraid of them,
for I am with you to protect you –
it is Yahweh who speaks!'

Then Yahweh put out his hand and touched my mouth and said to me:
'There! I am putting my words into your mouth.'
(Jeremiah 1:1–9)

The prophet is given the gift of divine speech; he is 'inspired' directly with words that are not his own, just as the Apostles were inspired at Pentecost. The prophet's role in Israel was not merely to foretell the future, but to speak 'for' God, to speak in his place and tell Israel what He, Yahweh, thought of her. Similarly, the poet often feels that he has a prophetic role in society, just as the holy men of all ages and of all religions have felt. Indeed, Czeslaw Milosz has recently said that a poet often has a good idea about what will happen in the future too, because of the special way he experiences reality, so that a poet can fulfil the prophetic role by foretelling the future as well as by speaking in the name of a greater Reality about the way things are going in society.

But although many holy men feel that they have a specially divine mission in society, they all feel content to withdraw, in some sense, from the world and seek a solitude. Only in solitude and silence can they meditate and reach that specially receptive state when they can 'receive', or be in touch with a greater Reality or with God. Poets, too, frequently need to withdraw from the world into some kind of solitude, whether they live as literal hermits or by some kind of internal withdrawal.

The first two poems in the section show the 'restlessness' that is felt before 'God' is encountered. The Sandpiper in Elizabeth Bishop's poem rushes about frantically trying to find meaning in the bewildering arbitrariness of his world. The religious man can say, with the Christ of Charles Causley's Normandy crucifix, that God or that meaning are present in the humdrum realities of daily life, but that man cannot make the break-through necessary to find it.

George Herbert, Henry Vaughan and Gerard Manley Hopkins all describe moments of religious 'conversion' that clearly illustrate the pattern we have noticed. All are wrought up to a considerable pitch of stress before they surrender to the experience of the Divine. Herbert hears the voice calling him 'Child!' after intense and furious anguish. Vaughan, on the other hand, has a moment of vision in a 'flash' that is no sooner seen than it disappears. It is interesting that his vision is not outside himself but within himself, within his own psyche. There is almost a Jungian quality to his vision, as though he had recessed back in his subconscious to an earlier period of human life. What he sees is 'of much antiquity', and 'scarce remembred'.

Religious poets like Solomon Ibn Gabirol or Herbert in 'Christmas' see their poetic vocation as a religious experience. Shelley, on the other hand, who was sent down from Oxford for his atheism, was certainly not a religious man, but his vocation to poetry follows the usual pattern of a religious conversion. There is the usual frantic search followed by sudden Ecstasy. The 'Hymn to Intellectual Beauty' concludes the quasi-religious experience with a 'vow', just as the religious man must respond to his 'vision' by some kind of resolution. Wordsworth's experience of a very similar occurrence is much calmer. He was 'worn out' with a worldly life that was uncongenial to him. There was some kind of buried conflict, and, after one night of revelry and 'dissipation', things came to a head, or rather the conflict rose to the surface in a type of vision. He too feels breathed upon, inspired, by something greater than himself ('I made no vows, but vows / Were then made for me') and his response is to make of himself a 'dedicated Spirit'. Coleridge's vision in 'Kubla Khan' is more other-worldly. The poet who has had such a visionary experience has fed on the 'honey-dew' and 'milk of Paradise', and he is now, because of this sacred experience, almost a taboo figure. Moses, after he had been with God on Mount Sinai, had to cover his face with a veil, because the light shining from his face was too great for people to look upon. Shelley too in 'Alastor, or The Spirit of Solitude' sees the poet as a terrifying figure, separated by the force of his experience from ordinary human beings, just as the people surrounding the poet in 'Kubla Khan' cry fearfully 'Beware! Beware!'

Keats, in the selections from 'The Fall of Hyperion', brings together many of the things we have been considering. He too sees the poet's vocation in religious terms among the traditional appurtenances of religion: a temple, a sacrifice, a priestess. The poem takes the form of 'A Dream', which is a traditional way of receiving a divine revelation in all religions. Keats is quite clear that he has a special vocation; not everybody is capable of this kind of activity. His dream, like Vaughan's, seems to tap some ancient level of mankind's experience. The poet's vision is compared to the religious fanatic or dogmatist who 'weaves a paradise for a sect'. The true poet is 'sage' and 'physician' of mankind.

Not all poets have a climactic experience of vocation. Their calling reveals itself in another way. We should not expect Pope to talk in terms of visions when he writes about his poetic vocation. In his 'An Epistle from Mr Pope to Dr Arbuthnot' he shows how poetry is a compulsion, something that he has to do, something, he continues in the *Imitations of Horace*, without which his life would be desolate. It supports him through 'the long disease' of his life in the way that some people's religious vision sustains them. Indeed, the anti-Catholic laws of the period that deprived Pope of an Oxford education and of public life separated him from 'the world' in a way that would have driven him mad, had it not been for his 'Muse'.

Part of the poetic vocation is a sense of having a special mission to the world. William Blake and Moses Ibn Ezra both see their poetry as fulfilling a religious function of healing – restoring the lost innocence and joy of the child – and Moses Ibn Ezra uses the words of Isaiah that Jesus quoted to prove his divine mission about the deaf hearing, the blind seeing and the grief-stricken made joyful once more. But even more frequent is the poet's adoption of the prophetic role. Milton in *Paradise Lost* is the clearest example. His Heavenly Muse is the Spirit of God who spoke to Moses on Mount Sinai. He is also aware that he is sharing in a spiritual creation of 'Things unattempted yet in Prose or Rime' in his attempt to 'justifie the wayes of God to men'. Blake too, in his mysterious poem exhorting the Earth to 'Hear the voice of the Bard!', insists that the poet sees things hidden from ordinary men, that he has been inspired by the 'Holy Word' and can perform a redemption: 'And fallen, fallen light renew!'

All religious men have sought solitude and a disciplined and ascetic lifestyle. The ideal is to withdraw from the confusions of the world, where the peace and the tranquillity required for meditation is impossible. The poet also obviously requires solitude for his creative activity. In the solitude of 'The

Garden' Marvell meditates not by communing with a reality outside himself, but by withdrawing into his mind like a yōgin. Such creative meditation leads to an almost religious 'transcendence' of this world. Solitude was, of course, an important ideal to the Romantic poets, and Shelley, in describing the poet's loneliness in 'Alastor, or The Spirit of Solitude', shows that his separation from other men is so profound that celibacy is a natural outcome. It has often been thought that celibacy was a part of the religious vocation, and celibacy also figures largely and pathetically in 'The Lady of Shalott'. The Lady is clearly a type of creative artist, weaving her tapestry that depicts all she sees in the world. But here something has happened to the solitude. It is no longer voluntarily and lovingly accepted, but forced on the artist by some arbitrary curse. The world is seen as inimical to the artist, for when the Lady does become involved with it, it destorys her. This neurotic hatred of the world parallels the rather unhealthy hatred of the world sometimes expressed by religious writers. Coleridge in 'This Lime-Tree Bower My Prison' helps to redress the balance. Enforced solitude can lead the poet to vision. Just as the religious man is never lonely, neither should the poet be. He should love the world, however solitary he is, not turn from it in hatred.

There is clearly an overlap in the experience of both poets and religious men in the experience of vocation to the religious and poetic way of life. Elizabeth Jennings explores this in her poem 'To a Friend with a Religious Vocation'. At first she stresses the differences between her vocation and that of a nun, but in her very arguments proving that her mode of life is different, we can sense what a deeply 'religious' act poetic creation is for her. The last two poems in the section draw together the ideas we have explored. Farídu'ddín 'Aṭṭár's description of the death of the Phoenix is part of his great religious poem *The Conference of the Birds*, which describes the Sufi Way. It is clearly a religious exhortation to solitude and a *memento mori*. Yet the Phoenix, which has to be solitary for it is unique, is also a poet, a poet like Orpheus in Rilke's sonnet. The 'creatures of silence' gather round the poet and the Phoenix, learn from them as they sing, and the poet takes them over the threshold of poetry to sense the silence that is religion.

ELIZABETH BISHOP

Sandpiper

The roaring alongside he takes for granted,
and that every so often the world is bound to shake.
He runs, he runs to the south, finical, awkward,
in a state of controlled panic, a student of Blake.

The beach hisses like fat. On his left, a sheet
of interrupting water comes and goes
and glazes over his dark and brittle feet.
He runs, he runs straight through it, watching his toes.

– Watching, rather, the spaces of sand between them,
where (no detail too small) the Atlantic drains
rapidly backwards and downwards. As he runs,
he stares at the dragging grains.

The world is a mist. And then the world is
minute and vast and clear. The tide
is higher or lower. He couldn't tell you which.
His beak is focussed; he is preoccupied,

looking for something, something, something.
Poor bird, he is obsessed!
The millions of grains are black, white, tan, and gray,
mixed with quartz grains, rose and amethyst.

EDWARD THOMAS

The Glory

The glory of the beauty of the morning, –
The cuckoo crying over the untouched dew;
The blackbird that has found it, and the dove
That tempts me on to something sweeter than love;
White clouds ranged even and fair as new-mown hay;

The heat, the stir, the sublime vacancy
Of sky and meadow and forest and my own heart: –
The glory invites me, yet it leaves me scorning
All I can ever do, all I can be,
Beside the lovely of motion, shape, and hue,
The happiness I fancy fit to dwell
In beauty's presence. Shall I now this day
Begin to seek as far as heaven, as hell,
Wisdom and strength to match this beauty, start
And tread the pale dust pitted with small dark drops,
In hope to find whatever it is I seek,
Hearkening to short-lived happy-seeming things
That we know naught of, in the hazel copse?
Or must I be content with discontent
As larks and swallows are perhaps with wings?
And shall I ask at the day's end once more
What beauty is, and what I can have meant
By happiness? And shall I let all go,
Glad, weary, or both? Or shall I perhaps know
That I was happy oft and oft before,
Awhile forgetting how I am fast pent,
How dreary-swift, with naught to travel to,
Is Time? I cannot bite the day to the core.

CHARLES CAUSLEY

I am the Great Sun

(From a Normandy crucifix of 1632)

I am the great sun, but you do not see me,
    I am your husband, but you turn away.
I am the captive, but you do not free me,
    I am the captain you will not obey.

I am the truth, but you will not believe me,
    I am the city where you will not stay,
I am your wife, your child, but you will leave me,
    I am that God to whom you will not pray.

I am your counsel, but you do not hear me,
I am the lover whom you will betray,
I am the victor, but you do not cheer me,
I am the holy dove whom you will slay.

I am your life, but you will not name me,
Seal up your soul with tears, and never blame me.

GEORGE HERBERT

The Collar

I struck the board, and cry'd, Nc more.
I will abroad.
What? shall I ever sigh and pine?
My lines and life are free; free as the rode,
Loose as the winde, as large as store.
Shall I be still in suit?
Have I no harvest but a thorn
To let me bloud, and not restore
What I have lost with cordiall fruit?
Sure there was wine
Before my sighs did drie it: there was corn
Before my tears did drown it.
Is the yeare onely lost to me?
Have I no bayes to crown it?
No flowers, no garlands gay? all blasted?
All wasted?
Not so, my heart: but there is fruit,
And thou hast hands.
Recover all thy sigh-blown age
On double pleasures: leave thy cold dispute
Of what is fit, and not. Forsake thy cage,
Thy rope of sands,
Which pettie thoughts have made, and made to thee
Good cable, to enforce and draw,
And be thy law,
While thou didst wink and wouldst not see.

Away; take heed:
I will abroad.
Call in thy deaths head there: tie up thy fears.
He that forbears
To suit and serve his need,
Deserves his load.
But as I rav'd and grew more fierce and wilde
At every word,
Me thoughts I heard one calling, *Child!*
And I reply'd, *My Lord.*

HENRY VAUGHAN

Vanity of Spirit

Quite spent with thoughts I left my Cell, and lay
Where a shrill spring tun'd to the early day.
I beg'd here long, and gron'd to know
Who gave the Clouds so brave a bow,
Who bent the spheres, and circled in
Corruption with this glorious Ring,
What is his name, and how I might
Descry some part of his great light.
I summon'd nature: peirc'd through all her store,
Broke up some seales, which none had touch'd before,
Her wombe, her bosome, and her head
Where all her secrets lay a bed
I rifled quite, and having past
Through all the Creatures, came at last
To search my selfe, where I did find
Traces, and sounds of a strange kind.
Here of this mighty spring, I found some drills,
With Ecchoes beaten from th'eternall hills;
Weake beames, and fires flash'd to my sight,
Like a young East, or Moone-shine night,
Which shew'd me in a nook cast by
A peece of much antiquity,
With Hyerogliphicks quite dismembred,
And broken letters scarce remembred.

I tooke them up, and (much Joy'd,) went about
T'unite those peeces, hoping to find out
The mystery; but this neer done,
That little light I had was gone:
It griev'd me much. At last, said I,
Since in these veyls my Ecclips'd Eye
May not approach thee, (for at night
Who can have commerce with the light?)
I'le disapparell, and to buy
But one half glaunce, most gladly dye.

GERARD MANLEY HOPKINS

From 'The Wreck of the Deutschland'

I

Thou mastering me
God! giver of breath and bread;
World's strand, sway of the sea;
Lord of living and dead;
Thou hast bound bones and veins in me, fastened me flesh,
And after it almost unmade, what with dread,
Thy doing: and dost thou touch me afresh?
Over again I feel thy finger and find thee.

II

I did say yes
O at lightning and lashed rod;
Thou heardst me truer than tongue confess
Thy terror, O Christ, O God;
Thou knowest the walls, altar and hour and night:
The swoon of a heart that the sweep and the hurl of thee trod
Hard down with a horror of height:
And the midriff astrain with leaning of, laced with fire of stress.

III

The frown of his face
Before me, the hurtle of hell
Behind, where, where was a, where was a place?

I whirled out wings that spell
And fled with a fling of the heart to the heart of the Host.
My heart but you were dovewinged, I can tell,
Carrier-witted, I am bold to boast,
To flash from the flame to the flame then, tower from the grace to the grace.

IV

I am soft sift
In an hourglass – at the wall
Fast, but mined with a motion, a drift,
And it crowds and it combs to the fall;
I steady as a water in a well, to a poise, to a pane,
But roped with, always, all the way down from the tall
Fells or flanks of the voel, a vein
Of the gospel proffer, a pressure, a principle, Christ's gift.

SOLOMON IBN GABIROL

In the Morning I Look for You

(translated by David Goldstein)

In the morning I look for you,
My rock and my tower.
I lay my prayers before you,
That day and night are in me.

Before your greatness, I stand,
And am unnerved,
Because your eye will see
The thoughts that are in me.

What is it that the heart
Or the tongue can do,
And what power is there
In the spirit that is in me?

But I know you are pleased
With the songs that men make,
And so I shall praise you
While the divine soul is in me.

GEORGE HERBERT

Christmas

All after pleasures as I rid one day,
My horse and I, both tir'd, bodie and minde,
With full crie of affections, quite astray,
I took up in the next inne I could finde.
There when I came, whom found I but my deare,
My dearest Lord, expecting till the grief
Of pleasures brought me to him, readie there
To be all passengers most sweet relief?
O Thou, whose glorious, yet contracted light,
Wrapt in nights mantle, stole into a manger;
Since my dark soul and brutish is thy right,
To Man of all beasts be not thou a stranger:
Furnish & deck my soul, that thou mayst have
A better lodging then a rack or grave.

The shepherds sing; and shall I silent be?
My God, no hymne for thee?
My soul's a shepherd too; a flock it feeds
Of thoughts, and words, and deeds.
The pasture is thy word: the streams, thy grace
Enriching all the place.
Shepherd and flock shall sing, and all my powers
Out-sing the day-light houres.
Then we will chide the sunne for letting night
Take up his place and right:
We sing one common Lord; wherefore he should
Himself the candle hold.
I will go searching, till I finde a sunne
Shall stay, till we have done;
A willing shiner, that shall shine as gladly,
As frost-nipt sunnes look sadly.
Then we will sing, and shine all our own day,
And one another pay:
His beams shall cheer my breast, and both so twine,
Till ev'n his beams sing, and my musick shine.

PERCY BYSSHE SHELLEY
Hymn to Intellectual Beauty

I

The awful shadow of some unseen Power
Floats though unseen among us, – visiting
This various world with as inconstant wing
As summer winds that creep from flower to flower, –
Like moonbeams that behind some piny mountain shower,
It visits with inconstant glance
Each human heart and countenance;
Like hues and harmonies of evening, –
Like clouds in starlight widely spread, –
Like memory of music fled, –
Like aught that for its grace may be
Dear, and yet dearer for its mystery.

II

Spirit of BEAUTY, that dost consecrate
With thine own hues all thou dost shine upon
Of human thought or form, – where art thou gone?
Why dost thou pass away and leave our state,
This dim vast vale of tears, vacant and desolate?
Ask why the sunlight not for ever
Weaves rainbows o'er yon mountain-river,
Why aught should fail and fade that once is shown,
Why fear and dream and death and birth
Cast on the daylight of this earth
Such gloom, – why man has such a scope
For love and hate, despondency and hope?

III

No voice from some sublimer world hath ever
To sage or poet these responses given –
Therefore the names of Demon, Ghost, and Heaven,
Remain the records of their vain endeavour,
Frail spells – whose uttered charm might not avail to sever,
From all we hear and all we see,
Doubt, chance, and mutability.

Thy light alone – like mist o'er mountains driven,
Or music by the night-wind sent
Through strings of some still instrument,
Or moonlight on a midnight stream,
Gives grace and truth to life's unquiet dream.

IV

Love, Hope, and Self-esteem, like clouds depart
And come, for some uncertain moments lent.
Man were immortal, and omnipotent,
Didst thou, unknown and awful as thou art,
Keep with thy glorious train firm state within his heart.
Thou messenger of sympathies,
That wax and wane in lovers' eyes –
Thou – that to human thought art nourishment,
Like darkness to a dying flame!
Depart not as thy shadow came,
Depart not – lest the grave should be,
Like life and fear, a dark reality.

V

While yet a boy I sought for ghosts, and sped
Through many a listening chamber, cave and ruin,
And starlight wood, with fearful steps pursuing
Hopes of high talk with the departed dead.
I called on poisonous names with which our youth is fed;
I was not heard – I saw them not –
When musing deeply on the lot
Of life, at that sweet time when winds are wooing
All vital things that wake to bring
News of birds and blossoming, –
Sudden, thy shadow fell on me;
I shrieked, and clasped my hands in ecstasy!

VI

I vowed that I would dedicate my powers
To thee and thine – have I not kept the vow?
With beating heart and streaming eyes, even now
I call the phantoms of a thousand hours
Each from his voiceless grave: they have in visioned bowers
Of studious zeal or love's delight

Outwatched with me the envious night –
They know that never joy illumed my brow
Unlinked with hope that thou wouldst free
This world from its dark slavery,
That thou – O awful LOVELINESS,
Wouldst give whate'er these words cannot express.

VII

The day becomes more solemn and serene
When noon is past – there is a harmony
In autumn, and a lustre in its sky,
Which through the summer is not heard or seen,
As if it could not be, as if it had not been!
Thus let thy power, which like the truth
Of nature on my passive youth
Descended, to my onward life supply
Its calm – to one who worships thee,
And every form containing thee,
Whom, SPIRIT fair, thy spells did bind
To fear himself, and love all human kind.

WILLIAM WORDSWORTH

From *The Prelude* Book IV ('Summer Vacation')

. . . that heartless chase
Of trivial pleasures was a poor exchange
For books and nature at that early age.
'Tis true, some casual knowledge might be gained
Of character or life; but at that time,
Of manners put to school I took small note,
And all my deeper passions lay elsewhere.
Far better had it been to exalt the mind
By solitary study, to uphold
Intense desire through meditative peace;
And yet, for chastisement of these regrets,
The memory of one particular hour
Doth here rise up against me. 'Mid a throng
Of maids and youths, old men, and matrons staid,

A medley of all tempers, I had passed
The night in dancing, gaiety and mirth,
With din of instruments and shuffling feet,
And glancing forms, and tapers glittering,
And unaimed prattle flying up and down;
Spirits upon the stretch, and here and there
Slight shocks of young love-liking interspersed,
Whose transient pleasure mounted to the head,
And tingled through the veins. Ere we retired,
The cock had crowed, and now the eastern sky
Was kindling, nor unseen, from humble copse
And open field, through which the pathway wound,
And homeward led my steps. Magnificent
The morning rose, in memorable pomp,
Glorious as e'er I had beheld – in front,
The sea lay laughing at a distance; near,
The solid mountains shone, bright as the clouds,
Grain-tinctured, drenched in empyrean light;
And in the meadows and the lower grounds
Was all the sweetness of a common dawn –
Dews, vapours, and the melody of birds,
And labourers going forth to till the fields.

Ah! need I say, dear Friend! that to the brim
My heart was full; I made no vows, but vows
Were then made for me; bond unknown to me
Was given, that I should be, else sinning greatly,
A dedicated Spirit. On I walked
In thankful blessedness, which yet survives.

SAMUEL TAYLOR COLERIDGE

From 'Kubla Khan'

A damsel with a dulcimer
In a vision once I saw:
It was an Abyssinian maid,
And on her dulcimer she played,
Singing of Mount Abora.

Could I revive within me
Her symphony and song,
To such a deep delight 'twould win me,
That with music loud and long,
I would build that dome in air,
That sunny dome! those caves of ice!
And all who heard should see them there,
And all should cry, Beware! Beware!
His flashing eyes, his floating hair!
Weave a circle round him thrice,
And close your eyes with holy dread,
For he on honey-dew hath fed,
And drunk the milk of Paradise.

PERCY BYSSHE SHELLEY

From 'Alastor, or The Spirit of Solitude'

. . . wildly he wandered on,
Day after day a weary waste of hours,
Bearing within his life the brooding care
That ever fed on its decaying flame.
And now his limbs were lean; his scattered hair
Sered by the autumn of strange suffering
Sung dirges in the wind; his listless hand
Hung like dead bone within its withered skin;
Life, and the lustre that consumed it, shone
As in a furnace burning secretly
From his dark eyes alone. The cottagers,
Who ministered with human charity
His human wants, beheld with wondering awe
Their fleeting visitant. The mountaineer,
Encountering on some dizzy precipice
That spectral form, deemed that the Spirit of wind
With lightning eyes, and eager breath, and feet
Disturbing not the drifted snow, had paused
In its career: the infant would conceal
His troubled visage in his mother's robe
In terror at the glare of those wild eyes,

To remember their strange light in many a dream
Of after-times; but youthful maidens, taught
By nature, would interpret half the woe
That wasted him, would call him with false names
Brother, and friend, would press his pallid hand
At parting, and watch, dim through tears, the path
Of his departure from their father's door.

JOHN KEATS

From 'The Fall of Hyperion'

A Dream

Fanatics have their dreams, wherewith they weave
A paradise for a sect; the savage too
From forth the loftiest fashion of his sleep
Guesses at Heaven; pity these have not
Trac'd upon vellum or wild Indian leaf
The shadows of melodious utterance.
But bare of laurel they live, dream, and die;
For Poesy alone can tell her dreams,
With the fine spell of words alone can save
Imagination from the sable charm
And dumb enchantment. Who alive can say,
'Thou art no Poet – may'st not tell thy dreams'?
Since every man whose soul is not a clod
Hath visions, and would speak, if he had loved,
And been well nurtured in his mother tongue.
Whether the dream now purpos'd to rehearse
Be poet's or fanatic's will be known
When this warm scribe my hand is in the grave.

. . .

How long I slumber'd 'tis a chance to guess.
When sense of life return'd, I started up
As if with wings; but the fair trees were gone,
The mossy mound and arbour were no more:

I look'd around upon the carved sides
Of an old sanctuary with roof august,
Builded so high, it seem'd that filmed clouds
Might spread beneath, as o'er the stars of heaven;
So old the place was, I remember'd none
The like upon the Earth: what I had seen
Of grey cathedrals, buttress'd walls, rent towers,
The superannuations of sunk realms,
Or Nature's rocks toil'd hard in waves and winds,
Seem'd but the faulture of decrepit things
To that eternal domed Monument. –

. . .

'Are there not thousands in the world,' said I,
Encouraged by the sooth voice of the shade,
'Who love their fellows even to the death,
'Who feel the giant agony of the world,
'And more, like slaves to poor humanity,
'Labour for mortal good? I sure should see
'Other men here; but I am here alone.'
'Those whom thou spak'st of are no vision'ries,'
Rejoined that voice – 'They are no dreamers weak,
'They seek no wonder but the human face;
'No music but a happy-noted voice –
'They come not here, they have no thought to come –
'And thou art here, for thou art less than they –
'What benefit canst thou, or all thy tribe,
'To the great world? Thou art a dreaming thing,
'A fever of thyself – think of the Earth;
'What bliss even in hope is there for thee?
'What haven? every creature hath its home;
'Every sole man hath days of joy and pain,
'Whether his labours be sublime or low –
'The pain alone; the joy alone; distinct:
'Only the dreamer venoms all his days,
'Bearing more woe than all his sins deserve.'

. . .

So answer'd I, continuing, 'If it please,
'Majestic shadow, tell me: sure not all
'Those melodies sung into the World's ear
'Are useless: sure a poet is a sage;
'A humanist, physician to all men.
'That I am none I feel, as vultures feel
'They are no birds when eagles are abroad.
'What am I then: Thou spakest of my tribe:
'What tribe?' The tall shade veil'd in drooping white
Then spake, so much more earnest, that the breath
Moved the thin linen folds that drooping hung
About a golden censer from the hand
Pendent – 'Art thou not of the dreamer tribe?
'The poet and the dreamer are distinct,
'Diverse, sheer opposite, antipodes.
'The one pours out a balm upon the World,
'The other vexes it.' Then shouted I
Spite of myself, and with a Pythia's spleen,
'Apollo! faded! O far flown Apollo!
'Where is thy misty pestilence to creep
'Into the dwellings, through the door crannies
'Of all mock lyrists, large self worshipers
'And careless Hectorers in proud bad verse.
'Though I breathe death with them it will be life
'To see them sprawl before me into graves.'

ALEXANDER POPE

From 'An Epistle from Mr Pope to Dr Arbuthnot'

Why did I write? what sin to me unknown
Dipt me in Ink, my Parents' or my own?
As yet a Child, nor yet a Fool to Fame,
I lisp'd in Numbers, for the Numbers came.
I left no Calling for this idle trade,
No Duty broke, no Father dis-obey'd.
The Muse but serv'd to ease some Friend, not Wife,
To help me thro' this long Disease, my Life.

From *Imitations of Horace*

The Second Epistle of the Second Book of Horace Imitated

Bred up at home, full early I begun
To read in Greek, the Wrath of Peleus' Son.
Besides, my Father taught me from a Lad,
The better Art to know the good from bad:
(And little sure imported to remove,
To hunt for Truth in *Maudlin*'s learned Grove.)
But knottier Points we knew not half so well,
Depriv'd us soon of our Paternal Cell;
And certain Laws, by Suff'rers thought unjust,
Deny'd all Posts of Profit or of Trust:
Hopes after Hopes of pious Papists fail'd,
While mighty WILLIAM's thundring Arm prevail'd.
For Right Hereditary tax'd and fin'd,
He stuck to Poverty with Peace of Mind;
And me, the Muses help'd to undergo it;
Convict a Papist He, and I a Poet.
But (thanks to *Homer*) since I live and thrive,
Indebted to no Prince or Peer alive,
Sure I should want the Care of ten *Monroes*,*
If I would scribble, rather than repose.
    Years foll'wing Years, steal something ev'ry day,
At last they steal us from our selves away;
In one our Frolicks, one Amusements end,
In one a Mistress drops, in one a Friend:
This subtle Thief of Life, this paltry Time,
What will it leave me, if it snatch my Rhime?
If ev'ry Wheel of that unweary'd Mill
That turn'd ten thousand Verses, now stands still.

* Dr Monroe was Physician to Bedlam Hospital.

WILLIAM BLAKE

Piping down the valleys wild,
Piping songs of pleasant glee,
On a cloud I saw a child,
And he laughing said to me:

'Pipe a song about a Lamb!'
So I piped with merry chear.
'Piper, pipe that song again;'
So I piped: he wept to hear.

'Drop thy pipe, thy happy pipe,
'Sing thy songs of happy chear:'
So I sung the same again,
While he wept with joy to hear.

'Piper, sit thee down and write
'In a book that all may read.'
So he vanish'd from my sight,
And I pluck'd a hollow reed,

And I made a rural pen,
And I stain'd the water clear,
And I wrote my happy songs
Every child may joy to hear.

MOSES IBN EZRA

The Garden of Song

(translated by David Goldstein)

All who are sick at heart and cry in bitterness,
Let not your soul complain in grief.
Enter the garden of my songs, and find balm
For your sorrow, and sing there with open mouth.
Honey compared with them is bitter to the taste,

And before their scent, flowing myrrh is rank.
Through them the deaf hear, the stutterers speak,
The blind see, and the halting run.
The troubled and grief-stricken rejoice in them,
All who are sick at heart, and cry in bitterness.

JOHN MILTON

From *Paradise Lost* Book I

Of Mans First Disobedience, and the Fruit
Of that Forbidd'n Tree, whose mortal tast
Brought death into the World, and all our woe,
With loss of *Eden*, till one greater Man
Restore us, and regain the blissful Seat,
Sing Heav'nly Muse, that on the secret top
Of *Oreb*, or of *Sinai*, didst inspire
That Shepherd, who first taught the chosen Seed,
In the Beginning how the Heav'ns and Earth
Rose out of *Chaos*: Or if *Sion* Hill
Delight thee more, and *Siloa's* Brook that flowd
Fast by the Oracle of God; I thence
Invoke thy aid to my adventrous Song,
That with no middle flight intends to soar
Above th' *Aonian* Mount; while it persues
Things unattempted yet in Prose or Rime.
And chiefly Thou O Spirit, that dost preferr
Before all Temples th'upright heart and pure,
Instruct me, for Thou know'st; Thou from the first
Wast present, and with mighty wings outspred
Dove-like satst brooding on the vast Abyss
And mad'st it pregnant: What in mee is dark
Illumin, what is low raise and support;
That to the highth of this great Argument
I may assert Eternal Providence,
And justifie the wayes of God to men.

WILLIAM BLAKE

Hear the voice of the Bard!
Who Present, Past, & Future, sees;
Whose ears have heard
The Holy Word
That walk'd among the ancient trees,

Calling the lapsèd Soul,
And weeping in the evening dew;
That might controll
The starry pole,
And fallen, fallen light renew!

'O Earth, O Earth, return!
'Arise from out the dewy grass;
'Night is worn,
'And the morn
'Rises from the slumberous mass.

'Turn away no more;
'Why wilt thou turn away?
'The starry floor,
'The wat'ry shore,
'Is given thee till the break of day.'

From the *Bhagavad-Gita*

Book VI (the 'Atmasanyamayōg')
(translated by Sir Edwin Arnold)

The sovereign soul
Of him who lives self-governed and at peace
Is centred in itself, taking alike
Pleasure and pain; heat, cold; glory and shame.
He is the Yōgi, he is *Yukta*, glad
With joy of light and truth; dwelling apart

Upon a peak, with senses subjugate
Whereto the clod, the rock, the glistering gold
Show all as one. By this sign is he known
Being of equal grace to comrades, friends,
Chance-comers, strangers, lovers, enemies,
Aliens and kinsmen; loving all alike,
Evil or good.
    Sequestered should he sit,
Steadfastly meditating, solitary,
His thoughts controlled, his passions laid away,
Quit of belongings. In a fair, still spot
Having his fixed abode, – not too much raised,
Nor yet too low, – let him abide, his goods
A cloth, a deerskin, and the Kuśa-grass.
There, setting hard his mind upon The One,
Restraining heart and senses, silent, calm,
Let him accomplish Yōga, and achieve
Pureness of soul, holding immovable
Body and neck and head, his gaze absorbed
Upon his nose-end, rapt from all around,
Tranquil in spirit, free of fear, intent
Upon his Brahmacharya vow, devout,
Musing on Me, lost in the thought of Me.
That Yōgin, so devoted, so controlled,
Comes to the peace beyond, – My peace, the peace
Of high Nirvana!

GERARD MANLEY HOPKINS

Heaven-Haven

(A nun takes the veil)

    I have desired to go
        Where springs not fail,
To fields where flies no sharp and sided hail
    And a few lilies blow.

And I have asked to be
Where no storms come,
Where the green swell is in the havens dumb,
And out of the swing of the sea.

ALEXANDER POPE

From *Imitations of Horace*

The Second Epistle of the Second Book of Horace Imitated

But grant I may relapse, for want of Grace,
Again to rhime, can *London* be the Place?
Who there his Muse, or Self, or Soul attends?
In Crouds and Courts, Law, Business, Feasts and Friends?
My Counsel sends to execute a Deed:
A Poet begs me, I will hear him read:
In Palace-Yard at Nine you'll find me there –
At Ten for certain, Sir, in Bloomsb'ry-Square –
Before the Lords at Twelve my Cause comes on –
There's a Rehearsal, Sir, exact at One. –
'Oh but a Wit can study in the Streets,
And raise his Mind above the Mob he meets.'
Not quite so well however as one ought;
A Hackney-Coach may chance to spoil a Thought,
And then a nodding Beam, or Pig of Lead,
God knows, may hurt the very ablest Head.
Have you not seen at Guild-hall's narrow Pass,
Two Aldermen dispute it with an Ass?
And Peers give way, exalted as they are,
Ev'n to their own S-r-v- -nce* in a Carr?
Go, lofty Poet! and in such a Croud,
Sing thy sonorous Verse – but not aloud.
Alas! to Grotto's and to Groves we run,
To Ease and Silence, ev'ry Muse's Son.

* S-r-v- -nce: Sir-reverence, i.e. human excrement.

ANDREW MARVELL

The Garden

I

How vainly men themselves amaze
To win the Palm, the Oke, or Bayes;
And their incessant Labours see
Crown'd from some single Herb or Tree,
Whose short and narrow verged Shade
Does prudently their Toyles upbraid;
While all Flow'rs and all Trees do close
To weave the Garlands of repose.

II

Fair quiet, have I found thee here,
And Innocence thy Sister dear!
Mistaken long, I sought you then
In busie Companies of Men.
Your sacred Plants, if here below,
Only among the Plants will grow.
Society is all but rude,
To this delicious Solitude.

III

No white nor red was ever seen
So am'rous as this lovely green.
Fond Lovers, cruel as their Flame,
Cut in these Trees their Mistress name.
Little, Alas, they know, or heed,
How far these Beauties Hers exceed!
Fair Trees! where s'eer your barkes I wound,
No Name shall but your own be found.

IV

When we have run our Passions heat,
Love hither makes his best retreat.
The *Gods*, that mortal Beauty chase
Still in a Tree did end their race.
Apollo hunted *Daphne* so,

Only that She might Laurel grow.
And *Pan* did after *Syrinx* speed,
Not as Nymph, but for a Reed.

V

What wond'rous Life is this I lead!
Ripe Apples drop about my head;
The Luscious Clusters of the Vine
Upon my Mouth do crush their Wine;
The Nectaren, and curious Peach,
Into my hands themselves do reach;
Stumbling on Melons, as I pass,
Insnar'd with Flow'rs, I fall on Grass.

VI

Mean while the Mind, from pleasure less,
Withdraws into its happiness:
The Mind, that Ocean where each kind
Does streight its own resemblance find;
Yet it creates, transcending these,
Far other Worlds, and other Seas;
Annihilating all that's made
To a green Thought in a green Shade.

VII

Here at the Fountains sliding foot,
Or at some Fruit-trees mossy root,
Casting the Bodies Vest aside,
My Soul into the boughs does glide:
There like a Bird it sits, and sings,
Then whets, and combs its silver Wings;
And, till prepar'd for longer flight,
Waves in its Plumes the various Light.

VIII

Such was that happy Garden-state,
While Man there walk'd without a Mate:
After a Place so pure and sweet,
What other Help could yet be meet!
But 'twas beyond a Mortal's share
To wander solitary there:

Two Paradises 'twere in one
To live in Paradise alone.

IX

How well the skilful Gardner drew
Of flow'rs and herbes this Dial new;
Where from above the milder Sun
Does through a fragrant Zodiack run;
And, as it works, th' industrious Bee
Computes its time as well as we.
How could such sweet and wholsome Hours
Be reckon'd but with herbs and flow'rs!

PERCY BYSSHE SHELLEY

From 'Alastor, or The Spirit of Solitude'

There was a Poet whose untimely tomb
No human hands with pious reverence reared,
But the charmed eddies of autumnal winds
Built o'er his mouldering bones a pyramid
Of mouldering leaves in the waste wilderness: –
A lovely youth, – no mourning maiden decked
With weeping flowers, or votive cypress wreath,
The lone couch of his everlasting sleep: –
Gentle and brave, and generous, – no lorn bard
Breathed o'er his dark fate one melodious sigh:
He lived, he died, he sung, in solitude.
Strangers have wept to hear his passionate notes,
And virgins, as unknown he passed, have pined
And wasted for fond love of his wild eyes.
The fire of those soft orbs has ceased to burn,
And Silence, too enamoured of that voice,
Locks its mute music in her rugged cell.

ALFRED, LORD TENNYSON

The Lady of Shalott

I

On either side the river lie
Long fields of barley and of rye,
That clothe the wold and meet the sky;
And thro' the field the road runs by
    To many-tower'd Camelot;
And up and down the people go,
Gazing where the lilies blow
Round an island there below,
    The island of Shalott.

Willows whiten, aspens quiver,
Little breezes dusk and shiver
Thro' the wave that runs for ever
By the island in the river
    Flowing down to Camelot.
Four gray walls and four gray towers,
Overlook a space of flowers,
And the silent isle imbowers
    The Lady of Shalott.

By the margin, willow-veil'd,
Slide the heavy barges trail'd
By slow horses; and unhail'd
The shallop flitteth silken-sail'd
    Skimming down to Camelot:
But who hath seen her wave her hand?
Or at the casement seen her stand?
Or is she known in all the land,
    The Lady of Shalott?

Only reapers, reaping early
In among the bearded barley,
Hear a song that echoes cheerly
From the river winding clearly,
    Down to tower'd Camelot:

And by the moon the reaper weary,
Piling sheaves in uplands airy,
Listening, whispers, ''Tis the fairy
  Lady of Shalott.'

II

There she weaves by night and day
A magic web with colours gay.
She has heard a whisper say,
A curse is on her if she stay
  To look down to Camelot.
She knows not what the curse may be,
And so she weaveth steadily,
And little other care hath she,
  The Lady of Shalott.

And moving thro' a mirror clear
That hangs before her all the year,
Shadows of the world appear.
There she sees the highway near
  Winding down to Camelot:
There the river eddy whirls,
And there the surly village-churls,
And the red cloaks of market girls,
Pass onward from Shalott.

Sometimes a troop of damsels glad,
An abbot on an ambling pad,
Sometimes a curly shepherd-lad,
Or long-hair'd page in crimson clad,
  Goes by to tower'd Camelot;
And sometimes thro' the mirror blue
The knights come riding two and two:
She hath no loyal knight and true,
  The Lady of Shalott.

But in her web she still delights
To weave the mirror's magic sights,
For often thro' the silent nights
A funeral, with plumes and lights

And music, went to Camelot;
Or when the moon was overhead,
Came two young lovers lately wed;
'I am half sick of shadows,' said
The Lady of Shalott.

III

A bow-shot from her bower-eaves,
He rode between the barley-sheaves,
The sun came dazzling thro' the leaves,
And flamed upon the brazen greaves
Of bold Sir Lancelot.
A red-cross knight for ever kneel'd
To a lady in his shield,
That sparkled on the yellow field,
Beside remote Shalott.

The gemmy bridle glitter'd free,
Like to some branch of stars we see
Hung in the golden Galaxy.
The bridle bells rang merrily
As he rode down to Camelot:
And from his blazon'd baldric slung
A mighty silver bugle hung,
And as he rode his armour rung,
Beside remote Shalott.

All in the blue unclouded weather
Thick-jewell'd shone the saddle-leather,
The helmet and the helmet-feather
Burn'd like one burning flame together,
As he rode down to Camelot.
As often thro' the purple night,
Below the starry clusters bright,
Some bearded meteor, trailing light,
Moves over still Shalott.

His broad clear brow in sunlight glow'd;
On burnish'd hooves his war-horse trode;
From underneath his helmet flow'd
His coal-black curls as on he rode,

As he rode down to Camelot.
From the bank and from the river
He flash'd into the crystal mirror,
'Tirra lirra,' by the river
Sang Sir Lancelot.

She left the web, she left the loom,
She made three paces thro' the room,
She saw the water-lily bloom,
She saw the helmet and the plume,
She look'd down to Camelot.
Out flew the web and floated wide;
The mirror crack'd from side to side;
'The curse is come upon me,' cried
The Lady of Shalott.

IV

In the stormy east-wind straining,
The pale yellow woods were waning,
The broad stream in his banks complaining,
Heavily the low sky raining
Over tower'd Camelot;
Down she came and found a boat
Beneath a willow left afloat,
And round about the prow she wrote
The Lady of Shalott.

And down the river's dim expanse
Like some bold seër in a trance,
Seeing all his own mischance –
With a glassy countenance
Did she look to Camelot.
And at the closing of the day
She loosed the chain, and down she lay;
The broad stream bore her far away,
The Lady of Shalott.

Lying, robed in snowy white
That loosely flew to left and right –
The leaves upon her falling light –

Thro' the noises of the night
    She floated down to Camelot:
And as the boat-head wound along
The willowy hills and fields among,
They heard her singing her last song,
    The Lady of Shalott.

Heard a carol, mournful, holy,
Chanted loudly, chanted lowly,
Till her blood was frozen slowly,
And her eyes were darken'd wholly,
    Turn'd to tower'd Camelot.
For ere she reach'd upon the tide
The first house by the water-side,
Singing in her song she died,
    The Lady of Shalott.

Under tower and balcony,
By garden-wall and gallery,
A gleaming shape she floated by,
Dead-pale between the houses high,
    Silent into Camelot.
Out upon the wharfs they came,
Knight and burgher, lord and dame,
And round the prow they read her name,
    The Lady of Shalott.

Who is this? and what is here?
And in the lighted palace near
Died the sound of royal cheer;
And they cross'd themselves for fear,
    All the knights of Camelot:
But Lancelot mused a little space;
He said, 'She has a lovely face;
God in his mercy lend her grace,
    The Lady of Shalott.'

SAMUEL TAYLOR COLERIDGE

This Lime-Tree Bower My Prison

(In June of 1797 some long-expected friends paid a visit to the author's cottage; and on the morning of their arrival, he met with an accident, which disabled him from walking during the whole time of their stay. One evening, when they had left him for a few hours, he composed the following lines in the garden-bower.)

Well, they are gone, and here must I remain,
This lime-tree bower my prison! I have lost
Beauties and feelings, such as would have been
Most sweet to my remembrance even when age
Had dimm'd mine eyes to blindness! They, meanwhile,
Friends, whom I never more may meet again,
On springy heath along the hill-top edge,
Wander in gladness, and wind down, perchance,
To that still roaring dell, of which I told;
The roaring dell, o'erwooded, narrow, deep,
And only speckled by the mid-day sun;
Where its slim trunk the ash from rock to rock
Flings arching like a bridge; – that branchless ash,
Unsunn'd and damp, whose few poor yellow leaves
Ne'er tremble in the gale, yet tremble still,
Fann'd by the water-fall! and there my friends
Behold the dark green file of long lank weeds,
That all at once (a most fantastic sight!)
Still nod and drip beneath the dripping edge
Of the blue clay-stone.

Now, my friends emerge
Beneath the wide wide Heaven – and view again
The many-steepled tract magnificent
Of hilly fields and meadows, and the sea,
With some fair bark, perhaps, whose sails light up
The slip of smooth clear blue betwixt two Isles
Of purple shadow! Yes! they wander on
In gladness all; but thou, methinks, most glad,

My gentle-hearted Charles! for thou hast pined
And hunger'd after Nature, many a year,
In the great City pent, winning thy way
With sad yet patient soul, through evil and pain
And strange calamity! Ah! slowly sink
Behind the western ridge, thou glorious Sun!
Shine in the slant beams of the sinking orb,
Ye purple heath-flowers! richlier burn, ye clouds!
Live in the yellow light, ye distant groves!
And kindle, thou blue Ocean! So my friend
Struck with deep joy may stand, as I have stood,
Silent with swimming sense; yea, gazing round
On the wide landscape, gaze till all doth seem
Less gross than bodily; and of such hues
As veil the Almighty Spirit, when yet he makes
Spirits perceive his presence.

A delight
Comes sudden on my heart, and I am glad
As I myself were there! Nor in this bower,
This little lime-tree bower, have I not mark'd
Much that has sooth'd me. Pale beneath the blaze
Hung the transparent foliage; and I watch'd
Some broad and sunny leaf, and lov'd to see
The shadow of the leaf and stem above
Dappling its sunshine! And that walnut-tree
Was richly ting'd, and a deep radiance lay
Full on the ancient ivy, which usurps
Those fronting elms, and now, with blackest mass
Makes their dark branches gleam a lighter hue
Through the late twilight: and though now the bat
Wheels silent by, and not a swallow twitters,
Yet still the solitary humble-bee
Sings in the bean-flower! Henceforth I shall know
That Nature ne'er deserts the wise and pure;
No plot so narrow, be but Nature there,
No waste so vacant, but may well employ
Each faculty of sense, and keep the heart
Awake to Love and Beauty! and sometimes
'Tis well to be bereft of promis'd good,
That we may lift the soul and contemplate

With lively joy the joys we cannot share.
My gentle-hearted Charles! when the last rook
Beat its straight path along the dusky air
Homewards, I blest it! deeming its black wing
(Now a dim speck, now vanishing in light)
Had cross'd the mighty Orb's dilated glory,
While thou stood'st gazing; or, when all was still,
Flew creeking o'er thy head, and had a charm
For thee, my gentle-hearted Charles, to whom
No sound is dissonant which tells of Life.

ELIZABETH JENNINGS

To a Friend with a Religious Vocation

(For C.)

Thinking of your vocation, I am filled
With thoughts of my own lack of one. I see
Within myself no wish to breed or build
Or take the three vows ringed by poverty.
    And yet I have a sense,
Vague and inchoate, with no symmetry,
Of purpose. Is it merely a pretence,

A kind of scaffolding which I erect
Half out of fear, half out of laziness?
The fitful poems come but can't protect
The empty areas of loneliness.
    You know what you must do,
So that mere breathing is a way to bless.
Dark nights, perhaps, but no grey days for you.

Your vows enfold you. I must make my own;
Now this, now that, each one empirical.
My poems move from feelings not yet known,
And when the poem is written I can feel
    A flash, a moment's peace.
The curtain will be drawn across your grille.
My silences are always enemies.

Yet with the same convictions that you have
(It is but your vocation that I lack),
I must, like you, believe in perfect love.
It is the dark, the dark that draws me back
Into a chaos where
Vocations, visions fail, the will grows slack
And I am stunned by silence everywhere.

FARİDU'DDİN 'AṬṬĀR

From *The Conference of the Birds*

(translated by Afkham Darbandi and Dick Davis)

In India lives a bird that is unique:
The lovely phoenix has a long, hard beak
Pierced with a hundred holes, just like a flute –
It has no mate, its reign is absolute.
Each opening has a different sound; each sound
Means something secret, subtle and profound –
And as these shrill, lamenting notes are heard,
A silence falls on every listening bird;
Even the fish grow still. It was from this
Sad chant a sage learnt music's artifice.
The phoenix' life endures a thousand years
And, long before, he knows when death appears;
When death's sharp pangs assail his tiring heart,
And all signs tell him he must now depart,
He builds a pyre from logs and massy trees
And from this centre sings sad threnodies –
Each plaintive note trills out, from each pierced hole
Comes evidence of his untarnished soul –
Now like a mourner's ululating cries,
Now with an inward care the cadence dies –
And as he sings of death, death's bitter grief
Thrills through him and he trembles like a leaf.
Then drawn to him by his heart-piercing calls
The birds approach, and savage animals –
They watch, and watching grieve; each in his mind
Determines he will leave the world behind.

Some weep in sympathy and some grow faint;
Some die to hear his passionate complaint.
So death draws near, and as the phoenix sings
He fans the air with his tremendous wings,
A flame darts out and licks across the pyre –
Now wood and phoenix are a raging fire,
Which slowly sinks from that first livid flash
To soft, collapsing charcoal, then to ash:
The pyre's consumed – and from the ashy bed
A little phoenix pushes up its head.
What other creature can – throughout the earth –
After death takes him, to himself give birth?
If you were given all the phoenix' years,
Still you would have to die when death appears.
For years he sings in solitary pain
And must companionless, unmated, reign;
No children cheer his age and at his death
His ash is scattered by the wind's cold breath.
Now understand that none, however sly,
Can slip past death's sharp claws – we all must die;
None is immortal in the world's vast length;
This wonder shows no creature has the strength
To keep death's ruthless vehemence in check –
But we must soften his imperious neck;
Though many tasks will fall to us, this task
Remains the hardest that the Way will ask.

RAINER MARIA RILKE

From *Sonnets to Orpheus*

First Part, I
(translated by J. B. Leishman)

A tree ascending there. O pure transcension!
O Orpheus sings! O tall tree in the ear!
All noise suspended, yet in that suspension
what new beginning, beckoning, change, appear!

Creatures of silence pressing through the clear
disintricated wood from lair and nest;
and neither cunning, it grew manifest,
had made them breathe so quietly, nor fear,

but only hearing. Roar, cry, bell they found
within their hearts too small. And where before
less than a hut had harboured what came thronging,

a refuge tunnelled out of dimmest longing
with lowly entrance through a quivering door,
you built them temples in their sense of sound.

4.
SEX AND RELIGION

Christianity has always been hostile to sex, and so in the West we tend to separate sex and religion. Yet, in its condemnation of sex, Christianity is unusual. In the last section we touched briefly on celibacy, which is often seen as part of the mystical calling and a help to meditation. This is not universal, however. Judaism, being a religion based upon race, has no time for celibacy. Indeed, it used to be the case that before a Jew was allowed to embark on the mystical study of the *Kaballah*, it was considered essential that he was married, so that his libido was not unhealthily suppressed, which could be a danger on the mystical journey. The lives of some of the Christian saints certainly bear witness to the dangers of repression when it is combined with intensive meditation. As we have seen, the confrontation with the subconscious is dangerous unless the mystic is a balanced person. It could clearly be emphasized if there were some kind of sexual disturbance. Mohammad encouraged marriage and sexual intercourse; he said that there was to be 'no monkery in Islam'. Celibacy is not binding on the Sufi, and indeed the Sufis have always used the image of sexual love as an image of man's union with Allah. Some forms of Buddhism and Hinduism have used sex as a help to meditation and yōga. Today, a Buddhist who is intensely occupied in meditation might abandon sex for a time. Some Buddhists find that it is incompatible with meditation or that meditation is so enjoyable in itself that they don't need sex any more. But no Buddhist would impose celibacy on another. A choice of celibacy must come from within or it will be useless, and certainly any sexual guilt or unhealthy repression would be an 'unskilful state', embedding man firmly in the ego.

Why Christianity, of all the religions of the world, is so hostile to sexuality is a complicated question. Sex came to be seen as linked in some way with Original Sin, and so full of evil. The theologians who were most opposed to sex – Jerome, Augustine and Luther, for example – were all men who had had violent and passionate conversions of the type we have been considering in this book. This type of personality William James calls the 'twice-born' mentality. They have been 'born again' to a new life at their conversion. People who have had this kind of violent experience, James says, tend to be more unbalanced than those whose religion has developed peacefully without any emotional storms. Certainly one could say this of Augustine, Jerome and Luther. Most of these 'twice-born' theologians had a problem with sex and regarded their sexual past with loathing. In the desert when he was a hermit, Jerome was plagued by visions of naked ladies; Augustine's conversion troubles were nearly all sexual. It is also true that 'twice-born' theologians tend to adopt theologies that are fundamentalist, dogmatic and rigidly opposed to opposition. They are, therefore, for all their intensive spirituality, very far from the agnosticism of the mystical ideal. It is also true that unfortunately 'twice-born' people are often extremely brilliant, extremely forceful and have had, therefore, an enormous influence on Christianity. It is interesting that the rigid, dogmatic outlook that is a characteristic of Sectarian religion should be associated with sexual repression.

It is easy to see how sexuality could, provided it is not grasping and selfish, be a help to spirituality. The religious man seeks to break through the limitations of his ego, to transcend himself. He wants to experience God as He is, not as the ego thinks He ought to be. Sexual passion does give us a momentary transcendence. Even in unhappy love, we feel the limitations of our being and long to transcend them to be one with the beloved. Simone Weil has said that love is the 'sudden realization that somebody else absolutely exists'. When the lover realizes somebody's absolute existence, he does not love that person simply because he or she has qualities that suit his ego.

In the first two poems of the section, Blake shows us the repressions of Christianity, repressions that can lead to the sickness and perversion described by M. G. Mainwaring. In *Paradise Lost* Milton insists that before the Fall, Adam and Eve certainly had sex, whatever the hypocrites say about 'puritie and place and innocence'. Not only did unfallen man enjoy sex, Milton says, the angels do too. It is difficult to imagine how, as they have no bodies, and Adam is clearly perplexed and Raphael blushes with embarrassment and confusion. Nevertheless, they agree that love 'Leads up to Heav'n, is both the way and guide'. Sex is not merely something permitted – it can actually be conducive to religious experience. In 'The Everlasting Gospel' Blake denounces what Milton had called the hypocrisy of the Christian disapproval of sexuality. It is an hypocrisy that is clearly shown by the Bishop in Yeats's 'Crazy Jane' poem. The Bishop shows absolutely no Christian charity; he is extremely unkind in his condemnation of Jane's sexuality. Jane, however, proudly replies that 'fair needs foul'. St Augustine had also said that the place of Love was 'the place of excrement' to make Christians ashamed of their sexuality, but for Crazy Jane nothing can be 'spiritual' or 'holy' unless it has been smashed open and invaded by passion.

Love poems show us how religion and passion are allied. In Thomas Hardy's fourth 'She to Him' sonnet, the rejected woman shows the selflessness that belongs to great love. Love has helped her to transcend herself; her being is 'Fused from its separateness by ecstasy'. On the other hand, the difficulty we have in sustaining this transcendence in love can make us appreciate how earth-bound and limited we are, in a way that we perhaps might not have realized before. In 'Two in the Campagna' Browning wants to leave himself behind and be fused with the beloved totally, but he can't. He is left only with an acute realization of 'the pain / Of finite hearts'. But sometimes the self feels that it has escaped itself and fused with another, as Donne wittily explains in 'The Extasie', playing with the ideal of religious ecstasy when the soul leaves the body. In 'The Dreame' he even goes so far as to hint that love is in some way a revelation of the divine.

This last idea might seem blasphemous, but it is one that has constantly been used in religion. Both the Jewish and the Christian Scriptures have been quite happy to include 'The Song of Solomon', which is (despite the pious exegesis that makes of it an allegory of Christ's love for the Church) simply a secular love poem. The 'Song' has constantly been used by mystics to illustrate the union of Christ and the soul. We can see this in Teresa of Avila's 'I gave myself to Love Divine', though in this poem I feel a little worry about some kind of imaginative compensation going on. Teresa of Avila lived in sixteenth-century Spain, and was therefore much influenced by both Moorish and Arab poetry. Islam has always made a strong use of the imagery of sexual passion in describing the Love of God. Ḥafíẓ, in 'Love's hidden pearl is shining yet', shows how in passion man transcends his own individual feelings and joins the great universal emotions that are ineffable and cannot be 'divined' or conceived.

To abstract sexuality from life is impossible. D. M. Thomas shows this clearly in 'The Puberty Tree'; he suggests that his poetic imagination is almost literally rooted in his sexuality, and that both are intimately linked with a sense of mystery in the dark night. Instead of being renounced should not the erotic be used creatively? The Sanskrit poem 'When he saw her' rather wittily makes the point that sex can lead us directly to the contemplation of the divine. The great sixteenth-century Persian mystic Jámí is quite clear in his poem 'Even from earthly love thy face avert not' that to have experienced sexual love is a prerequisite for the spiritual life. Sufi mysticism is deeply sensual. So passionate were the poems of the Sufi mystic Ibnu 'l-'Arabí that he had quite a job persuading fellow-Sufis that poems like 'O her beauty – the tender maid!' really *were* religious, and had to write lengthy commentaries to prove that this was so.

It could be said that the erotic and the mystical are inseparable. To look at a pretty girl, as D. H. Lawrence suggests, can shatter the musings of dogmatic theology. Milosz, in the poem '*Esse*', shows how contemplation has an erotic dimension. Gazing at a girl on the Metro, the poet is 'dumbfounded' by her absolute reality: '*I am, she is.*' He is caught beyond the desire to possess or to grasp selfishly to an appreciation of the 'immensity of existing things' and a new appreciation of the confines of the ego and his separation from reality. It is the sort of 'love' that Simone Weil writes about. Milosz himself says of this poem that the title '*Esse*' has a religious dimension. God is Himself Existence, Being. To be forced beyond selfishness into an apprehension of being, however it comes, is to contemplate the Divine. That this contemplation is erotic should not be surprising. What is religion but the intercourse of God and man?

WILLIAM BLAKE

The Garden of Love

I went to the Garden of Love,
And saw what I never had seen:
A Chapel was built in the midst,
Where I used to play on the green.

And the gates of this Chapel were shut,
And 'Thou shalt not' writ over the door;
So I turn'd to the Garden of Love
That so many sweet flowers bore;

And I saw it was filled with graves,
And tomb-stones where flowers should be;
And Priests in black gowns were walking their rounds,
And binding with briars my joys & desires.

Ah! Sun-flower

Ah, Sun-flower! weary of time,
Who countest the steps of the Sun,
Seeking after that sweet golden clime
Where the traveller's journey is done:

Where the Youth pined away with desire,
And the pale Virgin shrouded in snow
Arise from their graves, and aspire
Where my Sun-flower wishes to go.

M. G. MAINWARING

Gothic columns of petrified motion
bursting into static fountains of stone
strive to raise cathedrals to heaven.
Above their spires, in the serene anguish
of azure skies, the buzzard circles
in long, dizzy, languid spirals
with his eye fixed on the earth below.

Worthy as monuments to the endless quest
to harvest blue roses, they are also
the tombs of the animating force
exhausting itself in a lost cause;
Cenotaphs built before the final count
they will survive the last knight errant
pursuing his own shadow into oblivion.

A sparrow trapped in the twilight of an attic
unsettles the dust with its demented flight
before succumbing to the fatal stillness.
The flesh is purged . . . and the residual bone
moulded by the tongue of patient decay
eerily gleams in some dark recess,
a banished memory refusing to die.

And thus lingered on the wasted spirit
in the empty splendour of its own mausoleum,
honing its teeth on the numb stone,
gnawing at the trailing hem of a shadow;
the itch in the knotted breast of Christ
trapped in the wooden gesture of hope
with the edge of a scream carved on his lips.

'*Eli, eli, lama sabacthani*', pierced
the smoke hanging over Gehenna.
The high priest felt a cold wind pass
and hid his face in the folds of his robe;
the still flame sank back into the wax;
the darkness rustled, and the veil
of the temple was rent in twain.

And now, like a madman patrolling the kingdom
of his cell, all night it roams the vaulted dark
awaiting the ritual of a brief resurrection.
Then – in the furtive light of a false dawn
when the fox returns to the wood's dark shore,
they come – a stealthy procession of hooded ghosts,
the unravished brides of an impotent God.

At first they crouch in secret prayer
suckling at their milkless breasts
the stillborn dream of an hermetic passion;
and then they raise their jealous gaze
to she whose high immaculate purity
is beyond emulation, for chastity can't heal
the dumb craving of the hidden wound.

And though the blood will continue to drip
until the flesh begins to fail, it is no more
than a twist of red, fading in polluted water,
returning to the earth that which it gave;
a hideous parable of the captive spirit
languishing in a sterile cell, a weary flame
drowning in a bed of pious ash.

Yet never to drown for nothing can rid
the flesh of its burden; not hands clasped
in silent prayer, nor pale lips parted
in vain petition to that smug eidolon;
for I have heard high above the hollow
purity of their song, an irreligious descant,
the sound of wailing from the stairless tower.

JOHN MILTON

From *Paradise Lost* Book IV

. . . into thir inmost bower
Handed they went; and eas'd the putting off
These troublesom disguises which wee wear,
Strait side by side were laid, nor turnd I weene
Adam from his fair Spouse, nor *Eve* the Rites
Mysterious of connubial Love refus'd:
Whatever Hypocrits austerely talk
Of puritie and place and innocence,
Defaming as impure what God declares
Pure, and commands to som, leaves free to all.
Our Maker bids increase, who bids abstain
But our Destroyer, foe to God and Man?
Haile wedded Love, mysterious Law, true sourse
Of human ofspring, sole proprietie
In Paradise of all things common else.
By thee adulterous lust was driv'n from men
Among the bestial herds to raunge, by thee
Founded in Reason, Loyal, Just, and Pure,
Relations dear, and all the Charities
Of Father, Son, and Brother first were known.
Farr be it, that I should write thee sin or blame,
Or think thee unbefitting holiest place,
Perpetual Fountain of Domestic sweets,
Whose Bed is undefil'd and chast pronounc't,
Present, or past, as Saints and Patriarchs us'd.
Here Love his gold'n shafts imploies, here lights
His constant Lamp, and waves his purple wings,
Reigns here and revels; not in the bought smile
Of Harlots, loveless, joyless, unindeard,
Casual fruition, nor in Court Amours,
Mixt Dance, or wanton Mask, or Midnight Ball,
Or Seranate, which the starv'd Lover sings
To his proud fair, best quitted with disdain.
These lulld by Nightingales imbraceing slept,
And on thir naked limbs the flourie roof
Showrd Roses, which the Morn repaird. Sleep on,

Blest pair; and O yet happiest if ye seek
No happier state, and know to know no more.

From *Paradise Lost* Book VIII

[Adam in conversation with the Archangel Raphael]

Love thou saist
Leads up to Heav'n, is both the way and guide;
Bear with me then, if lawful what I ask;
Love not the heav'nly Spirits, and how thir Love
Express they, by looks onely, or do they mix
Irradiance, virtual or immediat touch?
To whom the Angel with a smile that glowd
Celestial rosie red, Loves proper hue,
Answerd. Let it suffice thee that thou know'st
Us happie, and without Love no happiness.
Whatever pure thou in the body enjoy'st
(And pure thou wert created) wee enjoy
In eminence, and obstacle find none
Of membrane, joint, or limb, exclusive barrs:
Easier then Air with Air, if Spirits embrace,
Total they mix, Union of Pure with Pure
Desiring; nor restraind conveyance need
As Flesh to mix with Flesh, or Soul with Soul.

WILLIAM BLAKE

From 'The Everlasting Gospel'

Was Jesus Chaste? or did he
Give any Lessons of Chastity?
The morning blush'd fiery red:
Mary was found in Adulterous bed;
Earth groan'd beneath, & Heaven above
Trembled at discovery of Love.

Jesus was sitting in Moses' Chair,
They brought the trembling Woman There.
Moses commands she be stoned to death,
What was the sound of Jesus' breath?
He laid His hand on Moses' Law:
The Ancient Heavens, in Silent Awe
Writ with Curses from Pole to Pole,
All away began to roll:
The Earth trembling & Naked lay
In secret bed of Mortal Clay,
On Sinai felt the hand divine
Putting back the bloody shrine,
And she heard the breath of God
As she heard by Eden's flood:
'Good & Evil are no more!
'Sinai's trumpets, cease to roar!
'Cease, finger of God, to write!
'The Heavens are not clean in thy Sight.
'Thou art Good, & Thou Alone;
'Nor may sinner cast one stone.
'To be Good only, is to be
'A God or else a Pharisee.
'Thou Angel of the Presence Divine
'That didst create this Body of Mine,
'Wherefore hast thou writ these Laws
'And Created Hell's dark jaws?
'My Presence I will take from thee:
'A Cold Leper thou shalt be.
'Tho' thou wast so pure & bright
'That Heaven was Impure in thy Sight,
'Tho' thy Oath turn'd Heaven Pale,
'Tho' thy Covenant built Hell's Jail,
'Tho' thou didst all to Chaos roll
'With the Serpent for its soul,
'Still the breath Divine does move
'And the breath Divine is Love.
'Mary, Fear Not! Let me see
'The Seven Devils that torment thee:
'Hide not from my Sight thy Sin,
'That forgiveness thou maist win.
'Has no Man Condemned thee?'

'No Man, Lord:' 'then what is he
'Who shall Accuse thee? Come Ye forth,
'Fallen fiends of Heav'nly birth
'That have forgot your Ancient love
'And driven away my trembling Dove
'You shall bow before her feet;
'You shall lick the dust for Meat;
'And tho' you cannot Love, but Hate,
'Shall be beggars at Love's Gate.
'What was thy love? Let me see it;
'Was it love or dark deceit?'
'Love too long from Me has fled;
''Twas dark deceit, to Earn my bread;
''Twas Covet, or 'twas Custom, or
'Some trifle not worth caring for;
'That they may call a shame & Sin
'Love's temple that God dwelleth in,
'And his in secret hidden Shrine
'The Naked Human form divine,
'And render that a Lawless thing
'On which the Soul Expands its wing.
'But this, O Lord, this was my Sin
'When first I let these Devils in
'In dark pretence to Chastity:
'Blaspheming Love, blaspheming thee.
'Thence Rose Secret Adulteries,
'And thence did Covet also rise.
'My sin thou hast forgiven me,
'Canst thou forgive my Blasphemy?
'Canst thou return to this dark Hell,
'And in my burning bosom dwell?
'And canst thou die that I may live?
'And canst thou Pity & forgive?'
Then Roll'd the shadowy Man away
From the Limbs of Jesus, to make them his prey,
An Ever devouring appetite
Glittering with festering Venoms bright,
Crying, 'Crucify this cause of distress,
'Who don't keep the secrets of Holiness!
'All Mental Power by Diseases we bind,
'But he heals the deaf & the Dumb & the Blind.

'Whom God has afflicted for Secret Ends,
'He Comforts & Heals & calls them Friends.'
But, when Jesus was Crucified,
Then was perfected his glitt'ring pride:
In three Nights he devour'd his prey,
And still he devours the Body of Clay;
For dust & Clay is the Serpent's meat,
Which never was made for Man to Eat.

*

I am sure This Jesus will not do
Either for Englishman or Jew.
Seeing this False Christ, In fury & Passion
I made my Voice heard all over the Nation.

. . .

Was Jesus Born of a Virgin Pure
With narrow Soul & looks demure?
If he intended to take on Sin
The Mother should an Harlot been,
Just such a one as Magdalen
With seven devils in her Pen;
Or were Jew Virgins still more Curst,
And more sucking devils nurst?
Or what was it which he took on
That he might bring Salvation?
A Body subject to be Tempted,
From neither pain nor grief Exempted?
Or such a body as might not feel
The passions that with Sinners deal?
Yes, but they say he never fell.
Ask Caiaphas; for he can tell.
'He mock'd the Sabbath, & he mock'd
'The Sabbath's God, & he unlock'd
'The Evil spirits from their Shrines,
'And turn'd Fishermen to Divines;
'O'erturn'd the Tent of Secret Sins,
'& its Golden cords & Pins –
''Tis the bloody Shrine of War

'Pinn'd around from Star to Star,
'Halls of justice, hating Vice,
'Where the devil Combs his lice.
'He turn'd the devils into Swine
'That he might tempt the Jews to dine;
'Since which, a Pig has got a look
'That for a Jew may be mistook.
'"Obey your parents." – What says he?
'"Woman, what have I to do with thee?
'"No Earthly Parents I confess:
'"I am doing my Father's Business."
'He scorn'd Earth's Parents, scorn'd Earth's God,
'And mock'd the one & the other's Rod;
'His Seventy Disciples sent
'Against Religion & Government:
'They by the Sword of Justice fell
'And him their Cruel Murderer tell.
'He left his Father's trade to roam
'A wand'ring Vagrant without Home;
'And thus he others' labour stole
'That he might live above Controll.
'The Publicans & Harlots he
'Selected for his Company,
'And from the Adulteress turn'd away
'God's righteous Law, that lost its Prey.'

W. B. YEATS

Crazy Jane Talks with the Bishop

I met the Bishop on the road
And much said he and I.
'Those breasts are flat and fallen now,
Those veins must soon be dry;
Live in a heavenly mansion,
Not in some foul sty.'

'Fair and foul are near of kin,
And fair needs foul,' I cried.

'My friends are gone, but that's a truth
Nor grave nor bed denied,
Learned in bodily lowliness
And in the heart's pride.

'A woman can be proud and stiff
When on love intent;
But Love has pitched his mansion in
The place of excrement;
For nothing can be sole or whole
That has not been rent.'

THOMAS HARDY

She to Him

IV

This love puts all humanity from me;
I can but maledict her, pray her dead,
For giving love and getting love of thee –
Feeding a heart that else mine own had fed!

How much I love I know not, life not known,
Save as one unit I would add love by;
But this I know, my being is but thine own –
Fused from its separateness by ecstasy.

And thus I grasp thy amplitudes, of her
Ungrasped, though helped by nigh-regarding eyes;
Canst thou then hate me as an envier
Who see unrecked what I so dearly prize?
Believe me, Lost One, Love is lovelier
The more it shapes its moan in selfish-wise.

ROBERT BROWNING

Two in the Campagna

I wonder do you feel to-day
As I have felt since, hand in hand,
We sat down on the grass, to stray
In spirit better through the land,
This morn of Rome and May?

For me, I touched a thought, I know,
Has tantalized me many times,
(Like turns of thread the spiders throw
Mocking across our path) for rhymes
To catch at and let go.

Help me to hold it! First it left
The yellowing fennel, run to seed
There, branching from the brickwork's cleft,
Some old tomb's ruin: yonder weed
Took up the floating weft,

Where one small orange cup amassed
Five beetles, – blind and green they grope
Among the honey-meal: and last,
Everywhere on the grassy slope
I traced it. Hold it fast!

The champaign with its endless fleece
Of feathery grasses everywhere!
Silence and passion, joy and peace,
An everlasting wash of air –
Rome's ghost since her decease.

Such life here, through such lengths of hours,
Such miracles performed in play,
Such primal naked forms of flowers,
Such letting nature have her way
While heaven looks from its towers!

How say you? Let us, O my dove,
    Let us be unashamed of soul,
As earth lies bare to heaven above!
    How is it under our control
To love or not to love?

I would that you were all to me,
    You that are just so much, no more.
Nor yours nor mine, nor slave nor free!
    Where does the fault lie? What the core
O' the wound, since wound must be?

I would I could adopt your will,
    See with your eyes, and set my heart
Beating by yours, and drink my fill
    At your soul's springs, – your part my part
In life, for good and ill.

No. I yearn upward, touch you close,
    Then stand away. I kiss your cheek,
Catch your soul's warmth – I pluck the rose
    And love it more than tongue can speak –
Then the good minute goes.

Already how am I so far
    Out of that minute? Must I go
Still like the thistle-ball, no bar,
    Onward, whenever light winds blow,
Fixed by no friendly star?

Just when I seemed about to learn!
    Where is the thread now? Off again!
The old trick! Only I discern –
    Infinite passion, and the pain
Of finite hearts that yearn.

JOHN DONNE
The Extasie

Where, like a pillow on a bed,
    A Pregnant banke swel'd up, to rest
The violets reclining head,
    Sat we two, one anothers best.
Our hands were firmely cimented
    With a fast balme, which thence did spring,
Our eye-beames twisted, and did thred
    Our eyes, upon one double string;
So to'entergraft our hands, as yet
    Was all the meanes to make us one,
And pictures in our eyes to get
    Was all our propagation.
As 'twixt two equal Armies, Fate
    Suspends uncertaine victorie,
Our soules, (which to advance their state,
    Were gone out,) hung 'twixt her, and mee.
And whil'st our soules negotiate there,
    Wee like sepulchrall statues lay;
All day, the same our postures were,
    And wee said nothing, all the day.
If any, so by love refin'd,
    That he soules language understood,
And by good love were growen all minde,
    Within convenient distance stood,
He (though he knew not which soule spake,
    Because both meant, both spake the same)
Might thence a new concoction take,
    And part farre purer then he came.
This Extasie doth unperplex
    (We said) and tell us what we love,
Wee see by this, it was not sexe,
    Wee see, we saw not what did move:
But as all severall soules containe
    Mixture of things, they know not what,
Love, these mixt soules doth mixe againe,
    And makes both one, each this and that.

A single violet transplant,
The strength, the colour, and the size,
(All which before was poore, and scant,)
Redoubles still, and multiplies.
When love, with one another so
Interinanimates two soules,
That abler soule, which thence doth flow,
Defects of lonelinesse controules.
Wee then, who are this new soule, know,
Of what we are compos'd, and made,
For, th'Atomies of which we grow,
Are soules, whom no change can invade.
But O alas, so long, so farre
Our bodies why doe wee forbeare?
They'are ours, though they'are not wee, Wee are
The intelligences, they the spheare.
We owe them thankes, because they thus,
Did us, to us, at first convay,
Yeelded their forces, sense, to us,
Nor are drosse to us, but allay.
On man heavens influence workes not so,
But that it first imprints the ayre,
Soe soule into the soule may flow,
Though it to body first repaire.
As our blood labours to beget
Spirits, as like soules as it can,
Because such fingers need to knit
That subtile knot, which makes us man:
So must pure lovers soules descend
T'affections, and to faculties,
Which sense may reach and apprehend,
Else a great Prince in prison lies.
To'our bodies turne wee then, that so
Weake men on love reveal'd may looke;
Loves mysteries in soules doe grow,
But yet the body is his booke.
And if some lover, such as wee,
Have heard this dialogue of one,
Let him still marke us, he shall see
Small change, when we'are to bodies gone.

The Dreame

Deare love, for nothing lesse then thee
Would I have broke this happy dreame,
    It was a theame
For reason, much too strong for phantasie,
Therefore thou wakd'st me wisely; yet
My Dreame thou brok'st not, but continued'st it,
Thou art so truth, that thoughts of thee suffice,
To make dreames truths; and fables histories;
Enter these armes, for since thou thoughtst it best
Not to dreame all my dreame, let's act the rest.

As lightning, or a Tapers light,
Thine eyes, and not thy noise wak'd mee;
    Yet I thought thee
(For thou lovest truth) an Angell, at first sight,
But when I saw thou sawest my heart,
And knew'st my thoughts, beyond an Angels art,
When thou knew'st what I dreamt, when thou knew'st when
Excesse of joy would wake me, and cam'st then,
I must confesse, it could not chuse but bee
Prophane, to thinke thee any thing but thee.

Comming and staying show'd thee, thee,
But rising makes me doubt, that now,
    Thou art not thou.
That love is weake, where feare's as strong as hee;
'Tis not all spirit, pure and brave,
If mixture it of *Feare*, *Shame*, *Honor*, have.
Perchance as torches which must ready bee,
Men light and put out, so thou deal'st with mee,
Thou cam'st to kindle, goest to come; Then I
Will dreame that hope againe, but else would die.

From 'The Song of Solomon'

(Authorized Version)

I am come into my garden, my sister, my spouse,
I have gathered my Myrrhe with my spice,
I have eaten my honiecombe with my hony,
I have drunke my wine with my milke:
eate, O friends, drinke, yea drinke abundantly, O beloved!

I sleepe, but my heart waketh: it is the voyce of my beloved that knocketh,
saying, Open to me, my sister, my love, my dove, my undefiled:
for my head is filled with dewe, and my lockes with the drops of the night.

I have put off my coate,
how shall I put it on?
I have washed my feete,
how shall I defile them?

My beloved put in his hand by the hole of the dore,
and my bowels were moved for him.
I rose up to open to my beloved,
and my hands dropped with myrrhe,
and my fingers with sweete smelling myrrhe,
upon the handles of the locke.

I opened to my beloved, but my beloved had with drawen himselfe,
and was gone:
my soule failed when hee spake:
I sought him, but I could not find him:
I called him, but he gave me no answere.

The watchmen that went about the citie, found me,
they smote me, they wounded me,
the keepers of the walles tooke away my vaile from me.

I charge you, O daughters of Ierusalem,
if ye find my beloved,
that ye tell him, that I am sick of love.

What is thy beloved more then another beloved,
O thou fairest among women?
what is thy beloved more then another beloved,
that thou doest so charge us?

My beloved is white and ruddy,
the chiefest among tenne thousand.
His head is as the most fine gold,
his locks are bushy, and blacke as a Raven.
His eyes are as the eyes of doves by the rivers of water,
washed with milk and fitly set.
His cheekes are as a bed of spices,
as sweete flowers:
his lippes like lillies,
dropping sweete smelling myrrhe.
His hands are as gold rings set with the Berill:
His belly is as bright ivorie, overlayd with Saphires.
His legges are as pillars of marble, set upon sockets of fine gold:
his countenance is as Lebanon, excellent as the Cedars.
His mouth is most sweete, yea he is altogether lovely.
This is my beloved, and this is my friend,
O daughters of Ierusalem.

Whither is thy beloved gone?
O thou fairest among women,
whither is thy beloved turned aside?
that we may seeke him with thee.

My beloved is gone downe into his garden, to the beds of spices,
to feede in the gardens, and to gather lillies.

I am my beloveds, & my beloved is mine:
he feedeth among the lillies.

. . .

O that thou wert as my brother that sucked the brests of my mother,
when I should find thee without, I would kisse thee,
yet I should not be despised.
I would leade thee and bring thee into my mothers house,
who would instruct me:

I would cause thee to drinke of spiced wine,
of the iuice of my pomegranate.
His left hand should be under my head,
and his right hand should embrace me.

I charge you, O daughters of Ierusalem,
that ye stirre not up, nor awake my love untill he please.

(Who is this that commeth up from the wildernesse,
leaning upon her beloved?)

I raised thee up under the apple tree:
there thy mother brought thee forth,
there she brought thee forth that bare thee.

Set mee as a seale upon thy heart,
as a seale upon thine arme:
for love is strong as death,
iealousie is cruel as the grave:
the coales thereof are coals of fire, which hath a most vehement flame.
Many waters cannot quench love,
neither can the floods drowne it:
if a man would give all the substance of his house for love,
it would utterly be condemned.

TERESA OF AVILA

(translated by E. Allison Peers)

I gave myself to Love Divine,
And lo! my lot so changèd is
That my Beloved One is mine
And I at last am surely His.

When that sweet Huntsman from above
First wounded me and left me prone,
Into the very arms of Love
My stricken soul forthwith was thrown.
Since then my life's no more my own

And all my lot so changèd is
That my Beloved One is mine
And I at last am surely His.

The dart wherewith He wounded me
Was all embarbèd round with love,
And thus my spirit came to be
One with its Maker, God above.
No love but this I need to prove:
My life to God surrender'd is
And my Beloved One is mine
And I at last am surely His.

ḤAFÍẒ

(translated by R. A. Nicholson)

Love's hidden pearl is shining yet,
And Love's sealed casket bears the same device
As it bore of old;
The tears with which mine eyes are wet
Roll, as yesterday they rolled,
Roll, as they shall roll to-morrow,
Fraught with blood of sacrifice,
From the same fountain of eternal sorrow.

Ah, could my heart but speak
Or thou divine
What passion-flower is this
That lent its colour to those lips of thine!
What ruby blushes o'er thy lovely cheek,
Dreaming of the sun's hot kiss
In the darkness of the mine!
Ah, could my heart but speak
Or thou divine!

D. M. THOMAS

The Puberty Tree

My puberty tree swayed big, saw-edged leaves
by the open window, and rustled in my sleep
and when I lay awake on the drenched sheet,
for the nights were hot.

I stared at it, whether I woke or slept:
huge black saw-edged leaves against the moonlight.
It pulsed secretly. An immense spider crept
out of it in the dark

and dropped with a light swish into my room:
the Moon-spider, mother of the soft
harmless tarantulas that came inside indeed,
sometimes, and to which

I'd wake in the pale-green dawn or when the fierce
sun was already striking. The puberty tree
spun these black substances out into me,
and also a white

sticky gum I'd find on my chest and belly
in the middle of the night, when my saviour the cool
dawn was a silver-fish in the wall-crack of
a black airless room;

and I lay throbbing, terrified, exalted, strangled,
waiting for the spider-shape to loom.
Night by night the tree went on spinning black
and white substances into me;

now it is wholly inside me: my groin the root,
the slender bough my spine, the saw-edged leaves
my imagination; and the tree sways between
the dark, the light.

From *The Paddhati of Śārṅgadhara: A Sanskrit Anthology*

(translated by John Brough)

When he saw her,
He was struck by the arrows of love.
Nor could he save himself by shutting his eyes:
For he was a young man of an enquiring
And philosophical turn of mind.
And so he was forced to examine the problem
In greater detail
Of how the Creator
Had come to make
A figure like hers.

NÚRU'DDÍN 'ABDU 'R-RAḤMÁN JÁMÍ

(translated by E. G. Browne)

Even from earthly love thy face avert not,
Since to the Real it may serve to raise thee.
Ere A, B, C, are rightly apprehended,
How canst thou con the pages of thy Koran?
A sage (so heard I), unto whom a student
Came craving counsel on the course before him,
Said, 'If thy steps be strangers to love's pathways,
Depart, learn love, and then return before me!
For, shouldst thou fear to drink wine from Form's flagon,
Thou canst not drain the draught of the Ideal.
But yet beware! Be not by Form belated:
Strive rather with all speed the bridge to traverse.
If to the bourne thou fain wouldst bear thy baggage,
Upon the bridge let not thy footsteps linger.'

DHU 'L-NÚN

(translated by A. J. Arberry)

I die, and yet not dies in me
The ardour of my love for Thee,
Nor hath Thy Love, my only goal,
Assuaged the fever of my soul.

To Thee alone my spirit cries;
In Thee my whole ambition lies,
And still Thy Wealth is far above
The poverty of my small love.

I turn to Thee in my request,
And seek in Thee my final rest;
To Thee my loud lament is brought,
Thou dwellest in my secret thought.

However long my sickness be,
This wearisome infirmity,
Never to men will I declare
The burden Thou hast made me bear.

To Thee alone is manifest
The heavy labour of my breast,
Else never kin nor neighbours know
The brimming measure of my woe.

A fever burns below my heart
And ravages my every part;
It hath destroyed my strength and stay,
And smouldered all my soul away.

IBNU 'L-'ARABÍ

(translated by R. A. Nicholson)

Oh, her beauty – the tender maid! Its brilliance gives light
like lamps to one travelling in the dark.
She is a pearl hidden in a shell of hair as black as jet,
A pearl for which thought dives and remains unceasingly
in the deeps of that ocean.
He who looks upon her deems her to be a gazelle of the sandhills,
because of her shapely neck and the loveliness of her gestures.

D. H. LAWRENCE

The Man of Tyre

The man of Tyre went down to the sea
pondering, for he was a Greek, that God is one and
all alone and ever more shall be so.
And a woman who had been washing clothes in the pool of rock
where a stream came down to the gravel of the sea and sank in,
who had spread white washing on the gravel banked above the bay,
who had lain her shift on the shore, on the shingle slope,
who had waded to the pale green sea of evening, out to a shoal,
pouring sea-water over herself
now turned, and came slowly back, with her back to the evening sky.

Oh lovely, lovely with the dark hair piled up, as she went
deeper, deeper down the channel, then rose shallower, shallower,
with the full thighs slowly lifting of the wader wading shorewards
and the shoulders pallid with light from the silent sky behind
both breasts dim and mysterious, with the glamorous kindness
of twilight between them
and the dim notch of black maidenhair like an indicator,
giving a message to the man –

So in the cane-brake he clasped his hands in delight
that could only be god-given, and murmured:

Lo! God is one god! But here in the twilight
godly and lovely comes Aphrodite out of the sea
towards me!

CZESLAW MILOSZ

Esse

I looked at that face, dumbfounded. The lights of Metro stations flew by; I didn't notice them. What can be done, if our sight lacks absolute power to devour objects ecstatically, in an instant, leaving nothing more than the void of an ideal form, a sign like a hieroglyph simplified from the drawing of an animal or bird. A slightly snub nose, a high brow with sleekly brushed-back hair, the line of the chin – but why isn't the power of sight absolute? – and in a whiteness tinged with pink two sculpted holes, containing a dark, lustrous lava. To absorb that face but to have it simultaneously against the background of all spring boughs, walls, waves, in its weeping, its laughter, moving it back fifteen years, or ahead thirty. To have. It is not even a desire. Like a butterfly, a fish, the stem of a plant, only more mysterious. And so it befell me that after so many attempts at naming the world, I am able only to repeat, harping on one string, the highest, the unique avowal beyond which no power can attain: *I am, she is*. Shout, blow the trumpets, make thousands-strong marches, leap, rend your clothing, repeating only: *is!*

She got out at Raspail. I was left behind with the immensity of existing things. A sponge, suffering because it cannot saturate itself; a river, suffering because reflections of clouds and trees are not clouds and trees.

JOHN DONNE

Holy Sonnet XIV

Batter my heart, three person'd God; for, you
As yet but knocke, breathe, shine, and seeke to mend;
That I may rise, and stand, o'erthrow mee,'and bend
Your force, to breake, blowe, burn and make me new.
I, like an usurpt towne, to'another due,

Labour to'admit you, but Oh, to no end,
Reason your viceroy in mee, mee should defend,
But is captiv'd, and proves weake or untrue.
Yet dearely'I love you,'and would be loved faine,
But am betroth'd unto your enemie:
Divorce mee,'untie, or breake that knot againe,
Take mee to you, imprison mee, for I
Except you'enthrall mee, never shall be free,
Nor ever chast, except you ravish mee.

5.
WISE PASSIVENESS

Nor less I deem that there are Powers
Which of themselves our minds impress;
That we can feed this mind of ours
In a wise passiveness.
Wordsworth, 'Expostulation and Reply'

In all religions, contemplation and meditation are crucial. It is the process in which the mystic enters into himself and, by various well-tried techniques, induces in himself a state of calm receptiveness. Instead of churning with exciting ideas, the mind calms down, deliberately silences the aggressive critical faculty and attains, gradually, a state of calm happiness and peace. Different interpretations are given of the activity of meditation, but the phenomenon is much the same in all religions. A Sufi and a Christian would both say that they were encountering God in the soul. They would say that they could not do anything without the help of Allah, of Christ or the Holy Spirit, who carries them along without their knowing what is happening on this spiritual journey. The states of calm peace or ecstatic joy they achieve they would attribute to union with God. The Buddhist would, of course, say none of these things, but it must be remembered that these states of mind are far beyond the limits of rational concepts, so that rational interpretations are irrelevant and unsatisfactory. All traditions stress the importance of stilling the rational critical faculty, because God cannot be thought, he can only be loved, as *The Cloud of Unknowing* insists. The poet also often shows that he too contemplates in a remarkably similar way to the mystic. He too descends into his mind and often there encounters a reality that seems to spring out at him unbidden, as though it were apart from him. This is often the source of a poem, which has come upon the poet with such force that it seems 'given', just as the mystic seems to encounter another being in his mind. Other poets talk about 'inspiration', about being taken over by a 'muse' or 'daimon' that almost dictates the poem to him, just as the mystic feels himself directly guided by 'God'. Yet again there seems to be a remarkable similarity between the mystic and the poetic states of mind.

The first three poems in the section could be described as examples of 'how not to do it', and sadly they often closely resemble the prayers of those people who are religious but not mystics. Very often instead of laying the aggressive ego aside in prayer, we bring it right with us into the heart of prayer. The lady in John Betjeman's poem 'In Westminster Abbey' assumes that God shares her political and social views, with ludicrous results. The lady's views are now an object of mirth in themselves for many people. Yet the reason the poem succeeds is not because it is a caricature of a now outdated attitude, but because it is a caricature of a sort of prayer that is a constant temptation. If the lady were uttering pure Thatcherism or impeccable socialism, if her sentiments were Republican or Democrat, her mistake would be to assume that God shares them. She has forgotten that God might well prove to be a pretty horrible shock, and that she is trying to encounter a reality that must transcend all human boundaries. One of the most ironic lines in the poem is 'What a treat to hear Thy Word', because the lady has not been listening, but talking non-stop. This again is quite contrary to the practice of meditation, in which one doesn't talk to God but listens in silence to Him. Johnannes Agricola, in Browning's poem, seems to be on the right path: at least he's meditating. However, we soon get very disturbed by the use of the words 'I' and 'me', which crop up with extreme frequency. By degrees we realize that Agricola is a monstrous egotist, with appalling views about predestination. Both the lady and Agricola are simply using 'God' to prop up their own egos. Neither has any intention of losing his or her ego in Him.

Betjeman and Browning are, of course, writing dramatic monologues; we are supposed to condemn the speakers out of their own mouths. However, Wesley's famous poem 'Wrestling Jacob'. is sincerely written as a genuine religious poem and, as such, is loved by many people. There is a rather disturbing egotism about it all the same. There is an overwhelming element of grabbing at a religious experience. The poet is grappling and 'wrestling' with God, forcing him to reveal himself. He wants to 'prevail over' him. It is quite the opposite to Moses' experience of the burning bush. There, when Moses asked God to reveal himself, God refused. To reveal his name would, according to Semitic belief, have given man power over God. When asked who He was and what was His name, God replied 'I am what I am' – refusing to reveal his name and nature. It is precisely God's name and nature that the poet is determined to wrest from God at all costs. It is rather disturbingly reminiscent of the sort of religion of which Wesleyism is an example. It depends entirely on a 'feeling' of conversion, of having been saved, and people wrestle with themselves to drum up an experience in some way. It can clearly lead to abuse and hysteria. William Cowper, when the feeling of salvation left him, assumed he was damned and went mad. This type of wrestling with God to get an experience is not mysticism. Despite all its talk of weakness (which smacks of emotional blackmail) the poem is really about power.

The best and simplest example of the receptive attitude of the mystic is given by Wordsworth in his two poems 'Expostulation and Reply' and 'The Tables Turned'. Wordsworth was a mystic, even though his views do not coincide with any theological orthodoxy. He calls the frame of mind he is enjoying 'wise passiveness'. It is calm and peaceful – no anguished wrestling or straining is involved. It has nothing to do with reason and intellect, which all too often can only 'meddle' with experience by analysing and dissecting it. The mystic has to lay aside all intellectual striving and approach reality with a heart 'That watches and receives'.

Mystics and poets would all agree with Rábi'a, the great woman mystic of Islam, that to think about God is 'selfish'. The mystic knows that none of his own efforts can help him; it is God, Allah or Reality that must possess him and guide him, taking over all his faculties. God or Reality must always elude our intellectual concepts and boundaries, which can only limit us in ourselves and distort the true reality of God. Jewish mysticism is rather different from other religions, however, in that it is more 'intellectual'. The mystic does not seek to attain to unity with God, but, as it were, to 'see' him with the eyes of the soul. To be united with such a majestic God would seem blasphemous to the Jew. Nevertheless, the mystical path of the *Kaballah* certainly does not follow the ordinary paths of logic, and is incomprehensible to the uninitiated. Moses Ibn Ezra speaks of knowing God in 'The Sources of my Being', but by the end of the poem it is clear that it is a very comprehensive form of knowledge, including an emotional joy and a spiritually dynamic sense of connection with 'the wisdom of the departed'. Given the remote and majestic nature of the God of Judaism, it might seem remarkable that he discovers that 'within me there was God', but it has constantly been taught by the mystics that the search is within. The *Bhagavad-Gita* sees the meditative and mystical discipline as a contemplation of the self. Krishna explains that He imbues the self and its moods and experiences, as he imbues the whole of reality. To encounter Krishna and to rest in him, the mystic must learn how to discipline the mind and heart in contemplation. It is a 'toil' and requires constant watchfulness to achieve the 'wise passiveness' of concentrated meditation. The pain of mysticism is humorously brought out by the Dervish in Farídu'ddín 'Aṭṭár's poem *The Conference of the Birds*, but he is aware, as a good Sufi, that Allah is there within him and in all his strivings on the Way. The Zen cultivation of concentrated balance is evoked by Aleksander Wat. The goal of the mystical life and the means of achieving it are all one: 'The target tells arrow, bowstring, hand and eye: . . . I am Thou.' It is a mistake to separate the means from the end of the mystical Way.

John of the Cross' great poem, 'Song of the Soul that Rejoices in Knowing God through Faith', sums up the state of the wise passiveness of meditation. The mystic encounters the sourceless source of reality in a darkness. He both longs for it and sees it plain. He knows it well, even though it is night and he can never understand or 'see' all its paradoxes. The night is not frightening but a source of great joy and peace. It is a state that is enjoyed not only by religious mystics, but by poets too.

In 'The Counterpart' Elizabeth Jennings sees that the poet must encounter a 'darkness' and 'stillness' that is enigmatic and paradoxical. In 'Frost at Midnight' we overhear Coleridge's silent and solitary meditation. The image of icicles at the very end of the poem sums up the mystical state of mind. It is a state of 'active passivity': the icicles are both receiving the light of the moon and at the same time shining quietly back at the source of light. Keats in the 'Ode to Psyche' plunges into 'some untrodden region' of his mind. It is, he says, a new type of religious experience in the depths of the psyche. The days of organized religions of creeds, temples and sacrifices are now over, he suggests.

In the wood of his mind, Keats encountered Psyche and Cupid unexpectedly, and when we descend into the subconscious in trance or dream, we never quite know what we will find there. The most famous example of a poem springing unbidden from the subconscious is surely Coleridge's 'Kubla Khan'. Coleridge himself tells the story:

> **In the summer of the year 1797, the Author, then in ill health, had retired to a lonely farm-house between Porlock and Linton, on the Exmoor confines of Somerset and Devonshire. In consequence of a slight indisposition, an anodyne had been prescribed, from the effects of which he fell asleep in his chair at the moment that he was reading the following sentence, or words of the same substance, in 'Purchas's Pilgrimage': 'Here the Khan Kubla commanded a palace to be built, and a stately garden thereunto. And thus ten miles of fertile ground were inclosed with a wall.' The Author continued for about three hours in a profound sleep, at least of the external senses, during which time he has the most vivid confidence, that he could not have composed less than from two to three hundred lines; if that indeed can be called composition in which all the images rose up before him as *things*, with a parallel production of the correspondent expressions, without any sensation or consciousness of effort. On awaking he appeared to himself to have a distinct recollection of the whole and taking his pen, ink and paper, instantly and eagerly wrote down the lines that are here preserved. At this moment he was unfortunately called out by a person on business from Porlock, and detained by him above an hour, and on his return to his room, found, to his no small surprise and mortification, that though he still retained some vague and dim recollection of the general purport of the vision, yet with the exception of some eight or ten scattered lines and images, all the rest had passed away like the images on the surface of a stream into which a stone has been cast, but, alas! without the after restoration of the latter . . . Yet from the still surviving recollections in his mind, the Author has frequently purposed to finish for himself what had been originally, as it were, given to him.**

Even though we are now much more familiar with the effect of drugs in releasing imagery in the subconscious, it is still a remarkable story, all the more remarkable for not being unique. The following poems in the section all deal, in one way or another, with poems or images or beings violently erupting or lurking in the depths of the subconscious. The act of poetic composition is seen as a process of hauling something up from these depths, so that at the end there is a new reality, a new creation that the poet has fathered ('Marina' by T. S. Eliot) or of 'coming awake' (Peter Levi). It is particularly interesting that one of these poems, Robert Frost's 'The Most of It', sees a strange erupting image, which appears unbidden, almost as the answer to a religious problem, an 'answer to a prayer'. Poets, we can see, are not shy of talking about their experience of composition in religious terms.

Other poets have more of a sense of being possessed by something from without, just as the mystic feels himself 'inspired' by God on his mystical quest. Wordsworth, in the two extracts from *The Prelude* in this section, sees himself as 'co-operating' with nature in composition. The first 'poetic spirit of our human life' is the imagination of the child who is making himself at home in the universe and is 'creator and receiver both', working 'in alliance' with surrounding nature. The auxiliar light that springs from the poet's mind similarly works in alliance with nature, creating new realities by

. . . observation of affinities
In objects where no brotherhood exists
To passive minds.

Milton, like Coleridge, feels himself inspired by the muse in his sleep, and his Muse is none other than the Holy Spirit Itself.

Wordsworth is clear that poetic composition has nothing at all to do with rational activity, any more than his mystical contemplation had. The mystic and the poet both seem to be using much the same kind of 'wise passiveness'. Both of them seem, at times, to encounter something that seems like another 'being' or presence – something that inspires or that reveals itself apparently unbidden with a strange authority. The passiveness may be divorced from the more aggressive rational powers of the mind, but that is not to say that it has to be unintelligent. Wordsworth is clear that it has to be 'wise'. To achieve it and to be able to sustain this receptive state of mind demands a considerable amount of intelligence and self-discipline. What is achieved, as John of the Cross says in his poem 'Stanzas Concerning an Ecstasy Experienced in High Contemplation', is a state where 'great things' are understood without using any of the usual means of arriving at knowledge. What is understood is 'secret'; it leaves the mystic 'stammering' and deprived of his senses. It is an 'understanding while not understanding', and in this state of absorption in the mind, the mystic is 'Transcending all knowledge'. It is a state where the ego is lost, the mystic 'Cuts free from himself', and all that he knew before 'Now seems worthless'. It is a form of death to one part of the mind and a new life of another kind of mentality hitherto unsuspected.

JOHN BETJEMAN

In Westminster Abbey

Let me take this other glove off
    As the *vox humana* swells,
And the beauteous fields of Eden
    Bask beneath the Abbey bells.
Here, where England's statesmen lie,
Listen to a lady's cry.

Gracious Lord, oh bomb the Germans.
    Spare their women for Thy Sake,
And if that is not too easy
    We will pardon Thy Mistake.
But, gracious Lord, whate'er shall be,
Don't let anyone bomb me.

Keep our Empire undismembered
    Guide our Forces by Thy Hand,
Gallant blacks from far Jamaica,
    Honduras and Togoland;
Protect them Lord in all their fights,
And, even more, protect the whites.

Think of what our Nation stands for,
    Books from Boots' and country lanes,
Free speech, free passes, class distinction,
    Democracy and proper drains.
Lord, put beneath Thy special care
One-eighty-nine Cadogan Square.

Although dear Lord I am a sinner,
I have done no major crime;
Now I'll come to Evening Service
Whensoever I have the time.
So, Lord, reserve for me a crown,
And do not let my shares go down.

I will labour for Thy Kingdom,
Help our lads to win the war,
Send white feathers to the cowards
Join the Women's Army Corps,
Then wash the Steps around Thy Throne
In the Eternal Safety Zone.

Now I feel a little better,
What a treat to hear Thy Word,
Where the bones of leading statesmen,
Have so often been interr'd.
And now, dear Lord, I cannot wait
Because I have a luncheon date.

ROBERT BROWNING
Johannes Agricola in Meditation

There's heaven above, and night by night
I look right through its gorgeous roof;
No suns and moons though e'er so bright
Avail to stop me; splendour-proof
I keep the broods of stars aloof:
For I intend to get to God,
For 'tis to God I speed so fast,
For in God's breast, my own abode,
Those shoals of dazzling glory, passed,
I lay my spirit down at last.
I lie where I have always lain,
God smiles as he has always smiled;
Ere suns and moons could wax and wane,
Ere stars were thundergirt, or piled

The heavens, God thought on me his child;
Ordained a life for me, arrayed
Its circumstances every one
To the minutest; ay, God said
This head this hand should rest upon
Thus, ere he fashioned star or sun.
And having thus created me,
Thus rooted me, he bade me grow,
Guiltless for ever, like a tree
That buds and blooms, nor seeks to know
The law by which it prospers so:
But sure that thought and word and deed
All go to swell his love for me,
Me, made because that love had need
Of something irreversibly
Pledged solely its content to be.
Yes, yes, a tree which must ascend,
No poison-gourd foredoomed to stoop!
I have God's warrant, could I blend
All hideous sins, as in a cup,
To drink the mingled venoms up;
Secure my nature will convert
The draught to blossoming gladness fast:
While sweet dews turn to the gourd's hurt,
And bloat, and while they bloat it, blast,
As from the first its lot was cast.
For as I lie, smiled on, full-fed
By unexhausted power to bless,
I gaze below on hell's fierce bed,
And those its waves of flame oppress,
Swarming in ghastly wretchedness;
Whose life on earth aspired to be
One altar smoke, so pure! – to win
If not love like God's love for me,
At least to keep his anger in;
And all their striving turned to sin.
Priest, doctor, hermit, monk grown white
With prayer, the broken-hearted nun,
The martyr, the wan acolyte,
The incense-swinging child, – undone
Before God fashioned star or sun!

God, whom I praise; how could I praise,
If such as I might understand,
Make out and reckon on his ways,
And bargain for his love, and stand,
Paying a price, at his right hand?

CHARLES WESLEY

Wrestling Jacob

Come, O thou Traveller unknown,
Whom still I hold but cannot see,
My company before is gone,
And I am left alone with thee,
With thee all night I mean to stay,
And wrestle till the break of day.

I need not tell thee who I am,
My misery, or sin declare,
Thyself hast called me by my name,
Look on thy hands, and read it there,
But who, I ask thee, who art thou?
Tell me thy name, and tell me now.

In vain thou strugglest to get free,
I never will unloose my hold:
Art thou the Man that died for me?
The secret of thy love unfold.
Wrestling I will not let thee go,
Till I thy name, thy nature know.

Wilt thou not yet to me reveal
Thy new, unutterable name?
Tell me, I still beseech thee, tell;
To know it now resolved I am.
Wrestling I will not let thee go,
Till I thy name, thy nature know.

'Tis all in vain to hold thy tongue,
Or touch the hollow of my thigh:
Though every sinew be unstrung,
Out of my arms thou shalt not fly.
Wrestling I will not let thee go,
Till I thy name, thy nature know.

What though my shrinking flesh complain,
And murmur to contend so long,
I rise superior to my pain,
When I am weak then I am strong,
And when my all of strength shall fail,
I shall with the God-Man prevail.

My strength is gone, my nature dies,
I sink beneath thy weighty hand,
Faint to revive, and fall to rise;
I fall, and yet by faith I stand,
I stand, and will not let thee go,
Till I thy name, thy nature know.

Yield to me now – for I am weak;
But confident in self-despair:
Speak to my heart, in blessings speak,
Be conquered by my instant prayer,
Speak, or thou never hence shalt move,
And tell me, if thy name is Love.

'Tis Love, 'tis Love! Thou diedst for me,
I hear thy whisper in my heart.
The morning breaks, the shadows flee:
Pure Universal Love thou art;
To me, to all, thy bowels move,
Thy nature and thy name is Love.

My prayer hath power with God; the Grace
Unspeakable I now receive,
Through Faith I see thee face to face,
I see thee face to face, and live:
In vain I have not wept, and strove,
Thy nature and thy name is Love.

I know thee, Saviour, who thou art,
Jesus, the feeble sinner's friend;
Nor wilt thou with the night depart,
But stay, and love me to the end;
Thy mercies never shall remove,
Thy nature and thy name is Love.

The Sun of Righteousness on me
Hath rose with healing in his wings,
Withered my nature's strength; from thee
My soul its life and succour brings,
My help is all laid up above;
Thy nature and thy name is Love.

Contented now upon my thigh
I halt, till life's short journey end;
All helplessness, all weakness I,
On thee alone for strength depend,
Nor have I power, from thee, to move;
Thy nature and thy name is Love.

Lame as I am, I take the prey,
Hell, earth, and sin with ease o'ercome;
I leap for joy, pursue my way,
And as a bounding hart fly home,
Through all eternity to prove
Thy nature and thy name is Love.

WILLIAM WORDSWORTH
Expostulation and Reply

'Why, William, on that old grey stone,
Thus for the length of half a day,
Why, William, sit you thus alone,
And dream your time away?

'Where are your books? – that light bequeathed
To Beings else forlorn and blind!
Up! up! and drink the spirit breathed
From dead men to their kind.

'You look round on your Mother Earth,
As if she for no purpose bore you;
As if you were her first-born birth,
And none had lived before you!'

One morning thus, by Esthwaite lake,
When life was sweet, I knew not why,
To me my good friend Matthew spake,
And thus I made reply:

'The eye – it cannot choose but see;
We cannot bid the ear be still;
Our bodies feel, where'er they be
Against or with our will.

'Nor less I deem that there are Powers
Which of themselves our minds impress;
That we can feed this mind of ours
In a wise passiveness.

'Think you, 'mid all this mighty sum
Of things for ever speaking,
That nothing of itself will come,
But we must still be seeking?

'– Then ask not wherefore, here, alone,
Conversing as I may,
I sit upon this old grey stone,
And dream my time away.'

The Tables Turned

(An evening scene on the same subject)

Up! up! my Friend, and quit your books;
Or surely you'll grow double:
Up! up! my Friend, and clear your looks;
Why all this toil and trouble?

The sun, above the mountain's head,
A freshening lustre mellow
Through all the long green fields has spread,
His first sweet evening yellow.

Books! 'tis a dull and endless strife:
Come, hear the woodland linnet,
How sweet his music! on my life,
There's more of wisdom in it.

And hark! how blithe the throstle sings!
He, too, is no mean preacher:
Come forth into the light of things,
Let Nature be your Teacher.

She has a world of ready wealth,
Our minds and hearts to bless –
Spontaneous wisdom breathed by health,
Truth breathed by cheerfulness.

One impulse from a vernal wood
May teach you more of man,
Of moral evil and of good,
Than all the sages can.

Sweet is the lore which Nature brings;
Our meddling intellect
Mis-shapes the beauteous forms of things: –
We murder to dissect.

Enough of Science and of Art;
Close up those barren leaves;

Come forth, and bring with you a heart
That watches and receives.

RÁBI'A

(translated by A. J. Arberry)

Two ways I love Thee: selfishly,
And next, as worthy is of Thee.
'Tis selfish love that I do naught
Save think on Thee with every thought.
'Tis purest love when Thou dost raise
The veil to my adoring gaze.
Not mine the praise in that or this:
Thine is the praise in both, I wis.

EMILY DICKINSON

The Wind – tapped like a tired Man –
And like a Host – 'Come in'
I boldly answered – entered then
My Residence within

A Rapid – footless Guest –
To offer whom a Chair
Were as impossible as hand
A Sofa to the Air –

No Bone had He to bind Him –
His Speech was like the Push
Of numerous Humming Birds at once
From a superior Bush –

His Countenance – a Billow –
His Fingers, as He passed
Let go a music – as of tunes
Blown tremulous in Glass –

He visited – still flitting –
Then like a timid Man
Again, He tapped – 'twas flurriedly
And I became alone –

GEORGE HERBERT
Prayer

Prayer the Churches banquet, Angels age,
    God's breath in man returning to his birth,
    The soul in paraphrase, heart in pilgrimage,
The Christian plummet sounding heav'n and earth;
Engine against th'Almightie, sinners towre,
    Reversed thunder, Christ-side-piercing spear,
    The six-daies world transposing in an houre,
A kinde of tune, which all things heare and fear;
Softnesse, and peace, and joy, and love, and blisse,
    Exalted Manna, gladnesse of the best,
    Heaven in ordinarie, man well drest,
The milkie way, the bird of Paradise,
    Church-bels beyond the starres heard, the souls bloud,
    The land of spices; something understood.

MOSES IBN EZRA
The Sources of my Being
(translated by David Goldstein)

I wakened my thoughts from slumber
To put to sleep the desire of my heart and eyes.
And the vagaries of Fortune I perused in my mind
To attune my ears to the events to come.
And the mouth of my thought told me great things,
And placed before me the wondrous deeds of my Lord,
And told me the inaccessible mysteries,
Until I thought I was neighbour to the sons on high.

A vision of the Almighty took hold of my mind,
And I knew that within me there was God.
His magnificent splendour was hidden,
But he was revealed in deed before the eyes of thought.
In my body he has kindled a lamp from his glory;
It tells me of the paths of the wise.
It is the light which shines in the days
Of youth, and grows brighter in old age.
Were it not derived from the mystery of his light
It would fail with my strength and my years.
With it I search out the chamber of wisdom,
And I climb with no ladder to the garden of delights.

My life he has set as nothing, and I shall walk
In the way that all walked before me.
I shall journey as my fathers journeyed.
I shall rest where my forebears rested.
And in all things will God bring me to judgement.
My deeds will be both witnesses and judge.
And so I despise to dwell in the world,
To be seduced and deceived by pride.
I forsake her, before she forsakes me,
Takes off my shoe and spits in my face.
Even if she made the sun my crown
And the moon to be my ornament
And the Great Bear a bracelet for my arm
And her young a necklace round my throat
I should not desire her strength,
Even if she housed me among the spheres of heaven.
But my desire is to fill my bowl
At the gate of instruction, and to dwell with the wise.
And how I yearn to turn their way,
But my feet are dragged by cords of iniquity
Among a people who do not know me.
I am not of them, and they are not mine.
When I speak, I give the kiss of peace,
And they believe I snap at them with my teeth.

The wisdom of the departed I regard as my portion,
And their writings are a balm to my sorrow,
And among them I hold sweet discourse,

Since they are the choicest of the faithful.
And when I swim in the sea of their wisdom
I gather pearls to embroider the days,
And in them is the delight of my eyes and heart,
And of them my jubilating lips will sing –
The light of my eyes, the song in my ears, the honey in my mouth,
And in my nostrils the scent of cinnamon.
And of them I shall muse, and be exalted all my days,
For in them are the sources of my being.

From the *Bhagavad-Gita*

Book VI (the 'Atmasanyamayōg')
(translated by Sir Edwin Arnold)

Steadfast a lamp burns sheltered from the wind;
Such is the likeness of the Yōgi's mind
Shut from sense-storms and burning bright to Heaven.
When mind broods placid, soothed with holy wont;
When Self contemplates self, and in itself
Hath comfort; when it knows the nameless joy
Beyond all scope of sense, revealed to soul –
Only to soul! and, knowing, wavers not,
True to the farther Truth; when, holding this,
It deems no other treasure comparable,
But, harboured there, cannot be stirred or shook
By any gravest grief, call that state 'peace',
That happy severance Yōga; call that man
The perfect Yōgin!
Steadfastly the will
Must toil thereto, till efforts end in ease,
And thought has passed from thinking.
Shaking off
All longings bred by dreams of fame and gain,
Shutting the doorways of the senses close
With watchful ward; so, step by step, it comes
To gift of peace assured and heart assuaged,
When the mind dwells self-wrapped, and the soul broods
Cumberless. But, as often as the heart
Breaks – wild and wavering – from control, so oft

Let him re-curb it, let him rein it back
To the soul's governance; for perfect bliss
Grows only in the bosom tranquillised,
The spirit passionless, purged from offence,
Vowed to the Infinite. He who thus vows
His soul to the Supreme Soul, quitting sin,
Passes unhindered to the endless bliss
Of unity with Brahma. He so vowed,
So blended, sees the Life-Soul resident
In all things living, and all living things
In that Life-Soul contained. And whoso thus
Discerneth Me in all, and all in Me,
I never let him go; nor looseneth he
Hold upon Me; but, dwell he where he may,
Whate'er his life, in Me he dwells and lives,
Because he knows and worships Me, Who dwell
In all which lives, and cleaves to Me in all.

FARĪDU'DDĪN 'AṬṬĀR

From *The Conference of the Birds*

(translated by Afkham Darbandi and Dick Davis)

A dervish wept to feel the violence of
The inextinguishable fires of love.
His spirit melted, and his soul became
A seething mass of incandescent flame;
He wept as he proceeded on his way,
And through his scalding tears was heard to say:
'For how much longer must I weep? Desire
Has burnt my life in its consuming fire.'
'What's all this boasting for?' a voice replied,
'Can you approach Him with such senseless pride?'
'And when did I approach Him?' asked the saint;
'No, He approaches me; that's my complaint –
How could a wretched thing like me pretend
To have the worth to claim Him as my friend?
Look – I do nothing; He performs all deeds
And He endures the pain when my heart bleeds.'

When He draws near and grants you audience
Should you hang back in tongue-tied diffidence?
When will your cautious heart consent to go
Beyond the homely boundaries you know?
O slave, if He should show His love to you,
Love which His deeds perpetually renew,
You will be nothing, you will disappear –
Leave all to Him who acts, and have no fear.
If there is any 'you', if any wraith
Of Self persists, you've strayed outside our faith.

TERESA OF AVILA

(translated by E. Allison Peers)

Soul, thou must seek thyself in Me
And thou must seek for Me in thee.

Such is the power of love's impress,
O soul, to grave thee on My heart,
That any craftsman must confess
He ne'er could have the like success,
Howe'er superlative his art.

It was by love that thou wert made
Lovely and beautiful to be;
So, if perchance thou shouldst have stray'd,
Upon My heart thou art portray'd.
Soul, thou must seek thyself in Me.

For well I know that thou wilt see
Thyself engraven on My breast –
An image vividly impressed –
And then thou wilt rejoice to be
So safely lodg'd, so highly blest.

And if perchance thou knowest not
Whither to go in quest of Me,
Go not abroad My face to see,

Roaming about from spot to spot,
For thou must seek for Me in thee.

For, soul, in thee I am confin'd,
Thou art My dwelling and My home;
And if one day I chance to find
Fast-clos'd the portals of thy mind
I ask for entrance when I come.

Oh, seek not for Me far away,
For, if thou wilt attain to Me,
Thou needest but My name to say
And I am there without delay,
For thou must seek for Me in thee.

ALEKSANDER WAT
Japanese Archery
(translated by Richard Lourie)

I

The hand tells the bowstring:
Obey me.

The bowstring answers the hand:
Draw Valiantly.

The bowstring tells the arrow:
O arrow, fly.

The arrow answers the bowstring:
Speed my flight.

The arrow tells the target:
Be my light.

The target answers the arrow:
Love me.

II

The target tells arrow, bowstring, hand and eye:
Ta twam asi.

Which means in a sacred tongue:
I am Thou.

III

(Footnote of a Christian:
O Mother of God,

watch over the target, the bow, the arrow
and the archer).

JOHN OF THE CROSS

Song of the Soul that Rejoices in Knowing God through Faith

(translated by K. Kavanaugh and O. Rodrigues)

That eternal spring is hidden,
For I know well where it has its rise,
Although it is night.

I do not know its origin, for it hasn't one,
But I know that every origin has come from it.
Although it is night.

I know that nothing else is so beautiful,
And that the heavens and the earth drink there
Although it is night.

I know well that it is bottomless
And that no one is able to cross it
Although it is night.

Its clarity is never darkened,
And I know that every light has come from it
Although it is night.

I know that its streams are so brimming
They water the lands of hell, the heavens, and earth,
Although it is night.

I know well the stream that flows from this spring
Is mighty in compass and power,
Although it is night.

I know that the stream proceeding from these two
Is preceded by neither of them,
Although it is night.

This eternal spring is hidden
In this living bread for our life's sake,
Although it is night.

It is here to call to creatures: and they
Are filled with this water, although in darkness,
Because it is night.

This living spring which I long for,
I see in this bread of life,
Although it is night.

ELIZABETH JENNINGS

The Counterpart

Since clarity suggests simplicity
And since the simple thing is here inapt,
I choose obscurities of tongue and touch,
The shadow side of language and the dark
Hinted in conversations close to quarrel,
Conceived within the mind in aftermaths.
The intellect no crystal is but swarming
Darkness on darkness, gently ruffled by
The senses as they draw an image home.

If art must be abstract that needs to speak
In honesty, in painful honesty,
Then every scene must be composed likewise,
Familiar objects turn to careful shapes,
Gestures be stiff, emotions emblematic.
So art makes peace with honesty and we
Detect a blazing, a Byzantine world,
A formal image shining from the dark
But no less enigmatic than the dark.

Only in such decorum can our pain
Survive without dilution or pretence.
The agony of loss, the potent thrust
Of seed that never will become a child
Need the severity of metaphor,
The symbol on the shield, the dove, the lion
Fixed in a stillness where the darkness folds
In pleated curtains, nothing disarranged:
And only then the eye begins to see.

SAMUEL TAYLOR COLERIDGE

Frost at Midnight

The Frost performs its secret ministry,
Unhelped by any wind. The owlet's cry
Came loud – and hark, again! loud as before.
The inmates of my cottage, all at rest,
Have left me to that solitude, which suits
Abstruser musings: save that at my side
My cradled infant slumbers peacefully.
'Tis calm indeed! so calm, that it disturbs
And vexes meditation with its strange
And extreme silentness. Sea, hill, and wood,
This populous village! Sea, and hill, and wood,
With all the numberless goings-on of life,
Inaudible as dreams! the thin blue flame
Lies on my low-burnt fire, and quivers not;

Only that film,* which fluttered on the grate,
Still flutters there, the sole unquiet thing.
Methinks, its motion in this hush of nature
Gives it dim sympathies with me who live,
Making it a companionable form,
Whose puny flaps and freaks the idling Spirit
By its own moods interprets, every where
Echo or mirror seeking of itself,
And makes a toy of Thought.
But O! how oft,
How oft, at school, with most believing mind,
Presageful have I gazed upon the bars,
To watch that fluttering *stranger*! and as oft
With unclosed lids, already had I dreamt
Of my sweet birthplace, and the old church-tower,
Whose bells, the poor man's only music, rang
From morn to evening, all the hot Fair-day,
So sweetly, that they stirred and haunted me
With a wild pleasure, falling on mine ear
Most like articulate sounds of things to come!
So gazed I, till the soothing things, I dreamt,
Lulled me to sleep, and sleep prolonged my dreams!
And so I brooded all the following morn,
Awed by the stern preceptor's face, mine eye
Fixed with mock study on my swimming book:
Save if the door half opened, and I snatched
A hasty glance, and still my heart leaped up,
For still I hoped to see the *stranger's* face,
Townsman, or aunt, or sister more beloved,
My play-mate when we both were clothed alike!

Dear Babe, that sleepest cradled by my side,
Whose gentle breathings, heard in this deep calm,
Fill up the interspersèd vacancies
And momentary pauses of the thought!
My babe so beautiful! it thrills my heart
With tender gladness, thus to look at thee,
And think that thou shalt learn far other lore,

* These films, Coleridge tells us, were called 'strangers' and were supposed to foretell the arrival of some absent friend.

And in far other scenes! For I was reared
In the great city, pent mid cloisters dim,
And saw nought lovely but the sky and stars.
But *thou*, my babe! shalt wander like a breeze
By lakes and sandy shores, beneath the crags
Of ancient mountain, and beneath the clouds,
Which image in their bulk both lakes and shores
And mountain crags: so shalt thou see and hear
The lovely shapes and sounds intelligible
Of that eternal language, which thy God
Utters, who from eternity doth teach
Himself in all, and all things in himself.
Great universal Teacher! he shall mould
Thy spirit, and by giving make it ask.

Therefore all seasons shall be sweet to thee,
Whether the summer clothe the general earth
With greenness, or the redbreast sit and sing
Betwixt the tufts of snow on the bare branch
Of mossy apple-tree, while the night thatch
Smokes in the sun-thaw; whether the eave-drops fall
Heard only in the trances of the blast,
Or if the secret ministry of frost
Shall hang them up in silent icicles,
Quietly shining to the quiet Moon.

ROBERT FROST

Stopping by Woods on a Snowy Evening

Whose woods these are I think I know.
His house is in the village, though;
He will not see me stopping here
To watch his woods fill up with snow.

My little horse must think it queer
To stop without a farmhouse near
Between the woods and frozen lake
The darkest evening of the year.

He gives his harness bells a shake
To ask if there is some mistake.
The only other sound's the sweep
Of easy wind and downy flake.

The woods are lovely, dark and deep,
But I have promises to keep,
And miles to go before I sleep
And miles to go before I sleep.

JOHN KEATS
Ode to Psyche

O Goddess! hear these tuneless numbers, wrung
    By sweet enforcement and remembrance dear,
And pardon that thy secrets should be sung
    Even into thine own soft-conched ear:
Surely I dreamt today, or did I see
    The winged Psyche with awaken'd eyes?
I wander'd in a forest thoughtlessly,
    And, on the sudden, fainting with surprise,
Saw two fair creatures, couched side by side
    In deepest grass, beneath the whisp'ring roof
    Of leaves and trembled blossoms, where there ran
        A brooklet, scarce espied:

'Mid hush'd, cool-rooted flowers, fragrant-eyed,
    Blue, silver-white, and budded Tyrian,
They lay calm-breathing on the bedded grass;
    Their arms embraced, and their pinions too;
    Their lips touch'd not, but had not bade adieu,
As if disjoined by soft-handed slumber,
And ready still past kisses to outnumber
    At tender eye-dawn of aurorean love:
        The winged boy I knew;
    But who wast thou, O happy, happy dove?
        His Psyche true!

O latest born and loveliest vision far
 Of all Olympus' faded hierarchy!
Fairer than Phœbe's sapphire-region'd star,
 Or Vesper, amorous glow-worm of the sky;
Fairer than these, though temple thou hast none,
  Nor altar heap'd with flowers;
Nor virgin-choir to make delicious moan
  Upon the midnight hours;
No voice, no lute, no pipe, no incense sweet
 From chain-swung censer teeming;
No shrine, no grove, no oracle, no heat
 Of pale-mouth'd prophet dreaming.

O brightest! though too late for antique vows,
 Too, too late for the fond believing lyre,
When holy were the haunted forest boughs,
 Holy the air, the water, and the fire;
Yet even in these days so far retir'd
 From happy pieties, thy lucent fans,
 Fluttering among the faint Olympians,
I see, and sing, by my own eyes inspir'd.
So let me be thy choir, and make a moan
  Upon the midnight hours;
Thy voice, thy lute, thy pipe, thy incense sweet
 From swinged censer teeming;
Thy shrine, thy grove, thy oracle, thy heat
 Of pale-mouth'd prophet dreaming.

Yes, I will be thy priest, and build a fane
 In some untrodden region of my mind,
Where branched thoughts, new grown with pleasant pain,
 Instead of pines shall murmur in the wind:
Far, far around shall those dark-cluster'd trees
 Fledge the wild-ridged mountains steep by steep;
And there by zephyrs, streams, and birds, and bees,
 The moss-lain Dryads shall be lull'd to sleep;
And in the midst of this wide quietness
A rosy sanctuary will I dress
With the wreath'd trellis of a working brain,
With buds, and bells, and stars without a name,
With all the gardener Fancy e'er could feign,

Who breeding flowers, will never breed the same:
And there shall be for thee all soft delight
That shadowy thought can win,
A bright torch, and a casement ope at night,
To let the warm Love in!

SAMUEL TAYLOR COLERIDGE

Kubla Khan

or, A Vision in a Dream

In Xanadu did Kubla Khan
A stately pleasure-dome decree:
Where Alph, the sacred river, ran
Through caverns measureless to man
Down to a sunless sea.
So twice five miles of fertile ground
With walls and towers were girdled round:
And there were gardens bright with sinuous rills,
Where blossomed many an incense-bearing tree;
And here were forests ancient as the hills,
Enfolding sunny spots of greenery.

But oh! that deep romantic chasm which slanted
Down the green hill athwart a cedarn cover!
A savage place! as holy and enchanted
As e'er beneath a waning moon was haunted
By woman wailing for her demon-lover!
And from this chasm, with ceaseless turmoil seething,
As if this earth in fast thick pants were breathing,
A mighty fountain momently was forced:
Amid whose swift half-intermitted burst
Huge fragments vaulted like rebounding hail,
Or chaffy grain beneath the thresher's flail:
And 'mid these dancing rocks at once and ever
It flung up momently the sacred river.
Five miles meandering with a mazy motion
Through wood and dale the sacred river ran,

Then reached the caverns measureless to man,
And sank in tumult to a lifeless ocean:
And 'mid this tumult Kubla heard from far
Ancestral voices prophesying war!
The shadow of the dome of pleasure
Floated midway on the waves;
Where was heard the mingled measure
From the fountain and the caves.
It was a miracle of rare device,
A sunny pleasure-dome with caves of ice!

A damsel with a dulcimer
In a vision once I saw:
It was an Abyssinian maid,
And on her dulcimer she played,
Singing of Mount Abora.
Could I revive within me
Her symphony and song,
To such a deep delight 'twould win me,
That with music loud and long,
I would build that dome in air,
That sunny dome! those caves of ice!
And all who heard should see them there,
And all should cry, Beware! Beware!
His flashing eyes, his floating hair!
Weave a circle round him thrice,
And close your eyes with holy dread,
For he on honey-dew hath fed,
And drunk the milk of Paradise.

R. S. THOMAS

A Person from Porlock

There came a knocking at the front door,
The eternal, nameless caller at the door;
The sound pierced the still hall,
But not the stillness about his brain.

It came again. He arose, pacing the floor
Strewn with books, his mind big with the poem
Soon to be born, his nerves tense to endure
The long torture of delayed birth.

Delayed birth: the embryo maimed in the womb
By the casual caller, the chance cipher that jogs
The poet's elbow, spilling the cupped dream.

The encounter over, he came, seeking his room;
Seeking the contact with his lost self;
Groping his way endlessly back
On the poem's path, calling by name
The foetus stifling in the mind's gloom.

ROBERT FROST

The Most Of It

He thought he kept the universe alone;
For all the voice in answer he could wake
Was but the mocking echo of his own
From some tree-hidden cliff across the lake.
Some morning from the boulder-broken beach
He would cry out on life, that what it wants
Is not its own love back in copy speech,
But counter-love, original response.
And nothing ever came of what he cried
Unless it was the embodiment that crashed
In the cliff's talus on the other side,
And then in the far distant water splashed,
But after a time allowed for it to swim,
Instead of proving human when it neared
And someone else additional to him,
As a great buck it powerfully appeared,
Pushing the crumpled water up ahead,
And landed pouring like a waterfall,
And stumbled through the rocks with horny tread,
And forced the underbush – and that was all.

WALLACE STEVENS
The Irish Cliffs of Moher

Who is my father in this world, in this house,
At the spirit's base?

My father's father, his father's father, his –
Shadows like winds

Go back to a parent before thought, before speech,
At the head of the past.

They go to the cliffs of Moher rising out of the mist,
Above the real,

Rising out of present time and place, above
The wet, green grass.

This is not landscape, full of the somnambulations
Of poetry

And the sea. This is my father or, maybe,
It is as he was,

A likeness, one of the race of fathers: earth
And sea and air.

ALFRED, LORD TENNYSON
The Kraken

Below the thunders of the upper deep;
Far, far beneath in the abysmal sea,
His ancient, dreamless, uninvaded sleep
The Kraken sleepeth: faintest sunlights flee
About his shadowy sides: above him swell
Huge sponges of millennial growth and height;

And far away into the sickly light,
From many a wondrous grot and secret cell
Unnumber'd and enormous polypi
Winnow with giant arms the slumbering green.
There hath he lain for ages and will lie
Battening upon huge seaworms in his sleep,
Until the latter fire shall heat the deep;
Then once by man and angels to be seen,
In roaring he shall rise and on the surface die.

T. S. ELIOT

Marina

Quis hic locus, quae
regio, quae mundi plaga?

What seas what shores what grey rocks and what islands
What water lapping the bow
And scent of pine and the woodthrush singing through the fog
What images return
O my daughter.
    Those who sharpen the tooth of the dog, meaning
Death
Those who glitter with the glory of the hummingbird, meaning
Death
Those who sit in the sty of contentment, meaning
Death
Those who suffer the ecstasy of the animals, meaning
Death

    Are become unsubstantial, reduced by a wind,
A breath of pine, and the woodsong fog
By this grace dissolved in place

    What is this face, less clear and clearer
The pulse in the arm, less strong and stronger –
Given or lent? more distant than stars and nearer than the eye

Whispers and small laughter between leaves and hurrying feet
Under sleep, where all the waters meet.
Bowsprit cracked with ice and paint cracked with heat.
I made this, I have forgotten
And remember.
The rigging weak and the canvas rotten
Between one June and another September,
Made this unknowing, half conscious, unknown, my own.
The garboard strake leaks, the seams need caulking.
This form, this face, this life
Living to live in a world of time beyond me; let me
Resign my life for this life, my speech for that unspoken,
The awakened, lips parted, the hope, the new ships.

What seas what shores what granite islands towards my timbers
And woodthrush calling through the fog
My daughter.

PETER LEVI

When does it end? When does a new poem
ever end? It ends with the island.

Boats, where green watered Puritanic sand
carries offshore beyond the twelve mile limit
yelp and squall of the wind, musk of the girls,
the sailor knew his sweetheart in that wind.

We move through sleep, silently and alone.
Then rises to the surface glowering
it is a tree growing
a lyric poem will have no deadline.

The wrapped roses smelling of paper
are pure explosions of reason
and have no end to them. Modern times;
we are some kind of lover in the end.

I love those most who have no role in life.
    Nothing awake.

Poetry is reason, a slow coming awake.
The world was waiting for lyric poems.
Reasons conjoined, work of the body,
and language cannot be sweetened
but freedom is the burning cigarette
on everyone's lips.
The word of reason when it is awake.

Time's harvest is not in the loose life of my dreams
island beyond island beyond island

when I am awake.

WILLIAM WORDSWORTH

From *The Prelude* Book II ('School-time')

                    Blest the infant Babe,
(For with my best conjecture I would trace
Our Being's earthly progress,) blest the Babe,
Nursed in his Mother's arms, who sinks to sleep,
Rocked on his Mother's breast; who with his soul
Drinks in the feelings of his Mother's eye!
For him, in one dear Presence, there exists
A virtue which irradiates and exalts
Objects through widest intercourse of sense.
No outcast he, bewildered and depressed:
Along his infant veins are interfused
The gravitation and the filial bond
Of nature that connect him with the world.
Is there a flower, to which he points with hand
Too weak to gather it, already love
Drawn from love's purest earthly fount for him
Hath beautified that flower; already shades
Of pity cast from inward tenderness
Do fall around him upon aught that bears

Unsightly marks of violence or harm.
Emphatically such a Being lives,
Frail creature as he is, helpless as frail,
An inmate of this active universe:
For feeling has to him imparted power
That through the growing faculties of sense
Doth like an agent of the one great Mind
Create, creator and receiver both,
Working but in alliance with the works
Which it beholds. – Such, verily, is the first
Poetic spirit of our human life,
By uniform control of after years,
In most, abated or suppressed; in some,
Through every change of growth and of decay,
Pre-eminent till death.

. . .

But let this
Be not forgotten, that I still retained
My first creative sensibility;
That by the regular action of the world
My soul was unsubdued. A plastic power
Abode with me; a forming hand, at times
Rebellious, acting in a devious mood;
A local spirit of his own, at war
With general tendency, but, for the most,
Subservient strictly to external things
With which it communed. An auxiliar light
Came from my mind, which on the setting sun
Bestowed new splendour; the melodious birds,
The fluttering breezes, fountains that run on
Murmuring so sweetly in themselves, obeyed
A like dominion, and the midnight storm
Grew darker in the presence of my eye:
Hence my obeisance, my devotion hence,
And hence my transport.

Nor should this, perchance,
Pass unrecorded, that I still had loved
The exercise and produce of a toil,
Than analytic industry to me

More pleasing, and whose character I deem
Is more poetic as resembling more
Creative agency. The song would speak
Of that interminable building reared
By observation of affinities
In objects where no brotherhood exists
To passive minds.

JOHN MILTON

From *Paradise Lost* Book VII

Descend from Heav'n *Urania*, by that name
If rightly thou art calld, whose Voice divine
Following, above th' *Olympian* Hill I soare,
Above the flight of *Pegasean* wing.
The meaning, not the Name I call: for thou
Nor of the Muses nine, nor on the top
Of old *Olympus* dwellst, but Heav'nlie borne,
Before the Hills appeerd, or Fountain flowd,
Thou with Eternal wisdom didst converse,
Wisdom thy Sister, and with her didst play
In presence of th' Almightie Father, pleas'd
With thy Celestial Song. Up led by thee
Into the Heav'n of Heav'ns I have presum'd,
An Earthlie Guest, and drawn Empyreal Aire,
Thy tempring; with like safetie guided down
Return me to my Native Element:
Least from this flying Steed unreind, (as once
Bellerophon, though from a lower Clime)
Dismounted, on th' *Aleain* Field I fall,
Erroneous there to wander and forlorne.
Half yet remaines unsung, but narrower bound
Within the visible Diurnal Spheare;
Standing on Earth, not rapt above the Pole,
More safe I Sing with mortal voice, unchang'd
To hoarce or mute, though fall'n on evil dayes,
On evil dayes though fall'n, and evil tongues;

In darkness, and with dangers compast round,
And solitude; yet not alone, while thou
Visitst my slumbers Nightly, or when Morn
Purples the East: still govern thou my Song,
Urania, and fit audience find, though few:
But drive farr off the barbarous dissonance
Of *Bacchus* and his Revellers, the Race
Of that wilde Rout that tore the *Thracian* Bard
In *Rhodope*, where Woods and Rocks had Eares
To rapture, till the savage clamor dround
Both Harp and Voice; nor could the Muse defend
Her Son. So fail not thou, who thee implores:
For thou art Heav'nlie, shee an empty dreame.

From *Paradise Lost* Book IX

No more of talk where God or Angel Guest
With Man, as with his Friend, familiar us'd
To sit indulgent, and with him partake
Rural repast, permitting him the while
Venial discourse unblam'd: I now must change
Those Notes to Tragic; foul distrust, and breach
Disloyal on the part of Man, revolt,
And disobedience: On the part of Heav'n
Now alienated, distance and distaste,
Anger and just rebuke, and judgement giv'n,
That brought into this World a world of woe,
Sin and her shadow Death, and Miserie
Deaths Harbinger: Sad task, yet argument
Not less but more Heroic then the wrauth
Of stern *Achilles* or his Foe persu'd
Thrice Fugitive about *Troy* Wall; or rage
Of *Turnus* for *Lavinia* disespous'd,
Or *Neptun*'s ire or *Juno*'s, that so long
Perplexd the *Greek* and *Cytherea*'s Son;
If answerable stile I can obtaine
Of my Celestial Patroness, who deignes
Her nightly visitation unimplor'd,

And dictates to me slumbring, or inspires
Easie my unpremeditated Verse:
Since first this Subject for Heroic Song
Pleas'd me long choosing, and beginning late;
Not sedulous by Nature to indite
Warrs, hitherto the onely Argument
Heroic deemd, chief maistrie to dissect
With long and tedious havoc fabl'd Knights
In Battels feignd; the better fortitude
Of Patience and Heroic Martyrdom
Unsung; or to describe Races and Games,
Or tilting Furniture, emblazond Shields,
Impreses quaint, Caparisons and Steeds;
Bases and tinsel Trappings, gorgious Knights
At Joust and Torneament; then marshald Feast
Serv'd up in Hall with Sewers, and Seneshals;
The skill of Artifice or Office mean,
Not that which justly gives Heroic name
To person or to Poem. Mee of these
Nor skilld nor studious, higher Argument
Remaines, sufficient of it self to raise
That name, unless an age too late, or cold
Climat, or Years damp my intended wing
Deprest; and much they may, if all be mine,
Not Hers who brings it nightly to my Ear.

JOHN OF THE CROSS

Stanzas Concerning an Ecstasy Experienced in High Contemplation

(translated by K. Kavanaugh and O. Rodrigues)

I entered into unknowing,
And there I remained unknowing,
Transcending all knowledge.

I entered into unknowing
Yet when I saw myself there
Without knowing where I was
I understood great things;
I shall not say what I felt
For I remained in unknowing
Transcending all knowledge.

That perfect knowledge
Was of peace and holiness
Held at no remove
In profound solitude;
It was something so secret
That I was left stammering,
Transcending all knowledge.

I was so whelmed,
So absorbed and withdrawn,
That my senses were left
Deprived of all their sensing,
And my spirit was given
An understanding while not understanding,
Transcending all knowledge.

He who truly arrives there
Cuts free from himself;
All that he knew before
Now seems worthless,
And his knowledge so soars
That he is left in unknowing
Transcending all knowledge.

The higher he ascends
The less he understands,
Because the cloud is dark
Which lit up the night;
Whoever knows this
Remains always in unknowing
Transcending all knowledge.

This knowledge in unknowing
Is so overwhelming
That wise men disputing
Can never overthrow it,
For their knowledge does not reach
To the understanding of not-understanding,
Transcending all knowledge.

And this supreme knowledge
Is so exalted
That no power of man or learning
Can grasp it;
He who masters himself
Will, with knowledge in unknowing,
Always be transcending.

And if you should want to hear:
This highest knowledge lies
In the loftiest sense
Of the essence of God;
This is a work of His mercy,
To leave one without understanding,
Transcending all knowledge.

6.
DYING INTO LIFE

Religion often speaks of a process of dying to achieve a richer and more satisfying existence. John of the Cross can say that he is plunged into a dark night, and that everything he has known before is now without value. The Sufi achieves the state of *faná'*, an annihilation of the self in God. We find the poet speaking of a similar process. It is not a masochistic search for suffering for its own sake – though the lives of some of the saints have manifested a desire for making life as unpleasant as possible with hair-raising mortifications. If the Sufi is annihilated, he also in the process discovers himself more fully. The Christian rises again with Christ – death and resurrection are written into the heart of the religion. So too the Buddhist. When the Enlightened man attains Nirvana he is annihilated and his ego disappears, releasing him from the cycle of suffering. But even though the Buddha refused to speak of the possibility of an after-life, we have seen that Nirvana is, mysteriously, something much greater than non-being, something that is positive and that is spoken of in much the same way as a Jew or a Christian speaks of the 'Holy City' or of God.

The first poem of the section shows the process of death as expressed in the doctrine of the Resurrection, but in Marvell's 'The Coronet' and Phineas Fletcher's poem, we have a more inward and mystical idea of a moral and spiritual death; it is only Christ who can 'shatter' the self and loosen the bonds. Emily Dickinson's Martyrs have to travel 'Through the strait pass of suffering'; like the mystic, they journey inexorably and in faith through a darkness and deprivation, through 'polar Air'.

What exactly does the mystic mean when he says that he is no longer living? 'I live now, not I, but Christ lives in me', wrote St Paul. One would be tempted to see this as some kind of delusion or mania, were it not such a universal process. It must describe some kind of human experience that seems common to religious and to creative activity. One of the things that a mystic experiences is the suffering of life without God. Both John of the Cross and Teresa of Avila speak of dying 'because I do not die'. Without God a mystic is a fish out of water. His life is 'no life at all', a 'prison', albeit a prison of love. The Christian mystic believes that total union can only come after death, so 'The waiting-time is hard to bear'. There is a certain amount of egotism in this, perhaps, but it also illustrates the compulsion that must exist in the mystic. As part of his nature he is impelled to the life of meditation and death to self. It is not something that he can will himself to do, any more than a poet can be forced to write a poem. Mysticism is something that he *has* to do, and the compulsion he feels is something that the ordinary man who is content to keep his religion to Sunday morning, for example, just doesn't share.

In *The Conference of the Birds*, Farídu'ddín 'Aṭṭár explains that although the end of the mystical journey is an annihilation, it is only by becoming Nothing that the mystic can recover his true self. All the Sufi's ecstasies and visions were only glimpses of this fully realized Self that has fused with the Divine. Rúmí's joyous poem shows us this enhanced existence – he has escaped the narrow confines of the self, so that he is now identified with every lover, every believer of whatever creed, with good and evil, with Paradise and Hell. How can the mystic be confined to one set of man-made beliefs? He has achieved such an enriched state of being that the boundaries men use to define themselves and prop themselves up no longer have any meaning.

Poets constantly speak of this process of death and renewal. In 'The Fall of Hyperion' Keats himself sees the poetic vocation as a dying into life that is very similar to the mystical process. Like the mystic he is consumed by a restlessness. But after the pain and agony of dying, the poet too gains an enhanced existence, 'A power within me of enormous ken'; like the mystic he sees 'as a god sees'. It is a transformation that Seamus Heaney shares as he concludes his long pilgrimage to Station Island by comparing his vocation as poet to the Christian vocation. He is in a state of 'trance' that renders the commonplace road into an archetypal road of the spirit. Speaking in the persona of Sweeney, the seventh-century Ulster king who was, Heaney says, 'transformed into a bird-man and exiled to the trees by the curse of St Ronan', he achieves at the end of the poem a liberation. He is no longer the bird-man flapping uneasily around the Church 'scaling heaven by superstition'. Rather, he has entered himself, entered deep into a cliff, a cave, and by contemplation of 'a stone-faced vigil', he will find his 'long dumbfounded spirit' breaking cover. The deer's expectancy, its long wait for the water that is and must ever be dried up, is an image of the perseverance and death that the religious man and the poet must be prepared to face in the cavern of the self. Only in 'the font of exhaustion' can he share that universal process deep within the psyche of renewal and new life.

GEORGE HERBERT

Easter-wings

Lord, who createdst man in wealth and store,
Though foolishly he lost the same,
Decaying more and more,
Till he became
Most poore:
With thee
O let me rise
As larks, harmoniously,
And sing this day thy victories:
Then shall the fall further the flight in me.

My tender age in sorrow did beginne:
And still with sicknesses and shame
Thou didst so punish sinne,
That I became
Most thinne.
With thee
Let me combine
And feel this day thy victorie:
For, if I imp my wing on thine,
Affliction shall advance the flight in me.

ANDREW MARVELL

The Coronet

When for the Thorns with which I long, too long,
With many a piercing wound,
My Saviours head have crown'd,
I seek with Garlands to redress that Wrong:
Through every Garden, every Mead,
I gather flow'rs (my fruits are only flow'rs)
Dismantling all the fragrant Towers
That once adorned my Shepherdesses head.

And now when I have summ'd up all my store,
    Thinking (so I my self deceive)
    So rich a Chaplet thence to weave
As never yet the king of Glory wore:
    Alas I find the Serpent old
    That, twining in his speckled breast,
    About the flow'rs disguis'd does fold,
    With wreaths of Fame and Interest.
Ah, foolish Man, that would'st debase with them
And mortal Glory, Heaven's Diadem!
But thou who only could'st the Serpent tame,
Either his slipp'ry knots at once untie,
And disintangle all his winding Snare:
Or shatter too with him my curious frame:
And let these wither, so that he may die,
Though set with Skill and chosen out with Care.
That they, while Thou on both their Spoils dost tread,
May crown thy Feet, that could not crown thy Head.

PHINEAS FLETCHER

        Me, Lord? Canst thou mispend
    One word, misplace one look on me?
        Call'st me thy Love, thy Friend?
    Can this poor soul the object be
Of these love-glances, those life-kindling eyes?
What? I the centre of thy arms' embraces?
    Of all thy labour I the prize?
    Love never mocks, Truth never lies.
Oh how I quake: Hope fear, fear hope displaces:
I would, but cannot hope: such wondrous love amazes.

        See, I am black as night,
    See, I am darkness: dark as hell.
        Lord, thou more fair than light;
    Heaven's sun thy shadow: can suns dwell
With shades? 'twixt light and darkness what commerce?

True: thou art darkness, I thy Light: my ray
Thy mists and hellish fogs shall pierce.
With me, black soul, with me converse;
I make the foul December flowery May.
Turn thou thy night to me: I'll turn thy night to day.

See, Lord, see, I am dead:
Tombed in myself: myself my grave.
A drudge: so born, so bred:
Myself even to myself a slave.
Thou Freedom, Life: can Life and Liberty
Love bondage, death? *Thy Freedom I: I tied*
To loose thy bonds: be bound to me:
My yoke shall ease, my bonds shall free.
Dead soul, thy Spring of life, my dying side:
There die with me to live: to live in thee I died.

EMILY DICKINSON

Through the strait pass of suffering –
The Martyrs – even – trod.
Their feet – upon Temptation –
Their faces – upon God –

A stately – shriven – Company
Convulsion – playing round
Harmless – as streaks of Meteor –
Upon a Planet's Bond –

Their faith – the everlasting troth –
Their Expectation – fair –
The Needle – to the North Degree –
Wades – so – thro' polar Air!

TERESA OF AVILA

I Die because I Do Not Die

(translated by E. Allison Peers)

I live, yet no true life I know,
And, living thus expectantly,
I die because I do not die.

Since this new death-in-life I've known,
Estrang'd from self my life has been,
For now I live a life unseen:
The Lord has claim'd me as His own.
My heart I gave Him for His throne,
Whereon he wrote indelibly:
'I die because I do not die.'

Within this prison-house divine,
Prison of love whereby I live,
My God Himself to me doth give,
And liberate this heart of mine.
And, as with love I yearn and pine,
With God my prisoner, I sigh:
'I die because I do not die.'

How tedious is this life below,
This exile, with its griefs and pains,
This dungeon and these cruel chains
In which the soul is forced to go!
Straining to leave this life of woe,
With anguish sharp and deep I cry:
'I die because I do not die.'

How bitter our existence ere
We come at last the Lord to meet!
For, though the soul finds loving sweet,
The waiting-time is hard to bear.
Oh, from this leaden weight of care,
My God, relieve me speedily,
Who die because I do not die.

I only live because I know
That death's approach is very sure,
And hope is all the more secure
Since death and life together go.
O death, thou life-creator, lo!
I wait upon thee, come thou nigh:
I die because I do not die.

Consider, life, love's potency,
And cease to cause me grief and pain.
Reflect, I beg, that, thee to gain,
I first must lose thee utterly.
Then, death, come pleasantly to me.
Come softly: undismay'd am I
Who die because I do not die.

That life, with life beyond recall,
Is truly life for evermore:
Until this present life be o'er
We cannot savour life at all.
So, death, retreat not at my call,
For life through death I can descry
Who die because I do not die.

O life, what service can I pay
Unto my God Who lives in me
Save if I first abandon thee
That I may merit thee for aye?
I'd win thee dying day by day,
Such yearning for my Spouse have I,
Dying because I do not die.

JOHN OF THE CROSS

Stanzas of the Soul that Suffers with Longing to See God

(translated by K. Kavanaugh and O. Rodrigues)

I live, but not in myself,
And I have such hope
That I die because I do not die.

I no longer live within myself
And I cannot live without God,
For if I have neither Him nor myself
What will life be?
It will be a thousand deaths,
Longing for my true life
And dying because I do not die.

This life that I live
Is no life at all,
And so I die continually
Until I live with You;
Hear me, my God:
I do not desire this life,
I am dying because I do not die.

When I am not with You
What life can I have
Except to endure
The bitterest death known?
I pity myself
For I go on and on living,
Dying because I do not die.

A fish that leaves the water
Has this relief:
The dying it endures
Ends at last in death.
What death can equal
My pitiful life?
For the longer I live, the more drawn out is my dying.

When I try to find relief
Beholding You in the Sacrament
I find this greater sorrow:
I cannot enjoy You wholly.
All things are affliction
Since I do not see You as I desire,
And I die because I do not die.

And if I rejoice, Lord,
In the hope of seeing You,
Yet seeing I can lose You
Doubles my sorrow.
Living in such fear
And hoping as I hope,
I die because I do not die.

Lift me from this death,
My God, and give me life;
Do not hold me bound
With these so strong bonds;
See how I long to see You;
I am so wholly miserable
That I die because I do not die.

I will cry out for death
And mourn my living
While I am held here
For my sins.
O my God, when will it be
That I can truly say:
Now I live because I do not die?

Commentary Applied to Spiritual Things

(translated by K. Kavanaugh and O. Rodrigues)

Without support and with support,
Living without light, in darkness,
I am wholly being consumed.

My soul is disentangled
From every created thing
And lifted above itself
In a life of delight
Supported only in God.
So can it not be said
That I most value this:
My soul now sees itself
Without support and with support.

And though I suffer darknesses
In this mortal life,
That is not so hard a thing;
For though I have no light
I have the life of heaven.
For the blinder love is
The more it gives such life,
Holding the soul surrendered,
Living without light, in darkness.

After I have known it
Love works so in me
That whether things go well or badly
Love turns all to one sweetness
Transforming the soul in itself.
And so in its delighting flame
Which I feel within me,
Swiftly, with nothing spared,
I am wholly being consumed.

JALÁLU'DDÍN RÚMÍ

(translated by R. A. Nicholson)

I died as mineral and became a plant,
I died as plant and rose to animal,
I died as animal and I was man.
Why should I fear? When was I less by dying?
Yet once more I shall die as man, to soar
With angels blest; but even from angelhood
I must pass on: all except God doth perish.
When I have sacrificed my angel soul,
I shall become what no mind e'er conceived.
Oh, let me not exist! for Non-existence
Proclaims in organ tones, '*To Him we shall return*.'*

* Koran 2:151

BÁBÁ KÚHÍ OF SHÍRÁZ

(translated by R. A. Nicholson)

In the market, in the cloister – only God I saw.
In the valley and on the mountain – only God I saw.
Him I have seen beside me oft in tribulation;
In favour and in fortune – only God I saw.
In prayer and fasting, in praise and contemplation,
In the religion of the Prophet – only God I saw.
Neither soul nor body, accident nor substance,
Qualities nor causes – only God I saw.
I oped mine eyes and by the light of His face around me
In all the eye discovered – only God I saw.
Like a candle I was melting in his fire:
Amidst the flames outlashing – only God I saw.
Myself with mine own eyes I saw most clearly,
But when I looked with God's eyes – only God I saw.
I passed away into nothingness, I vanished,
And lo, I was the All-living – only God I saw.

From the *Bhagavad-Gita*

Book IV (the 'Jnāna Yōg')
(translated by Sir Edwin Arnold)

Nay, but of such an one,
Whose crave is gone, whose soul is liberate,
Whose heart is set on truth – of such an one,
What work he does is work of sacrifice,
Which passeth purely into ash and smoke
Consumed upon the altar! All's then God!
The sacrifice is Brahm, the ghee and grain
Are Brahm, the fire is Brahm, the flesh it eats
Is Brahm; and unto Brahm attaineth he
Who, in such office, meditates on Brahm.
Some votaries there be who serve the gods
With flesh and altar-smoke; but other some
Who, lighting subtler fires, make purer rite
With will of worship. Of the which be they
Who, in white flame of continence, consume
Joys of the sense, delights of eye and ear,
Forgoing tender speech and sound of song:
And they who, kindling fires with torch of Truth,
Burn on a hidden altar-stone the bliss
Of youth and love, renouncing happiness:
And they who lay for offering there their wealth
Their penance, meditation, piety,
Their steadfast reading of the scrolls, their lore
Painfully gained with long austerities:
And they who, making silent sacrifice,
Draw in their breath to feed the flame of thought,
And breathe it forth to waft the heart on high,
Governing the ventage of each entering air
Lest one sigh pass which helpeth not the soul:
And they who, day by day denying needs,
Lay life itself upon the altar-flame,
Burning the body wan. Lo! all these keep
The rite of offering, as if they slew
Victims; and all thereby efface much sin.
Yea! and who feed on the immortal food
Left of such sacrifice, to Brahma pass,

To the Unending. But for him that makes
No sacrifice, he hath nor part nor lot
Even in the present world. How should he share
Another . . . ?

FARĪDU'DDĪN 'AṬṬĀR

From *The Conference of the Birds*

(translated by Afkham Darbandi and Dick Davis)

[The thirty birds reach the end of their pilgrimage and meet the King, the Simorgh]

Hallaj's* corpse was burnt and when the flame
Subsided, to the pyre a sufi came
Who stirred the ashes with his staff and said:
'Where has that cry "I am the Truth" now fled?
All that you cried, all that you saw and knew,
Was but the prelude to what now is true.
The essence lives; rise now and have no fear,
Rise up from ruin, rise and disappear –
All shadows are made nothing in the one
Unchanging light of Truth's eternal sun.'
A hundred thousand centuries went by,
And then those birds, who were content to die,
To vanish in annihilation, saw
Their Selves had been restored to them once more,
That after Nothingness they had attained
Eternal Life, and self-hood was regained.
This Nothingness, this Life, are states no tongue
At any time has adequately sung –
Those who can speak still wander far away
From that dark truth they struggle to convey,
And by analogies, they try to show
The forms men's partial knowledge cannot know . . .

* Hallaj, the Sufi mystic, was executed for blasphemy, and is a controversial figure in Islam. While in ecstasy he cried out, 'I am the Truth,' thus expressing his ecstatic sense of union with God.

Be nothing first! and then you will exist,
You cannot live whilst life and Self persist –
Till you reach Nothingness you cannot see
The Life you long for in eternity.

JALÁLU'DDÍN RÚMÍ

(translated by R. A. Nicholson)

If there be any lover in the world, O Moslems, 'tis I.
If there be any believer, infidel, or Christian hermit, 'tis I.
The wine-dregs, the cupbearer, the minstrel, the harp and the music,
The beloved, the candle, the drink and the joy of the drunken – 'tis I.
The two-and-seventy creeds and sects in the world
Do not really exist: I swear by God that every creed and sect – 'tis I.
Earth and air and water and fire – knowest thou what they are?
Earth and air and water and fire, nay, body and soul too – 'tis I.
Truth and falsehood, good and evil, ease and difficulty from first to last,
Knowledge and learning and asceticism and piety and faith – 'tis I.
The fire of Hell, be assured, with its flaming limbos,
Yes, and Paradise and Eden and the houris – 'tis I.
This earth and heaven with all that they hold,
Angels, peris, genies, and mankind – 'tis I.

PETER LEVI

In stone settlements when the moon is stone
and gardens have died back to the bare bone
the stars consume to frost, they have their wish,
they wither and flourish.

A wrinkled ocean washes out star-frost,
nothing survives in it, nothing is lost,
far deeper than the cold shadows of fish
I wither and flourish.

As the wild rose in winter is not seen,
the weak scent and the prickle and the green,
but hedges live, the sun is dragonish,
we wither and flourish.

JOHN KEATS

From 'The Fall of Hyperion'

A Dream

Towards the altar sober-paced I went,
Repressing haste, as too unholy there;
And, coming nearer, saw beside the shrine
One minist'ring; and there arose a flame. –
When in mid-May the sickening East wind
Shifts sudden to the south, the small warm rain
Melts out the frozen incense from all flowers,
And fills the air with so much pleasant health
That even the dying man forgets his shroud; –
Even so that lofty sacrificial fire,
Sending forth Maian incense, spread around
Forgetfulness of everything but bliss,
And clouded all the altar with soft smoke;
From whose white fragrant curtains thus I heard
Language pronounc'd: 'If thou canst not ascend
'These steps, die on that marble where thou art.
'Thy flesh, near cousin to the common dust,
'Will parch for lack of nutriment – thy bones
'Will wither in few years, and vanish so
'That not the quickest eye could find a grain
'Of what thou now art on that pavement cold.
'The sands of thy short life are spent this hour,
'And no hand in the universe can turn
'Thy hourglass, if these gummed leaves be burnt
'Ere thou canst mount up these immortal steps.'
I heard, I look'd: two senses both at once,
So fine, so subtle, felt the tyranny
Of that fierce threat and the hard task proposed.
Prodigious seem'd the toil; the leaves were yet

Burning – when suddenly a palsied chill
Struck from the paved level up my limbs
And was ascending quick to put cold grasp
Upon those streams that pulse beside the throat:
I shriek'd, and the sharp anguish of my shriek
Stung my own ears – I strove hard to escape
The numbness; strove to gain the lowest step.
Slow, heavy, deadly was my pace: the cold
Grew stifling, suffocating, at the heart;
And when I clasp'd my hands I felt them not.
One minute before death, my iced foot touch'd
The lowest stair; and as it touch'd, life seem'd
To pour in at the toes: I mounted up,
As once fair angels on a ladder flew
From the green turf to heaven – 'Holy Power,'
Cried I, approaching near the horned shrine,
'What am I that should so be saved from death?
'What am I that another death come not
'To choke my utterance sacrilegious, here?'
Then said the veiled shadow – 'Thou hast felt
'What 'tis to die and live again before
'Thy fated hour, that thou hadst power to do so
'Is thy own safety; thou hast dated on
'Thy doom.' – 'High Prophetess,' said I, 'purge off,
'Benign, if so it please thee, my mind's film.' –
'None can usurp this height,' return'd that shade,
'But those to whom the miseries of the world
'Are misery, and will not let them rest.
'All else who find a haven in the world,
'Where they may thoughtless sleep away their days,
'If by a chance into this fane they come,
'Rot on the pavement where thou rottedst half.' –

. . .

I look'd upon the altar, and its horns
Whiten'd with ashes, and its lang'rous flame,
And then upon the offerings again;
And so by turns – till sad Moneta cried,
'The sacrifice is done, but not the less
'Will I be kind to thee for thy good will.

'My power, which to me is still a curse,
'Shall be to thee a wonder; for the scenes
'Still swooning vivid through my globed brain,
'With an electral changing misery,
'Thou shalt with those dull mortal eyes behold,
'Free from all pain, if wonder pain thee not.'
As near as an immortal's sphered words
Could to a mother's soften, were these last:
And yet I had a terror of her robes,
And chiefly of the veils, that from her brow
Hung pale, and curtain'd her in mysteries,
That made my heart too small to hold its blood.
This saw that Goddess, and with sacred hand
Parted the veils. Then saw I a wan face,
Not pin'd by human sorrows, but bright-blanch'd
By an immortal sickness which kills not;
It works a constant change, which happy death
Can put no end to; deathwards progressing
To no death was that visage; it had past
The lilly and the snow; and beyond these
I must not think now, though I saw that face –
But for her eyes I should have fled away.
They held me back, with a benignant light,
Soft mitigated by divinest lids
Half-closed, and visionless entire they seem'd
Of all external things; – they saw me not,
But in blank splendor, beam'd like the mild moon,
Who comforts those she sees not, who knows not
What eyes are upward cast. As I had found
A grain of gold upon a mountain side,
And twing'd with avarice strain'd out my eyes
To search its sullen entrails rich with ore,
So at the view of sad Moneta's brow,
I ach'd to see what things the hollow brain
Behind enwombed: what high tragedy
In the dark secret chambers of her skull
Was acting, that could give so dread a stress
To her cold lips, and fill with such a light
Her planetary eyes; and touch her voice
With such a sorrow – 'Shade of Memory!' –
Cried I, with act adorant at her feet,

'By all the gloom hung round thy fallen house,
'By this last temple, by the golden age,
'By great Apollo, thy dear Foster Child,
'And by thyself, forlorn divinity,
'The pale Omega of a withered race,
'Let me behold, according as thou saidst,
'What in thy brain so ferments to and fro!'
No sooner had this conjuration pass'd
My devout lips, than side by side we stood
(Like a stunt bramble by a solemn pine)
Deep in the shady sadness of a vale,
Far sunken from the healthy breath of morn,
Far from the fiery noon and eve's one star.
Onward I look'd beneath the gloomy boughs,
And saw, what first I thought an image huge,
Like to the image pedestal'd so high
In Saturn's temple. Then Moneta's voice
Came brief upon mine ear – 'So Saturn sat
'When he had lost his Realms –' whereon there grew
A power within me of enormous ken
To see as a god sees, and take the depth
Of things as nimbly as the outward eye
Can size and shape pervade. The lofty theme
At those few words hung vast before my mind,
With half-unravel'd web. I set myself
Upon an eagle's watch, that I might see,
And seeing ne'er forget.

SEAMUS HEANEY

From *Station Island* 'On the Road'

The road ahead
kept reeling in
at a steady speed,
the verges dripped.

In my hands
like a wrested trophy,
the empty round
of the steering wheel.

The trance of driving
made all roads one:
the seraph-haunted, Tuscan
footpath, the green

oak-alleys of Dordogne
or that track through corn
where the rich young man
asked his question –

Master, what must I
do to be saved?
Or the road where the bird
with an earth-red back

and a white and black
tail, like parquet
of flint and jet,
wheeled over me

in visitation.
Sell all you have
and give to the poor.
I was up and away

like a human soul
that plumes from the mouth
in undulant, tenor
black-letter Latin.

I was one for sorrow,
Noah's dove,
a panicked shadow
crossing the deerpath.

If I came to earth
it would be by way of
a small east window
I once squeezed through,

scaling heaven
by superstition,
drunk and happy
on a chapel gable.

I would roost a night
on the slab of exile,
then hide in the cleft
of that churchyard wall

where hand after hand
keeps wearing away
at the cold, hard-breasted
votive granite.

And follow me.
I would migrate
through a high cave mouth
into an oaten, sun-warmed cliff,

on down the soft-nubbed,
clay-floored passage,
face-brush, wing-flap,
to the deepest chamber.

There a drinking deer
is cut into rock,
its haunch and neck
rise with the contours,

the incised outline
curves to a strained
expectant muzzle
and a nostril flared

at a dried-up source.
For my book of changes
I would meditate
that stone-faced vigil

until the long dumbfounded
spirit broke cover
to raise a dust
in the font of exhaustion.

7.
THE MEDDLING INTELLECT

Sweet is the lore which Nature brings
Our meddling intellect
Mis-shapes the beauteous forms of things: –
We murder to dissect

Wordsworth, 'The Tables Turned'

Although both true mysticism and poetry are activities that require a great deal of intelligence, both poets and mystics agree that their activity is not purely rational or logical. Wordsworth in 'The Tables Turned' said that for the mystic, the 'meddling intellect' can only destroy 'the beauteous shape of things' by analysing and dissecting them. Both seem to be using a type of consciousness that is receptive rather than aggressively rational. I use the word 'aggressive' because the analytical part of our minds that we all value so highly in Western society – and with good reason – does not peacefully receive the world as it is. It has to label, classify, compare, break things down, wrestle with the world in an attempt to understand it. Wordsworth said that we 'murder to dissect', and although that is putting things very strongly, it is true that we do not allow the 'shape of things' to remain intact when we assault them with our minds. Indeed, the mystics very often juxtapose 'thinking' with 'loving' as alternative activities. God 'may well be loved but not thought', said the author of *The Cloud of Unknowing*, and it is certainly true that those types of religion that have been analytic and dogmatic have been the most aggressive and unloving. When Christian murders Moslem, when Catholics and Protestants murder one another, when Congregationalists in New England murder Quakers, they are murdering because they are 'dissecting'. As Derek Walcott says in the poem from *Midsummer*, they murder 'for a noun'. By saying 'God is not this but that' and using a good deal of aggressive logic to prove their point, they are not experiencing 'God as He is', but creating a God in their own image and likeness. They are banking up their egos defensively by what they call 'God' and committing idolatry. This defensiveness and egotistical activity leads them into hostility that is the obverse of all that religion stands for.

We can see this alliance of aggression, cruelty and simple unkindness with dogmatic and analytic religion in the first poems in this section. As a contrast, Sidney Godolphin's 'Hymn' marks the alliance of simplicity with love. In 'Maximus' D. H. Lawrence knows very well that God cannot be described or conceived by man, but an act of love in inviting a stranger into his house reveals God to him. It is important too that what Lawrence says is 'Come in'. He is open and receptive in the way that all true contemplatives must be. Unlike Wesley in 'Wrestling Jacob', he gets no answer when he asks the stranger for his name, but a 'loveliness' enters him that is in some indefinable sense a vision of the divine. Faith is an emotion, not a logical argument, which gives the religious man like Tennyson a chance to 'dream', to dwell deep in his 'spirit'. Tennyson will not even give the Reality he chooses a name. John of the Cross also explains that what the mystic finds cannot be named. It is a reality that he has to call 'I-don't-know-what'. The mystic has to live 'Alone, mind empty of form and figure'. He can have no prop or support for the ego, can find 'no support or foothold'. What he has gained is beyond thought, beyond beauty, and he too realizes that there can be no end to his search. There can be no moment when he can reach a final position and say, 'I have found or experienced this and that.' He is always having to travel 'Towards greater heights'.

The Sufis are particularly prone to the real agnosticism of mysticism. Ḥafíẓ can find God equally well in a mosque or a tavern. He cannot be gained by ordinary endeavour, but the eye of the spirit has nothing to do with creed or form. Love can be found in a Christian convent or Church as well as in a mosque. Rúmí has got to the point where he has so lost his ego ('for I to myself am unknown') that he no longer has a position or creed. The usual categories that men use to define themselves and other people no longer apply to him. Ibnu 'l-'Arabí finds also that his 'heart is capable of every form', Jewish, Christian or Moslem. 'Form is not yours, O Monks!' the Buddha had announced. For the mystic to persecute people for holding different doctrinal views would be unthinkable once he has lost himself in Love.

Poets are also very clear that their activity owes little to reason. The poem on the Tanfield memorial in Burford church says that it was 'love' that made the Lady Tanfield, who is supposed to have written this, a poet. It was her 'harte' not her 'witt' that created. In 'Coleridge' R. S. Thomas sees a conflict in the poet's mind between his philosophy and his poetic nature. 'He felt his theories break and go' and he encounters a 'cloud of unknowing' in a 'nihilistic blue' sky that cannot be probed by human efforts. The poet must always have an inner ear that is receptive to the mysterious and the extraordinary. Shakespeare and Hardy both talk about folk laws and superstitions of Christmas that logically we know must be untrue. However, there is that in the poet that can 'in part' believe them, that 'hopes' that 'it might be so'. It may indeed be true, but true in an entirely different way from the truth of science and logic.

Blake and Hopkins were both mystics and poets. In 'The Tyger' Blake asks questions and expects no answers. It is a poem that consists entirely of questions. Religion tends to get into trouble when it tries to answer the sort of impossible questions that Blake asks here. For the mystic there can be no answers. When the author of *The Cloud of Unknowing* was asked, 'What is God?' he could only reply, 'I do not know.' This agnostic mood is powerfully evoked by Hopkins in the frightening vision of 'Spelt from Sybil's Leaves'. The night, the physical night, is descending, and in doing so, its darkness blurs all distinctions and obscures all categories that support us during the daylight. We can no longer prop up our infirm egos by analysing ourselves and defining other people, saying what is right and wrong, good and evil. The judging and critical faculty is no longer valid in the mystic night, which is a deliberate forgetting, 'Disremembering, dismembering'. It is a night that is a kind of death: 'Óur evening is over us; our night whélms, whélms, ánd will end us.' Hell is a state in which 'thoughts against thoughts in groans grind'. The poetic and the mystical minds have to be capable of the discipline and terror of this agnostic night, which brings about death of the ego. It was Keats who said that the poet was 'the most unpoetical thing in existence' because he has no identity. It was also Keats who makes what he calls 'negative capability' sound like a description of wise passiveness. 'It is when a man is capable of being in uncertainties, mysteries, doubts, without any irritable reaching after facts and reason.' Like Hopkins he felt the force of the dark night of the mystic when he writes of leaving what he calls 'the chamber of Maiden Thought':

> **. . . and at the same time on all sides of it many doors are set open – but all dark – all leading to dark passages – We see not the ballance of good and evil. We are in a Mist. *We* are now in that state – we feel 'the burden of the Mystery'.**

He was, he wrote to his brother, writing 'in the midst of a great darkness – without knowing the bearing of any one assertion of any one opinion'. Keats was not a religious man, but in his practice of poetry he was a mystic.

DEREK WALCOTT

From *Midsummer*

XXII

Rest, Christ! from tireless war. See, it's midsummer,
but what roars in the throat of the oaks is martial man,
the marching hosannas darken the wheat of Russia,
the coiled ram hides in the rocks of Afghanistan.
Crowned hydrants gush, baptizing the street urchins,
the water cannons blot their screams in mist,
but snow does not melt from the furnace brow of Mahomet,
or napkins hemorrhage from the brow of Christ.
Along the island the almonds seethe with anger,
the wind that churns these orchards of white surf
and whistles dervishes up from the hot sand
revolves this globe, this painted O that spins,
reciting as it moves, tribes, frontiers,
dots that are sounds, cities that love their names,

while weather vanes still scrape the sky for omens.
Though they have different sounds for 'God' or 'hunger',
the opposing alphabets in city squares
shout with one voice, nation takes on nation,
and, from their fury of pronunciation,
children lie torn on rubble for a noun.

ROBERT BROWNING

Soliloquy of the Spanish Cloister

Gr-r-r – there go, my heart's abhorrence!
    Water your damned flower-pots, do!
If hate killed men, Brother Lawrence,
    God's blood, would not mine kill you!
What? your myrtle-bush wants trimming?
    Oh, that rose has prior claims –
Needs its leaden vase filled brimming?
    Hell dry you up with its flames!

At the meal we sit together:
    Salve tibi! I must hear
Wise talk of the kind of weather,
    Sort of season, time of year:
Not a plenteous cork-crop: scarcely
    Dare we hope oak-galls, I doubt:
What's the Latin name for 'parsley'?
    What 's the Greek name for Swine's Snout?

Whew! We'll have our platter burnished,
    Laid with care on our own shelf!
With a fire-new spoon we're furnished,
    And a goblet for ourself,
Rinsed like something sacrificial
    Ere 'tis fit to touch our chaps –
Marked with L. for our initial!
    (He-he! There his lily snaps!)

Saint, forsooth! While brown Dolores
Squats outside the Convent bank
With Sanchicha, telling stories,
Steeping tresses in the tank,
Blue-black, lustrous, thick like horsehairs,
– Can't I see his dead eye glow,
Bright as 'twere a Barbary corsair's?
(That is, if he'd let it show!)

When he finishes refection,
Knife and fork he never lays
Cross-wise, to my recollection,
As I do, in Jesu's praise.
I the Trinity illustrate,
Drinking watered orange-pulp –
In three sips the Arian frustrate;
While he drains his at one gulp.

Oh, those melons? If he's able
We're to have a feast! so nice!
One goes to the Abbot's table,
All of us to get a slice.
How go on your flowers? None double?
Not one fruit-sort can you spy?
Strange! – And I, too, at such trouble,
Keep them close-nipped on the sly!

There's a great text in Galatians,
Once you trip on it, entails
Twenty-nine distinct damnations,
One sure, if another fails:
If I trip him just a-dying,
Sure of heaven as sure can be,
Spin him round and send him flying
Off to hell, a Manichee?

Or, my scrofulous French novel
On grey paper with blunt type!
Simply glance at it, you grovel
Hand and foot in Belial's gripe:
If I double down its pages

At the woeful sixteenth print,
When he gathers his greengages,
Ope a sieve and slip it in't?

Or, there's Satan! – one might venture
Pledge one's soul to him, yet leave
Such a flaw in the indenture
As he'd miss it, past retrieve,
Blasted lay that rose-acacia,
We're so proud of! *Hy, Zy, Hine* . . .
'St, there's Vespers! *Plena gratiâ*
Ave, Virgo! Gr-r-r – you swine!

WILLIAM BLAKE

A Little Boy Lost

'Nought loves another as itself,
'Nor venerates another so,
'Nor is it possible to Thought
'A greater than itself to know:

'And Father, how can I love you
'Or any of my brothers more?
'I love you like the little bird
'That picks up crumbs around the door.'

The Priest sat by and heard the child,
In trembling zeal he seiz'd his hair:
He led him by his little coat,
And all admir'd the Priestly care.

And standing on the altar high,
'Lo! what a fiend is here!' said he,
'One who sets reason up for judge
'Of our most holy Mystery.'

The weeping child could not be heard,
The weeping parents wept in vain;
They strip'd him to his little shirt,
And bound him in an iron chain;

And burn'd him in a holy place,
Where many had been burn'd before:
The weeping parents wept in vain.
Are such things done on Albion's shore?

PHILIP LARKIN
Days

What are days for?
Days are where we live.
They come, they wake us
Time and time over.
They are to be happy in:
Where can we live but days?

Ah, solving that question
Brings the priest and the doctor
In their long coats
Running over the fields.

SIDNEY GODOLPHIN
Hymn

Lord, when the wise men came from far,
Led to thy cradle by a star,
Then did the shepherds too rejoice,
Instructed by thy angel's voice.
Blest were the wise men in their skill,
And shepherds in their harmless will.

Wise men, in tracing Nature's laws,
Ascend unto the highest cause;
Shepherds with humble fearfulness
Walk safely, though their light be less.
Though wise men better know the way,
It seems no honest heart can stray.

There is no merit in the wise
But love, the shepherds' sacrifice.
Wise men, all ways of knowledge passed,
To the shepherds' wonder come at last.
To know can only wonder breed,
And not to know is wonder's seed.

A wise man at the altar bows,
And offers up his studied vows,
And is received. May not the tears,
Which spring too from a shepherd's fears,
And sighs upon his frailty spent,
Though not distinct, be eloquent?

'Tis true, the object sanctifies
All passions which within us rise,
But since no creature comprehends
The cause of causes, end of ends,
He who himself vouchsafes to know
Best pleases his creator so.

When then our sorrows we apply
To our own wants and poverty,
When we look up in all distress,
And our own misery confess,
Sending both thanks and prayers above,
Then, though we do not know, we love.

D. H. LAWRENCE
Maximus

God is older than the sun and moon
and the eye cannot behold him
nor voice describe him.

But a naked man, a stranger, leaned on the gate
with his cloak over his arm, waiting to be asked in.
So I called him: Come in, if you will! –
He came in slowly, and sat down by the hearth.
I said to him: And what is your name? –
He looked at me without answer, but such a loveliness
entered me, I smiled to myself, saying: He is God!
So he said: *Hermes!*

God is older than the sun and moon
and the eye cannot behold him
nor the voice describe him:
and still, this is the God Hermes, sitting by my hearth.

ALFRED, LORD TENNYSON
From *In Memoriam A. H. H.*

CXXIV

That which we dare invoke to bless;
    Our dearest faith; our ghastliest doubt;
    He, They, One, All; within, without;
The Power in darkness whom we guess;

I found Him not in world or sun,
    Or eagle's wing, or insect's eye;
    Nor thro' the questions men may try,
The petty cobwebs we have spun:

If e'er when faith had fall'n asleep,
I heard a voice 'believe no more'
And heard an ever-breaking shore
That tumbled in the Godless deep;

A warmth within the breast would melt
The freezing reason's colder part,
And like a man in wrath the heart
Stood up and answer'd 'I have felt.'

No, like a child in doubt and fear:
But that blind clamour made me wise;
Then was I as a child that cries,
But, crying, knows his father near;

And what I am beheld again
What is, and no man understands;
And out of darkness came the hands
That reach thro' nature, moulding men.

CXXIII

There rolls the deep where grew the tree.
O earth, what changes hast thou seen!
There, where the long street roars, hath been
The stillness of the central sea.

The hills are shadows, and they flow
From form to form, and nothing stands;
They melt like mist, the solid lands,
Like clouds they shape themselves and go.

But in my spirit will I dwell,
And dream my dream, and hold it true;
For tho' my lips may breathe adieu,
I cannot think the thing farewell.

JOHN OF THE CROSS

Commentary Applied to Spiritual Things

(translated by K. Kavanaugh and O. Rodrigues)

Not for all of beauty
Will I ever lose myself,
But for I-don't-know-what
Which is attained so gladly.

Delight in the world's good things
At the very most
Can only tire the appetite
And spoil the palate;
And so, not for all of sweetness
Will I ever lose myself,
But for I-don't-know-what
Which is so gladly found.

The generous heart
Never delays over easy things
But eagerly goes on
To more difficult ones.
Nothing satisfies it,
And its faith ascends so high
That it tastes I-don't-know-what
Which is so gladly found.

He who is sick with love,
Whom God Himself has touched,
Finds his tastes so changed
That they fall sway
Like a fevered man's
Who loathes any food he sees
And desires I-don't-know-what
Which is so gladly found.

Do not wonder
That the taste should be left like this,
For the cause of this sickness

Differs from all others;
And so he is withdrawn
From all creatures,
And tastes I-don't-know-what
Which is so gladly found.

For when once the will
Is touched by God Himself
It cannot be satisfied
Except by God;
But since His Beauty is open
To faith alone, the will
Tastes Him in I-don't-know-what
Which is so gladly found.

Tell me then, would you pity
A man so in love,
For he takes no delight
In all of creation;
Alone, mind empty of form and figure,
Finding no support or foothold,
He tastes there I-don't-know-what
Which is so gladly found.

Do not think that he who lives
The so precious inner life
Finds joy and gladness
In the sweetnesses of earth;
But there beyond all beauty
And what is and will be and was,
He tastes I-don't-know-what
Which is so gladly found.

The man who seeks to advance
Looks carefully to
What he has yet to gain
More than to what he has gained;
And so I will always tend
Toward greater heights;
Beyond all things, to I-don't-know-what
Which is so gladly found.

I will never lose myself
For that which the senses
Can take in here,
Nor for all the mind can hold,
No matter how lofty,
Nor for grace or beauty,
But only for I-don't-know-what
Which is so gladly found.

ḤAFÍẒ

(translated by R. A. Nicholson)

Mortal never won to view thee,
Yet a thousand lovers woo thee;
Not a nightingale but knows
In the rosebud sleeps the rose.

Love is where the glory falls
Of thy face: on convent walls
Or on tavern floors the same
Unextinguishable flame.

Where the turban'd anchorite
Chanteth Allah day and night,
Churchbells ring the call to prayer,
And the Cross of Christ is there.

JALÁLU'DDÍN RÚMÍ

(translated by R. A. Nicholson)

Lo, for I to myself am unknown, now in God's name what must I do?
I adore not the Cross or the Crescent, I am not a Giaour or a Jew.
East nor West, land nor sea is my home, I have kin nor with angel nor gnome,
I am wrought not of fire or of foam, I am shaped not of dust or of dew.
I was born not in China afar, not in Saḳsín and not in Bulghár;

Not in India, where five rivers are, or 'Irák̤ or Khurásán I grew.
Not in this world or that world I dwell, not in Paradise, neither in Hell;
Not from Eden and Riẓwán I fell, not from Adam my lineage I drew.
In a place beyond uttermost place, in a tract without shadow of trace,
Soul and body transcending I live in the soul of my Loved One anew!

IBNU 'L-'ARABÍ

(translated by R. A. Nicholson)

My heart is capable of every form:
A cloister for the monk, a fane for idols,
A pasture for gazelles, the votary's Ka'ba,
The tables of the Torah, the Koran.
Love is the faith I hold: wherever turn
His camels, still the one true faith is mine.

LADY TANFIELD

Here shadowe lie,
whilst life is sadd,
Still hopes to die,
to him she hadd.

In bliss is hee
whom I lovd best,
thrise happie shee,
with him to rest.

So shall I be
with him I love,
and he wth mee
and both vs blessed.

love made me poet
and this I writt,
my harte did do it,
and not my witt.

WILLIAM WORDSWORTH

From *The Prelude* Book II ('School-time')

But who shall parcel out
His intellect by geometric rules,
Split like a province into round and square?
Who knows the individual hour in which
His habits were first sown, even as a seed?
Who that shall point as with a wand and say
'This portion of the river of my mind
Came from yon fountain'? Thou, my Friend!* art one
More deeply read in thy own thoughts; to thee
Science appears but what in truth she is,
Not as our glory and our absolute boast,
But as a succedaneum, and a prop
To our infirmity. No officious slave
Art thou of that false secondary power
By which we multiply distinctions, then
Deem that our puny boundaries are things
That we perceive, and not that we have made.
To thee, unblinded by these formal arts,
The unity of all hath been revealed,
And thou wilt doubt, with me less aptly skilled
Than many are to range the faculties
In scale and order, class the cabinet
Of their sensations, and in voluble phrase
Run through the history and birth of each
As of a single independent thing.

* The 'Friend' Wordsworth addresses in *The Prelude* is Coleridge.

R. S. THOMAS

Coleridge

Walking often beside the waves'
Endless embroidery of the bare sand,
Coleridge never could understand,
Dazed by the knocking of the wind
In the ear's passage, the chorus
Of shrill voices from the sea
That mocked his vain philosophy
In salt accents. And at tide's retreat,
When the vexed ocean camping far
On the horizon filled the air
With dull thunder, ominous and low,
He felt his theories break and go
In small clouds about the sky,
Whose nihilistic blue repelled
The vain probing of his eye.

WILLIAM SHAKESPEARE

From *Hamlet* Act I, Scene 1

MARCELLUS:
It faded on the crowing of the cock.
Some say that ever 'gainst that season comes
Wherein our Saviour's birth is celebrated,
The bird of dawning singeth all night long,
And then, they say, no spirit dare stir abroad,
The nights are wholesome, then no planets strike,
No fairy takes nor witch hath power to charm.
So hallow'd and so gracious is that time.

HORATIO:
So have I heard and do in part believe it.

THOMAS HARDY

The Oxen

Christmas Eve, and twelve of the clock.
    'Now they are all on their knees,'
An elder said as we sat in a flock
    By the embers in hearthside ease.

We pictured the meek mild creatures where
    They dwelt in their strawy pen,
Nor did it occur to one of us there
    To doubt they were kneeling then.

So fair a fancy few would weave
    In these years! Yet, I feel,
If someone said on Christmas Eve,
    'Come; see the oxen kneel

'In the lonely barton by yonder coomb
    Our childhood used to know,'
I should go with him in the gloom,
    Hoping it might be so.

WILLIAM BLAKE

The Tyger

Tyger! Tyger! burning bright
In the forests of the night,
What immortal hand or eye
Could frame thy fearful symmetry?

In what distant deeps or skies
Burnt the fire of thine eyes?
On what wings dare he aspire?
What the hand dare sieze the fire?

And what shoulder, & what art,
Could twist the sinews of thy heart?
And when thy heart began to beat,
What dread hand? & what dread feet?

What the hammer? what the chain?
In what furnace was thy brain?
What the anvil? what dread grasp
Dare its deadly terrors clasp?

When the stars threw down their spears,
And water'd heaven with their tears,
Did he smile his work to see?
Did he who made the Lamb make thee?

Tyger! Tyger! burning bright
In the forests of the night,
What immortal hand or eye
Dare frame thy fearful symmetry?

GERARD MANLEY HOPKINS

Spelt from Sibyl's Leaves

Earnest, earthless, equal, attuneable, | vaulty, voluminous, . . . stupendous
Evening strains to be time's vást, | womb-of-all, home-of-all, hearse-of-all
 night.
Her fond yellow hornlight wound to the west, | her wild hollow hoarlight
 hung to the height
Waste; her earliest stars, earl-stars, | stárs principal, overbend us,
Fíre-féaturing heaven. For earth | her being has unbound, her dapple is at an
 end, as-
tray or aswarm, all throughther, in throngs; | self ín self steepèd and páshed –
 qúite
Disremembering, dísmémbering | áll now. Heart, you round me right
With: Óur évening is over us; óur night | whélms, whélms, ánd will end us.
Only the beak-leaved boughs dragonish | damask the tool-smooth bleak light;
 black,

Ever so black on it. Óur tale, O óur oracle! | Lét life, wáned, ah lét life wind
Off hér once skéined stained véined varíety | upon, áll on twó spools; párt, pen, páck
Now her áll in twó flocks, twó folds – black, white; | right, wrong; reckon but, reck but, mind
But thése two; wáre of a wórld where bút these | twó tell, each off the óther; of a rack
Where, selfwrung, selfstrung, sheathe- and shelterless, | thóughts agaínst thoughts ín groans grínd.

8.
VISION AND IMAGINATION

When we speak of 'vision' in a religious context, we tend to think of apparitions: of the Virgin Mary appearing to children at Fatima or Lourdes, or Jesus appearing to Margaret Mary Alacoque. These kind of visions happen spontaneously; the visionary has not usually prepared for them or even induced them deliberately in meditation. The sceptic might well question these kind of visions as purely hysterical hallucinations. The mind can do strange things. We are all hallucinating all the time, neurologists tell us. It is only the rational part of the brain that suppresses this image-making faculty, and it is possible that some kind of shock or mental change could trigger a conscious hallucination. The Venerable Sangharakshita told me that during his very early days of Buddhist meditation, he once had a vision of the Virgin Mary. He was not expecting this, obviously, because he doesn't 'believe in' the Virgin Mary as a Christian does. However, he did not decide that this vision of the Virgin was a proof of Christianity's claim. He was very interested in art, and the Virgin of his vision reminded Sangharakshita of a Murillo painting. What was happening was that in his meditations he had tapped some hidden but powerful reach of his subconscious.

It is possible, then, for man to create visions for himself, out of his needs, desires and beliefs. This is not necessarily a bad thing. When we speak of somebody having 'vision' not in a religious context, we mean that he has special insight that lifts him above other people. Theologians like John of the Cross usually decry the type of visions that happen at Fatima or Lourdes. They are not nearly as important as the cultivation of meditation and the stilling of the critical faculty, nor as important as the approaching of God in love, in a patient and unspectacular way. This experience is, as we have seen, ineffable. It cannot be described or defined. Visions of Jesus or of angels, on the other hand, are quite the reverse. They speak very comprehensible messages indeed. They are assertive, dogmatic and often tell us more about the visionaries than about Jesus or Mary. Instead of lifting above this world, they speak, judge and act very much in the spirit and mode of this world.

However, poets and mystics have had visions that have risen up from the subconscious with such authority that they seem given from outside. Mystics also encounter a 'presence' during meditation. It is with these states that I am concerned in this section of the anthology. Vision is simply a way of viewing reality. It is permeated by beliefs that we hold apart from the moment of vision. In a sense, the contemplative minds of both mystic and poet create vision for themselves, creatively and calmly. Poets have called this faculty imagination.

In the first two poems of the section we have examples of visions that fall upon the recipient unawares. 'The Burning Babe' appears to Southwell out of the blue, but he doesn't say that Jesus appeared to him, coming down specially to cheer him up one chilly Christmas night. The apparition could well be of the same order as Coleridge's in 'Kubla Khan'. Tennyson's sudden trance and vision are rather different. He is whirled out of himself, and what he 'sees' is not so much an image as an ineffable Reality. It seems likely that Tennyson was epileptic, which would physically dispose him to this type of experience, and this is a warning to us that there may well be a pathological explanation for much religious vision. Dostoyevsky in *The Idiot* has memorably described the sense of ecstasy and significance that floods the epileptic just before a *grand mal* attack, and as I myself suffer from Temporal Lobe Epilepsy, I can verify this. It seems like an experience of God, but it is in fact caused by some kind of electrical thunderstorm in the brain.

Mystical vision is something quite different from the visions of an epileptic or those of children who see the Virgin Mary and have long conversations with her. One kind of mystical vision suggests that the mystic makes the dogma of his religion his own, during the course of his meditation. In the poem by Ibnu 'l-Fáriḍ we see such a vision that is deeply linked to dogmatic belief. It is a passionate vision that has been carefully prepared for in silence and long meditation. When it comes, the poet does not attempt to describe this vision. All he will tell us is that it shows him the truth of the central belief of Islam, the Moslem's daily confession of faith: 'There is no God but He, and He is the most High.' The vision of God that Dante describes at the end of the *Divine Comedy* is really, I think, more of a theological meditation on the Trinity and the Incarnation than a mystic vision like 'l-Fáriḍ's. However, at the end the poet is suddenly rapt from his intellectual puzzlings and attains a sense of Oneness with the 'Love' that moves the sun and the stars. His intellectual beliefs have been removed from the sphere of mental gymnastics to ineffable experience, and the poet has become One with the Reality that his intellectual vision could only symbolize. He has made his belief his own.

Keats's vision in 'Ode to a Nightingale' and Wordsworth's vision on the Alps are different again, because they are not theologically earthed. They do not lead the poets to affirm the creeds and beliefs of a given religion, but they are certainly mystical experiences all the same. Keats's vision is imbued with nearly all the elements of mysticism that we have noted in the anthology. He is restless and yearning for the mystical experience. He is moved by his personal perception of existence as suffering to seek for an end or an escape from pain. He is quite aware that no amount of activity in 'the dull brain', which only 'perplexes and retards' the mystic, will be of any use to him at all. He enters into a 'dark night' of unknowing, very similar to the darkness described by John of the Cross. From this he passes away from himself to a vision of joy and eternity, which soon goes, leaving the poet alone. He has been summoned back 'to my sole self' and is left with the agnosticism of all true mystics; he will not classify his vision: 'Was it a vision, or a waking dream? . . . Do I wake or sleep?' Wordsworth's vision on the Alps is classic. It is a time when he sees not embodied forms of heavenly and supernatural beings, but 'into the life' of ordinary things around him. What happened to him was that a 'Power' rose from the depths of his mind ('from the mind's abyss')

> **. . . in such strength**
> **Of usurpation, when the light of sense**
> **Goes out, but with a flash that has revealed**
> **The invisible world, doth greatness make abode**

He could see the crags and waterfalls around him, but they were shot through with a new significance. In the Alpine landscape he saw a vision of paradox that is somehow reconciled: the 'woods decaying, never to be decayed', 'Tumult and peace, the darkness and the light'. All were 'Like workings of one mind'; it was a revelation (an 'Apocalypse') of some eternal reality greater than we normally see with 'the light of sense'. It is a truly mystical vision, but where a religious man would say that he had experienced God, perhaps, or would say that the vision came from outside himself, Wordsworth is quite clear that it comes from within. He has 'imagined' it all. But for Wordsworth and for the Romantic poets, the imagination is not something to be taken lightly. Keats said that it was 'creative of essential beauty'; that 'what the imagination seizes as beauty must be truth, whether it existed before or not', and these ideas are explored by both Shelley in the extract from *Prometheus Unbound* and by Peter Levi in his poem 'I imagine where God has never been'. What the poet imagines has its own truth; it is creative of a new and valuable reality. These mystical moments are for Wordsworth the source of his spiritual life; they give him that sense of infinitude without which man is nothing. They don't spring upon him unawares, for we have seen how he encouraged his mind to adopt the 'wise passiveness' of contemplation. Here the vision came when he was literally wrapt in a 'cloud of unknowing'. The mists swirled around him on the Alpine paths, and when he says 'I was lost', it is clear that he meant more than the literal fact that he had lost his way and didn't know where he physically was.

In Book III of *Paradise Lost* Milton also is tragically lost in his blindness, and prays that the Celestial Light will irradiate the eyes of his mind 'that I may see and tell / Of things invisible to mortal sight'. This is an excellent description of religious faith, which means that your mind has taken up a position that gives you a particular vision of the world. Hopkins too shows us that the poet's image-making can be used to reflect not just beliefs about religion, but can lead directly to God and Christ Himself. His vision of the Windhover is in no way supernatural – it is a real bird – but by contemplating it he can see it as a reflection of God. It is a means to God that has been called the Way of Affirmation by spiritual writers. Instead of saying, with the mystic, what God is not, you see God reflected and revealed in the things of this world. In 'Hurrahing in Harvest' Hopkins sees this affirmative vision as a dynamic force that 'hurls' the poet towards God once the two ingredients of God-given landscape and the beholder who can see that it is God-given come together. The poet sees more than ordinary people, as both Hardy and Dylan Thomas show in 'Afterwards' and 'Over Sir John's Hill'. Hopkins had conventional religious beliefs; Thomas had not, but he saw the poet 'fabling' like a young Aesop as performing an almost priestly role in commemorating the dead birds alongside 'saint heron'. Because the poet has this ability to see more deeply and more intensely than most of us, he can communicate his 'vision' to those of us who are not so alive to the power of images.

Imagination may also be of help to more ordinary believers as well as creating special mystical experiences. In 'Legend' Causley sees the myth-making powers of the imagination as redemptive; it can 'Put winter to flight!' He hints that without imagination, religion is powerless to comfort and redeem: the church steeple looks very 'brittle' and frail when threatened by the overwhelming powers of winter.

Myths are vitally important to us. They tell us stories about the world that comfort us and give us a sense of purpose and significance. They impose a form on the chaos and arbitrariness of what we see around us. Poetry and religion both create these myths for us, and religion must be poetical and imaginative. Every one of us has somehow to create a myth for himself about how he fits into the world. We tell ourselves stories about our own lives, interpreting and evaluating their events into some sort of order so that they acquire a shape and direction. Psychoanalysis is the new great myth of our time and deeply religious in its search for significance and private meaning. However, we don't have to resort to psychoanalysis to create these myths for ourselves. Wordsworth says that there are in all our lives 'spots of time', events that remain with us with the force of 'visions' in the religious sense. The images of desolation of the cold moorland scene when he got lost as a child, and of that afternoon while he was waiting to be taken home from school for the Christmas holidays have deep moral force. He returns to them again and again as to a fountain. They have acquired life-giving force, even though when the events were actually happening they seemed of little or of no significance. They lead Wordsworth to bow in reverence to God, but even more they show him the 'mystery of man' who can thus imaginatively create significance and beauty of such moral richness from the things he sees around him. The power is not God-given; it comes from man himself, from the 'hiding-places' of creative power deep within his mind. We are imaginative beings, and the only way we can live in the world is to work in alliance with the images we see. The poet and the mystic both see the dignity and mystery of the human mind, which is not just a receptacle of divine messages, but can be itself creative of essential meaning.

ROBERT SOUTHWELL

The Burning Babe

As I in hoary winter's night stood shivering in the snow,
Surprised I was with sudden heat which made my heart to glow;
And lifting up a fearful eye to view what fire was near,
A pretty Babe all burning bright did in the air appear;
Who, scorchèd with excessive heat, such floods of tears did shed,
As though his floods should quench his flames which with his tears were fed.

'Alas!' quoth he, 'but newly born in fiery heats I fry,
Yet none approach to warm their hearts or feel my fire but I.
My faultless breast the furnace is, the fuel wounding thorns;
Love is the fire, and sighs the smoke, the ashes shame and scorns;
The fuel justice layeth on, and mercy blows the coals;
The metal in this furnace wrought are men's defilèd souls:
For which, as now on fire I am to work them to their good,
So will I melt into a bath to wash them in my blood.'
With this he vanished out of sight and swiftly sunk away,
And straight I callèd unto mind that it was Christmas Day.

ALFRED, LORD TENNYSON

From *In Memoriam A. H. H.*

XCV

By night we linger'd on the lawn,
For underfoot the herb was dry;
And genial warmth; and o'er the sky
The silvery haze of summer drawn;

And calm that let the tapers burn
    Unwavering: not a cricket chirr'd:
    The brook alone far-off was heard,
And on the board the fluttering urn:

And bats went round in fragrant skies,
    And wheel'd or lit the filmy shapes
    That haunt the dusk, with ermine capes
And woolly breasts and beaded eyes;

While now we sang old songs that peal'd
    From knoll to knoll, where, couch'd at ease,
    The white kine glimmer'd, and the trees
Laid their dark arms about the field.

But when those others, one by one,
    Withdrew themselves from me and night,
    And in the house light after light
Went out, and I was all alone,

A hunger seized my heart; I read
    Of that glad year which once had been,
    In those fall'n leaves which kept their green,
The noble letters of the dead:

And strangely on the silence broke
    The silent-speaking words, and strange
    Was love's dumb cry defying change
To test his worth; and strangely spoke

The faith, the vigour, bold to dwell
    On doubts that drive the coward back,
    And keen thro' wordy snares to track
Suggestion to her inmost cell.

So word by word, and line by line,
    The dead man touch'd me from the past,
    And all at once it seem'd at last
The living soul was flash'd on mine,

And mine in this was wound, and whirl'd
About empyreal heights of thought,
And came on that which is, and caught
The deep pulsations of the world,

Æonian music measuring out
The steps of Time – the shocks of Chance –
The blows of Death. At length my trance
Was cancell'd, stricken thro' with doubt.

Vague words! but ah, how hard to frame
In matter-moulded forms of speech,
Or ev'n for intellect to reach
Thro' memory that which I became:

Till now the doubtful dusk reveal'd
The knolls once more where, couch'd at ease,
The white kine glimmer'd, and the trees
Laid their dark arms about the field:

And suck'd from out the distant gloom
A breeze began to tremble o'er
The large leaves of the sycamore,
And fluctuate all the still perfume,

And gathering freshlier overhead,
Rock'd the full-foliaged elms, and swung
The heavy-folded rose, and flung
The lilies to and fro, and said

'The dawn, the dawn,' and died away;
And East and West, without a breath,
Mixt their dim lights, like life and death,
To broaden into boundless day.

IBNU 'L-FÁRIḌ

(translated by R. A. Nicholson)

Let passion's swelling tide my senses drown!
Pity love's fuel, this long-smouldering heart,
Nor answer with a frown,
When I would fain behold Thee as Thou art,
*'Thou shalt not see Me.'** O my soul, keep fast
The pledge thou gav'st: endure unfaltering to the last!
For Love is life, and death in love the Heaven
Where all sins are forgiven.
To those before and after and of this day,
That witnesseth my tribulation, say,
'By me be taught, me follow, me obey,
And tell my passion's story through wide East and West.'
With my Beloved I alone have been
When secrets tenderer than evening airs
Passed, and the Vision blest
Was granted to my prayers,
That crowned me, else obscure, with endless fame,
The while amazed between
His beauty and His majesty
I stood in silent ecstasy,
Revealing that which o'er my spirit went and came.
Lo, in His face commingled
Is every charm and grace;
The whole of Beauty singled
Into a perfect face
Beholding Him would cry
'There is no God but He, and He is the most High!'

* As God said to Moses (Koran 7:139).

DANTE ALIGHIERI

From *Paradiso* Canto XXXIII

(translated by Dorothy L. Sayers and Barbara Reynolds)

The piercing brightness of the living ray
Which I endured, my vision had undone,
I think, if I had turned my eyes away.

And I recall this further led me on,
Wherefore my gaze more boldness yet assumed
Till to the Infinite Good it last had won.

O grace abounding, whereby I presumed
So deep the eternal light to search and sound
That my whole vision was therein consumed!

In that abyss I saw how love held bound
Into one volume all the leaves whose flight
Is scattered through the universe around;

How substance, accident, and mode unite
Fused, so to speak, together, in such wise
That this I tell of is one simple light.

Yea, of this complex I believe mine eyes
Beheld the universal form – in me,
Even as I speak, I feel such joy arise.

One moment brings me deeper lethargy
Than twenty-five centuries brought the quest that dazed
Neptune when Argo's shadow crossed the sea.

And so my mind, bedazzled and amazed,
Soon fixed in wonder, motionless, intent,
And still my wonder kindled as I gazed.

That light doth so transform a man's whole bent
That never to another sight or thought
Would he surrender, with his own consent;

For everything the will has ever sought
    Is gathered there, and there is every quest
    Made perfect, which apart from it falls short.

Now, even what I recall will be exprest
    More feebly than if I could wield no more
    Than a babe's tongue, yet milky from the breast;

Not that the living light I looked on wore
    More semblances than one, which cannot be,
    For it is always what it was before;

But as my sight by seeing learned to see,
    The transformation which in me took place
    Transformed the single changeless form for me.

That light supreme, within its fathomless
    Clear substance, showed to me three spheres, which bare
    Three hues distinct, and occupied one space;

The first mirrored the next, though it were
    Rainbow from rainbow, and the third seemed flame
    Breathed equally from each of the first pair.

How weak are words, and how unfit to frame
    My concept – which lags after what was shown
    So far, 'twould flatter it to call it lame!

Eternal light, that in Thyself alone
    Dwelling, alone dost know Thyself, and smile
    On Thy self-love, so knowing and so known!

The sphering thus begot, perceptible
    In Thee like mirrored light, now to my view –
    When I had looked on it a little while –

Seemed in itself, and in its own self-hue,
    Limned with our image; for which cause mine eyes
    Were altogether drawn and held thereto.

As the geometer his mind applies
  To square the circle, nor for all his wit
  Finds the right formula, howe'er he tries,

So strove I with that wonder – how to fit
  The image to the sphere; so sought to see
  How it maintained the point of rest in it.

Thither my own wings could not carry me,
  But that a flash my understanding clove,
  Whence its desire came to it suddenly.

High phantasy lost power and here broke off;
  Yet as a wheel moves smoothly, free from jars,
  My will and my desire were turned by love,

The love that moves the sun and the other stars.

JOHN KEATS

Ode to a Nightingale

I

My heart aches, and a drowsy numbness pains
  My sense, as though of hemlock I had drunk,
Or emptied some dull opiate to the drains
  One minute past, and Lethe-wards had sunk:
'Tis not through envy of thy happy lot,
  But being too happy in thine happiness, –
    That thou, light-winged Dryad of the trees,
      In some melodious plot
  Of beechen green, and shadows numberless,
    Singest of summer in full-throated ease.

II

O, for a draught of vintage! that hath been
  Cool'd a long age in the deep-delved earth,
Tasting of Flora and the country green,
  Dance, and Provençal song, and sunburnt mirth!
O for a beaker full of the warm South,

Full of the true, the blushful Hippocrene,
With beaded bubbles winking at the brim,
And purple-stained mouth;
That I might drink, and leave the world unseen,
And with thee fade away into the forest dim:

III

Fade far away, dissolve, and quite forget
What thou among the leaves hast never known,
The weariness, the fever, and the fret
Here, where men sit and hear each other groan;
Where palsy shakes a few, sad, last gray hairs,
Where youth grows pale, and spectre-thin, and dies;
Where but to think is to be full of sorrow
And leaden-eyed despairs,
Where Beauty cannot keep her lustrous eyes,
Or new Love pine at them beyond to-morrow.

IV

Away! away! for I will fly to thee,
Not charioted by Bacchus and his pards,
But on the viewless wings of Poesy,
Though the dull brain perplexes and retards:
Already with thee! tender is the night,
And haply the Queen-Moon is on her throne,
Cluster'd around by all her starry Fays;
But here there is no light,
Save what from heaven is with the breezes blown
Through verdurous glooms and winding mossy ways.

V

I cannot see what flowers are at my feet,
Nor what soft incense hangs upon the boughs
But in embalmed darkness, guess each sweet
Wherewith the seasonable month endows
The grass, the thicket, and the fruit-tree wild;
White hawthorn, and the pastoral eglantine;
Fast fading violets cover'd up in leaves;
And mid-May's eldest child,
The coming musk-rose, full of dewy wine,
The murmurous haunt of flies on summer eves.

VI

Darkling I listen; and, for many a time
I have been half in love with easeful Death,
Call'd him soft names in many a mused rhyme,
To take into the air my quiet breath;
Now more than ever seems it rich to die,
To cease upon the midnight with no pain,
While thou art pouring forth thy soul abroad
In such an ecstasy!
Still wouldst thou sing, and I have ears in vain –
To thy high requiem become a sod.

VII

Thou wast not born for death, immortal Bird!
No hungry generations tread thee down;
The voice I hear this passing night was heard
In ancient days by emperor and clown:
Perhaps the self-same song that found a path
Through the sad heart of Ruth, when, sick for home,
She stood in tears amid the alien corn;
The same that oft-times hath
Charm'd magic casements, opening on the foam
Of perilous seas, in faery lands forlorn.

VIII

Forlorn! the very word is like a bell
To toll me back from thee to my sole self!
Adieu! the fancy cannot cheat so well
As she is fam'd to do, deceiving elf.
Adieu! adieu! thy plaintive anthem fades
Past the near meadows, over the still stream,
Up the hill-side; and now 'tis buried deep
In the next valley-glades:
Was it a vision, or a waking dream?
Fled is that music: – Do I wake or sleep?

WILLIAM WORDSWORTH

From *The Prelude*

Book VI ('Cambridge and the Alps')

When from the Vallais we had turned, and clomb
Along the Simplon's steep and rugged road,
Following a band of muleteers, we reached
A halting-place, where all together took
Their noon-tide meal. Hastily rose our guide,
Leaving us at the board; awhile we lingered,
Then paced the beaten downward way that led
Right to a rough stream's edge, and there broke off;
The only track now visible was one
That from the torrent's further brink held forth
Conspicuous invitation to ascend
A lofty mountain. After brief delay
Crossing the unbridged stream, that road we took,
And clomb with eagerness, till anxious fears
Intruded, for we failed to overtake
Our comrades gone before. By fortunate chance,
While every moment added doubt to doubt,
A peasant met us, from whose mouth we learned
That to the spot which had perplexed us first
We must descend, and there should find the road,
Which in the stony channel of the stream
Lay a few steps, and then along its banks;
And, that our future course, all plain to sight,
Was downwards, with the current of that stream.
Loth to believe what we so grieved to hear,
For still we had hopes that pointed to the clouds,
We questioned him again, and yet again:
But every word that from the peasant's lips
Came in reply, translated by our feelings,
Ended in this, – *that we had crossed the Alps*.

Imagination – here the Power so called
Through sad incompetence of human speech,
That awful Power rose from the mind's abyss
Like an unfathered vapour that enwraps,

At once, some lonely traveller. I was lost;
Halted without an effort to break through;
But to my conscious soul I now can say –
'I recognise thy glory:' in such strength
Of usurpation, when the light of sense
Goes out, but with a flash that has revealed
The invisible world, doth greatness make abode,
There harbours; whether we be young or old,
Our destiny, our being's heart and home,
Is with infinitude, and only there;
With hope it is, hope that can never die,
Effort, and expectation, and desire,
And something evermore about to be
Under such banners militant, the soul
Seeks for no trophies, struggles for no spoils
That may attest her prowess, blest in thoughts
That are their own perfection and reward,
Strong in herself and in beatitude
That hides her, like the mighty flood of Nile
Poured from his fount of Abyssinian clouds
To fertilise the whole Egyptian plain.
The melancholy slackening that ensued
Upon those tidings by the peasant given
Was soon dislodged. Downwards we hurried fast,
And with the half-shaped road which we had missed,
Entered a narrow chasm. The brook and road
Were fellow-travellers in this gloomy strait,
And with them did we journey several hours
At a slow pace. The immeasurable height
Of woods decaying, never to be decayed,
The stationary blasts of waterfalls,
And in the narrow rent at every turn
Winds thwarting winds, bewildered and forlorn,
The torrents shooting from the clear blue sky,
The rocks that muttered close upon our ears,
Black drizzling crags that spake by the way-side
As if a voice were in them, the sick sight
And giddy prospect of the raving stream,
The unfettered clouds and region of the Heavens,
Tumult and peace, the darkness and the light –
Were all like workings of one mind, the features

Of the same face, blossoms upon one tree;
Characters of the great Apocalypse,
The types and symbols of Eternity,
Of first, and last, and midst, and without end.

PERCY BYSSHE SHELLEY

From *Prometheus Unbound*

A Spirit's Song

On a poet's lips I slept
Dreaming like a love-adept
In the sound his breathing kept;
Nor seeks nor finds he, mortal blisses,
But feeds on the aëreal kisses
Of shapes that haunt thought's wildernesses.
He will watch from dawn to gloom
The lake reflected sun illume
The yellow bees in the ivy-bloom,
Nor heed nor see, what things they be;
But from these create he can
Forms more real than living man,
Nurslings of immortality!

PETER LEVI

(for Joan)

I imagine where God has never been
and a landscape Adam has never seen,
say a broad estuary
crab-apple salty on the crooked bough
different from the places we live now;

and I imagine by that estuary
and grape colours and long tones of the sea
quite a new kind of poem
without excuses: thistle, sand and reed
are their own explanation like the creed.

Inland birds cannot enter the poem,
because they carry an intense light with them,
streams of old-fashioned skies;
and half human bird-noises will not fit:
night falls heavy, seabirds understand it.

JOHN MILTON

From *Paradise Lost* Book III

Hail holy Light, ofspring of Heav'n first-born,
Or of th' Eternal Coeternal beam
May I express thee unblam'd? since God is Light,
And never but in unapproached Light
Dwelt from Eternitie, dwelt then in thee,
Bright effluence of bright essence increate.
Or hear'st thou rather pure Ethereal stream,
Whose Fountain who shall tell? before the Sun,
Before the Heav'ns thou wert, and at the voice
Of God, as with a Mantle didst invest
The rising world of waters dark and deep,
Won from the void and formless infinite.
Thee I re-visit now with bolder wing,
Escap't the *Stygian* Pool, though long detaind
In that obscure sojourn, while in my flight
Through utter and through middle darkness borne
With other notes then to th' *Orphean* Lyre
I sung of *Chaos* and *Eternal Night*,
Taught by the heav'nly Muse to venture down
The dark descent, and up to reascend,
Though hard and rare: thee I revisit safe,
And feel thy sovran vital Lamp; but thou
Revisit'st not these eyes, that rowle in vain

To find thy piercing ray, and find no dawn:
So thick a drop serene hath quencht thir Orbs,
Or dim suffusion veild. Yet not the more
Cease I to wander where the Muses haunt
Cleer Spring, or shadie Grove, or Sunnie Hill,
Smit with the love of sacred Song; but chief
Thee *Sion* and the flowrie Brooks beneath
That wash thy hallowd feet, and warbling flow,
Nightly I visit: nor somtimes forget
Those other two equald with me in Fate,
So were I equald with them in renown,
Blind *Thamyris* and blind *Mœonides*,
And *Tiresias* and *Phineus* Prophets old:
Then feed on thoughts, that voluntarie move
Harmonious numbers; as the wakeful Bird
Sings darkling, and in shadiest Covert hid
Tunes her nocturnal Note. Thus with the Year
Seasons return, but not to mee returns
Day, or the sweet approach of Ev'n or Morn,
Or sight of vernal bloom, or Summers Rose,
Or flocks, or herds, or human face divine;
But cloud in stead, and ever-during dark
Surrounds me, from the chearful waies of men
Cut off, and for the Book of knowledg fair
Presented with a Universal blanc
Of Natures works to mee expung'd and ras'd,
And wisdom at one entrance quite shut out.
So much the rather thou Celestial Light
Shine inward, and the mind through all her powers
Irradiate, there plant eyes, all mist from thence
Purge and disperse, that I may see and tell
Of things invisible to mortal sight.

HENRY VAUGHAN
Religion

My God, when I walk in those groves,
And leaves thy spirit doth still fan,
I see in each shade that there grows
An Angel talking with a man.

Under a *juniper*, some house,
Or the cool *myrtle's* canopy,
Others beneath an oak's green boughs,
Or at some *fountain's* bubbling eye;

Here *Jacob* dreams and wrestles; there
Elias by a raven is fed,
Another time by the Angel, where
He brings him water with his bread;

In *Abraham's* tent the winged guests
(O how familiar then was heaven!)
Eat, drink, discourse, sit down, and rest
Until the cool, and shady *even*;

Nay thou thy self, my God, in *fire*,
Whirl-winds and *clouds*, and the *soft voice*
Speak'st there so much, that I admire
We have no conference in these days;

Is the truce broke? or 'cause we have
A mediator now with thee,
Dost thou therefore old treaties waive
And by appeals from him decree?

Or is't so, as some green heads say
That now all miracles must cease?
Though thou hast promised they should stay
The tokens of the Church, and peace;

No, no; Religion is a spring
That from some secret, golden mine
Derives her birth, and thence doth bring
Cordials in every drop, and wine;

But in her long, and hidden course
Passing through the earth's dark veins,
Grows still from better unto worse,
And both her taste, and colour stains,

Then drilling on, learns to increase
False *echoes*, and confused sounds,
And unawares doth often seize
On veins of *sulphur* under ground;

So poisoned, breaks forth in some clime,
And at first sight doth many please,
But drunk, is puddle, or mere slime
And 'stead of physic, a disease;

Just such a tainted sink we have
Like that *Samaritan's* dead *well*,
Nor must we for the kernel crave
because most voices like the *shell*.

Heal then these waters, Lord; or bring thy flock
Since these are troubled, to the springing rock,
Look down great Master of the feast; O shine,
And turn once more our *Water* into *Wine*!

Song of Solomon, IV, 12
My sister, my spouse is as a garden enclosed, as a spring shut up, and a fountain sealed up.

SAMUEL HA-NAGID

I Look Up to the Sky

(translated by David Goldstein)

I look up to the sky and its stars,
And down to the earth and the things that creep there.
And I consider in my heart how their creation
Was planned with wisdom in every detail.
See the heavens above like a tent,
Constructed with loops and with hooks,
And the moon with its stars, like a shepherdess
Driving her sheep to pasture;
The moon itself among the clouds,
Like a ship sailing under its banners;
The clouds like a girl in her garden
Moving, and watering the myrtle-trees;
The dew-mist – a woman shaking
Drops from her hair on the ground.
The inhabitants turn, like animals, to rest,
(Their palaces like their stables);
And all fleeing from the fear of death,
Like a dove pursued by the falcon.
And these are compared at the end to a plate
Which is smashed into innumerable sherds.

GERARD MANLEY HOPKINS

The Windhover

To Christ our Lord

I caught this morning morning's minion, king-
    dom of daylight's dauphin, dapple-dawn-drawn Falcon,
        in his riding
    Of the rolling level underneath him steady air, and striding
High there, how he rung upon the rein of a wimpling wing
In his ecstasy! then off, off forth on swing,

As a skate's heel sweeps smooth on a bow-bend: the hurl
and gliding
Rebuffed the big wind. My heart in hiding
Stirred for a bird, – the achieve of, the mastery of the thing!

Brute beauty and valour and act, oh, air, pride, plume here
Buckle! AND the fire that breaks from thee then, a billion
Times told lovelier, more dangerous, O my chevalier!

No wonder of it: shéer plód makes plough down sillion
Shine, and blue-bleak embers, ah my dear,
Fall, gall themselves and gash gold-vermilion.

Hurrahing in Harvest

Summer ends now; now, barbarous in beauty, the stooks arise
Around; up above, what wind-walks! what lovely behaviour
Of silk-sack clouds! has wilder, wilful-wavier
Meal-drift moulded ever and melted across skies?

I walk, I lift up, I lift up heart, eyes,
Down all that glory in the heavens to glean our Saviour;
And, éyes, heárt, what looks, what lips yet gave you a
Rapturous love's greeting of realer, of rounder replies?

And the azurous hung hills are his world-wielding shoulder
Majestic – as a stallion stalwart, very-violet-sweet! –
These things, these things were here and but the beholder
Wanting; which two when they once meet,
The heart réars wíngs bold and bolder
And hurls for him, O half hurls earth for him off under his feet.

THOMAS HARDY
Afterwards

When the Present has latched its postern behind my tremulous stay,
        And the May month flaps its glad green leaves like wings,
Delicate-filmed as new-spun silk, will the neighbours say,
        'He was a man who used to notice such things'?

If it be in the dusk when, like an eyelid's soundless blink,
        The dewfall-hawk comes crossing the shades to alight
Upon the wind-warped upland thorn, a gazer may think,
        'To him this must have been a familiar sight.'

If I pass during some nocturnal blackness, mothy and warm,
        When the hedgehog travels furtively over the lawn,
One may say, 'He strove that such innocent creatures should
                come to no harm,
        But he could do little for them; and now he is gone.'

If, when hearing that I have been stilled at last, they stand at the door,
        Watching the full-starred heavens that winter sees,
Will this thought rise on those who will meet my face no more,
        'He was one who had an eye for such mysteries'?

And will any say when my bell of quittance is heard in the gloom,
        And a crossing breeze cuts a pause in its outrollings,
Till they rise again, as they were a new bell's boom,
        'He hears it not now, but used to notice such things'?

DYLAN THOMAS
Over Sir John's Hill

Over Sir John's hill,
The hawk on fire hangs still;
In a hoisted cloud, at drop of dusk, he pulls to his claws
And gallows, up the rays of his eyes the small birds of the bay

And the shrill child's play
Wars
Of the sparrows and such who swansing, dusk, in wrangling hedges.
And blithely they squawk
To fiery tyburn over the wrestle of elms until
The flash the noosed hawk
Crashes, and slowly the fishing holy stalking heron
In the river Towy below bows his tilted headstone.

Flash, and the plumes crack,
And a black cap of jack-
Daws Sir John's just hill dons, and again the gulled birds hare
To the hawk on fire, the halter height, over Towy's fins,
In a whack of wind.
There
Where the elegiac fisherbird stabs and paddles
In the pebbly dab-filled
Shallow and sedge, and 'dilly dilly,' calls the loft hawk,
'Come and be killed,'
I open the leaves of the water at a passage
Of psalms and shadows among the pincered sandcrabs prancing

And read, in a shell,
Death clear as a buoy's bell:
All praise of the hawk on fire in hawk-eyed dusk be sung,
When his viperish fuse hangs looped with flames under the brand
Wing, and blest shall
Young
Green chickens of the bay and bushes cluck, 'dilly dilly,
Come let us die.'
We grieve as the blithe birds, never again, leave shingle and elm,
The heron and I,
I young Aesop fabling to the near night by the dingle
Of eels, saint heron hymning in the shell-hung distant

Crystal harbour vale
Where the sea cobbles sail,
And wharves of water where the walls dance and the white cranes stilt.
It is the heron and I, under judging Sir John's elmed
Hill, tell-tale the knelled
Guilt

Of the led-astray birds whom God, for their breast of whistles,
Have mercy on,
God in his whirlwind silence save, who marks the sparrows hail,
For their souls' song.
Now the heron grieves in the weeded verge. Through windows
Of dusk and water I see the tilting whispering

Heron, mirrored, go,
As the snapt feathers snow,
Fishing in the tear of the Towy. Only a hoot owl
Hollows, a grassblade blown in cupped hands, in the looted elms
And no green cocks or hens
Shout
Now on Sir John's hill. The heron, ankling the scaly
Lowlands of the waves,
Makes all the music; and I who hear the tune of the slow,
Wear-willow river, grave,
Before the lunge of the night, the notes on this time-shaken
Stone for the sake of the souls of the slain birds sailing.

CHARLES CAUSLEY

Legend

As I walked over the western plain
    The silent snow descending
I saw winter lean on the valley's edge
    His frozen medals spending.

Silent he lay, like Gulliver,
    Over the tiny town,
His heels kicking for cold at Brown Willy,
His loins on Wilsey Down.

I saw his three-cornered hat
    Making an alp of the sky,
The snow flossing his blue coat and his buckles,
    Drifting his lip and his eye.

Brittle O brittle hangs the steeple:
    A finger of white,
The insidious snow furling, whirling
    In the glass ball of night.

Set forth so, imagination!
    Loot the locked turrets of light,
Speak with the tongues of bandits and angels,
    Put winter to flight!

WILLIAM WORDSWORTH

From *The Prelude*

Book XII ('Imagination and Taste, how Impaired and Restored')

    There are in our existence spots of time,
That with distinct pre-eminence retain
A renovating virtue, whence, depressed
By false opinion and contentious thought,
Or aught of heavier or more deadly weight,
In trivial occupations, and the round
Of ordinary intercourse, our minds
Are nourished and invisibly repaired;
A virtue, by which pleasure is enhanced,
That penetrates, enables us to mount,
When high, more high, and lifts us up when fallen.
This efficacious spirit chiefly lurks
Among those passages of life that give
Profoundest knowledge to what point, and how,
The mind is lord and master – outward sense
The obedient servant of her will. Such moments
Are scattered everywhere, taking their date
From our first childhood. I remember well,
That once, while yet my inexperienced hand
Could scarcely hold a bridle, with proud hopes
I mounted, and we journeyed towards the hills:
An ancient servant of my father's house
Was with me, my encourager and guide:

We had not travelled long, ere some mischance
Disjoined me from my comrade; and, through fear
Dismounting, down the rough and stony moor
I led my horse, and, stumbling on, at length
Came to a bottom, where in former times
A murderer had been hung in iron chains.
The gibbet-mast had mouldered down, the bones
And iron case were gone; but on the turf,
Hard by, soon after that fell deed was wrought,
Some unknown hand had carved the murderer's name.
The monumental letters were inscribed
In times long past; but still, from year to year,
By superstition of the neighbourhood,
The grass is cleared away, and to this hour
The characters are fresh and visible:
A casual glance had shown them, and I fled,
Faltering and faint, and ignorant of the road:
Then, reascending the bare common, saw
A naked pool that lay beneath the hills,
The beacon on the summit, and, more near,
A girl, who bore a pitcher on her head,
And seemed with difficult steps to force her way
Against the blowing wind. It was, in truth,
An ordinary sight; but I should need
Colours and words that are unknown to man,
To paint the visionary dreariness
Which, while I looked all round for my lost guide,
Invested moorland waste, and naked pool,
The beacon crowning the lone eminence,
The female and her garments vexed and tossed
By the strong wind. When, in the blessèd hours
Of early love, the loved one at my side,
I roamed, in daily presence of this scene,
Upon the naked pool and dreary crags,
And on the melancholy beacon, fell
A spirit of pleasure and youth's golden gleam;
And think ye not with radiance more sublime
For these remembrances, and for the power
They had left behind? So feeling comes in aid
Of feeling, and diversity of strength
Attends us, if but once we have been strong.

Oh! mystery of man, from what a depth
Proceed thy honours. I am lost, but see
In simple childhood something of the base
On which thy greatness stands; but this I feel,
That from thyself it comes, that thou must give,
Else never canst receive. The days gone by
Return upon me almost from the dawn
Of life: the hiding-places of man's power
Open; I would approach them, but they close.
I see by glimpses now; when age comes on,
May scarcely see at all; and I would give,
While yet we may, as far as words can give,
Substance and life to what I feel, enshrining,
Such is my hope, the spirit of the Past
For future restoration. – Yet another
Of these memorials; –

One Christmas-time,
On the glad eve of its dear holidays,
Feverish, and tired, and restless, I went forth
Into the fields, impatient for the sight
Of those led palfreys that should bear us home;
My brothers and myself. There rose a crag,
That, from the meeting-point of two highways
Ascending, overlooked them both, far stretched;
Thither, uncertain on which road to fix
My expectation, thither I repaired,
Scout-like, and gained the summit; 'twas a day
Tempestuous, dark and wild, and on the grass
I sate half-sheltered by a naked wall;
Upon my right hand crouched a single sheep,
Upon my left a blasted hawthorn stood;
With those companions at my side, I watched,
Straining my eyes intensely, as the mist
Gave intermitting prospect of the copse
And plain beneath. Ere we to school returned, –
That dreary time, – ere we had been ten days
Sojourners in my father's house, he died,
And I and my three brothers, orphans then,
Followed his body to the grave. The event,
With all the sorrow that it brought, appeared
A chastisement; and when I called to mind

That day so lately past, when from the crag
I looked in such anxiety of hope;
With trite reflections of morality,
Yet in the deepest passion, I bowed low
To God, Who thus corrected my desires;
And, afterwards, the wind and sleety rain,
And all the business of the elements,
The single sheep, and the one blasted tree,
And the bleak music from that old stone wall,
The noise of wood and water, and the mist
That on the line of each of those two roads
Advanced in such indisputable shapes;
All these were kindred spectacles and sounds
To which I oft repaired, and thence would drink,
As at a fountain; and on winter nights,
Down to this very time, when storm and rain
Beat on my roof, or, haply, at noon day,
While in a grove I walk, whose lofty trees,
Laden with summer's thickest foliage, rock
In a strong wind, some working of the spirit,
Some inward agitations thence are brought,
Whate'er their office, whether to beguile
Thoughts over busy in the course they took,
Or animate an hour of vacant ease.

9.
DESOLATION AND ECSTASY

The poet and the mystic are both faced with a cloud of unknowing. Sometimes, in moments of vision, a ray of life pierces the obscurity, but for most of the time they are both left longing for the shaft of light. Humankind, says T. S. Eliot, 'cannot bear very much reality', and our moments of vision and ecstasy are necessarily short and transient. A long time is spent waiting for them in a period of wise passiveness. Often the waiting is extremely painful and the desolation, when the mystic is called back from the Reality he seeks to his 'sole self', is agonizing and painful. Spiritual writers speak of the aridity that fills the soul when God is absent and the Way seems intolerably difficult. Poets speak of their lack of inspiration as a painful block. Both poets and mystics write of these times of desolation in ways that are remarkably similar.

It is not just the mystic, but the ordinary religious man who feels this alternation of ecstasy and desolation in his religious life. Wesley and Cowper both write of the struggle it is sometimes to 'walk with God' when he seems absent and distant. The period of waiting can be painful and desolate, as both Hopkins and Emily Dickinson show in their poems in this section. There is a terrible, cold absence that is a deathlike distance, and that does us 'Heavenly Hurt'. It can lead to a sense of injustice – after all, the religious man is trying to please God, Hopkins cries, whereas sinners seem to prosper. It almost seems as though God could act no worse 'Wert thou my enemy, O thou my friend'. In the sonnet 'No worst, there is none', Hopkins evokes powerfully the horrors encountered in the 'no-man-fathomed' depths of the mind, while in 'Carrion Comfort' the desolation is felt as a powerful and hostile presence. Like Wesley in 'Wrestling Jacob', Hopkins recalls the story of Jacob, who spent a whole night wrestling with a mysterious stranger. Unlike Wesley, who was quite prepared to bludgeon this Stranger into some kind of revelation and comfort, Hopkins is filled with awe and terror at his temerity in wrestling 'with (my God!) my God'.

When the religious man is also a poet, the religious desolation he feels is closely linked with a sense of failure in poetic composition, not surprisingly as both proceed from the same state of mind. In 'Dejection: An Ode' Coleridge's problem is far more serious than it is for most poets. Unlike the religious poets, Coleridge feels that his poetic inspiration has gone for good, and we know that eventually he did stop writing poetry and turned to philosophy and criticism. He does not have the recourse of Herbert: he doesn't believe that a God will come from without and inspire him again. It is 'from the soul itself' that inspiration must come. His 'shaping spirit of Imagination' is a purely human gift that 'nature gave me at my birth'. The joyful communion that linked him with nature and produced his poetry comes, as we have seen, from the depths of his mind and now that his joy has failed, the whole world has become empty. He can see that nature is beautiful, as beautiful as ever, but he cannot feel it. Wordsworth replied to Coleridge's Dejection Ode with the famous Immortality Ode. He starts his poem by picking up those words of Coleridge's that referred to the happier past. 'There was a time' for Wordsworth too when there was vision and glory to be seen everywhere. This is something that we brought with us from a previous existence 'From God, who is our home'. As we get older the vision must fade, but Wordsworth is less subjective than Coleridge. He can still rejoice in nature, even though the glory and vision have faded for ever; he can still find 'Strength in what remains behind', and nourish himself also on his recollections of those 'spots of time' that are sources of inspiration and help. The idea that childhood is a specially privileged time is a common one to poets and religious people. Vaughan and Traherne both write in a similar vein about the loss of this childhood vision, while Rúmí feels that his mystical visions are what he has 'heard in Paradise'.

At Tintern Abbey Wordsworth speaks more optimistically about the passing of time; as he has grown older, he has learned to experience nature mystically and has felt an ecstatic presence that he can only call, with deliberate vagueness, 'something'. These moments of ecstasy, whether they come from Christians or Moslems, nature mystics like Wordsworth or Hindus, all have in common a sense of being at One with all things. The self fades away and becomes one with the 'something' that is encountered at the end of the mystical search. There is now no longer a division between the mystic and the reality he contemplates, however they might choose to describe this experience when they return back to earth. The mystic gives himself over to this vision and thus transcends himself.

Is there any way in which the poet can achieve a similar transcendence in the act of poetic composition? The last two poems in the section – Browning's 'Abt Vogler' and Seamus Heaney's poem from *Station Island* – suggest that there is. Abt Vogler laments that there is nothing left of his inspired improvisation, but he knows that he has touched Heaven, however briefly. He feels that the disappearance of the music he created is closer than poetry to the religious experience, because afterwards 'silence resumes her reign' and the essential ineffability of the ecstasy remains intact. Seamus Heaney's encounter with James Joyce on his pilgrimage to Station Island results in a liberation.

It was as if I had stepped free into space
alone with nothing that I had not known
already . . .

Every poet must, like Milton, strive towards 'Things unattempted yet in Prose or Rime'. This means that even things that they have valued in the past – special moments in Joyce's works for Heaney – must be cast under a 'thick cloud of forgetting'. It is a moment of poetic ecstasy, perhaps, as, at the end of the poem, the rain breaks and sizzles on the tarmac. In finding a new poetic voice, the poet has somehow transcended himself.

CHARLES WESLEY

Morning Hymn

Christ, whose glory fills the skies,
　　Christ the true, the only Light,
Sun of Righteousness, arise,
　　Triumph o'er the shades of night!
Day-spring from on high, be near!
Day-star, in my heart appear!

Dark and cheerless is the morn
　　Unaccompanied by thee;
Joyless is the day's return,
　　Till thy mercy's beams I see;
Till they inward light impart,
Glad my eyes, and warm my heart.

Visit then this soul of mine,
　　Pierce the gloom of sin and grief!
Fill me, Radiancy Divine,
　　Scatter all my unbelief!
More and more thyself display,
Shining to the perfect day.

WILLIAM COWPER
Walking with God

Oh! for a closer walk with God,
    A calm and heavenly frame;
A light to shine upon the road
    That leads me to the Lamb!

Where is the blessedness I knew
    When first I saw the Lord?
Where is the soul-refreshing view
    Of Jesus and his word?

What peaceful hours I once enjoyed!
    How sweet their memory still!
But they have left an aching void,
    The world can never fill.

Return, O holy Dove, return,
    Sweet messenger of rest;
I hate the sins that made thee mourn,
    And drove thee from my breast.

The dearest idol I have known,
    Whate'er that idol be;
Help me to tear it from thy throne,
    And worship only thee.

So shall my walk be close with God,
    Calm and serene my frame;
So purer light shall mark the road
    That leads me to the Lamb.

GEORGE HERBERT

The Bunch of Grapes

(Numbers 13: 17–27)

Joy, I did lock thee up: but some bad man
Hath let thee out again:
And now, me thinks, I am where I began
Sev'n yeares ago: one vogue and vein,
One aire of thoughts usurps my brain.
I did towards Canaan draw; but now I am
Brought back to the Red sea, the sea of shame.

For as the Jews of old by Gods command
Travell'd and saw no town;
So now each Christian hath his journeys spann'd:
Their storie pennes and sets us down.
A single deed is small renown.
Gods works are wide, and let in future times;
His ancient justice overflows our crimes.

Then we have too our guardian fires and clouds;
Our Scripture-dew drops fast:
We have our sands and serpents, tents and shrowds;
Alas! our murmurings come not last.
But where's the cluster? where's the taste
Of mine inheritance? Lord, if I must borrow,
Let me as well take up their joy, as sorrow.

But can he want the grape, who hath the wine?
I have their fruit and more.
Blessed be God, who prosper'd *Noahs* vine,
And made it bring forth grapes good store,
But much more him I must adore,
Who of the Laws sowre juice sweet wine did make,
Ev'n God himself being pressed for my sake.

EMILY DICKINSON

There's a certain Slant of light,
Winter Afternoons –
That oppresses, like the Heft
Of Cathedral Tunes –

Heavenly Hurt, it gives us –
We can find no scar,
But internal difference,
Where the Meanings, are –

None may teach it – Any –
'Tis the Seal Despair –
An imperial affliction
Sent us of the Air –

When it comes, the Landscape listens –
Shadows – hold their breath –
When it goes, 'tis like the Distance
On the look of Death –

GERARD MANLEY HOPKINS

Justus quidem tu es, Domine, si disputem tecum; verumtamen justa loquar ad te: Quare via impiorum prosperatur? &c.

Thou art indeed just, Lord, if I contend
With thee; but, sir, so what I plead is just.
Why do sinners' ways prosper? and why must
Disappointment all I endeavour end?
    Wert thou my enemy, O thou my friend,
How wouldst thou worse, I wonder, than thou dost
Defeat, thwart me? Oh, the sots and thralls of lust
Do in spare hours more thrive than I that spend,
Sir, life upon thy cause. See, banks and brakes
Now, leavèd how thick! lacèd they are again
With fretty chervil, look, and fresh wind shakes

Them; birds build – but not I build; no, but strain,
Time's eunuch, and not breed one work that wakes.
Mine, O thou lord of life, send my roots rain.

No worst, there is none. Pitched past pitch of grief,
More pangs will, schooled at forepangs, wilder wring.
Comforter, where, where is your comforting?
Mary, mother of us, where is your relief?
My cries heave, herds-long; huddle in a main, a chief
Woe, wórld-sorrow; on an áge-old anvil wince and sing –
Then lull, then leave off. Fury had shrieked 'No ling-
ering! Let me be fell: force I must be brief'.

O the mind, mind has mountains; cliffs of fall
Frightful, sheer, no-man-fathomed. Hold them cheap
May who ne'er hung there. Nor does long our small
Durance deal with that steep or deep. Here! creep,
Wretch, under a comfort serves in a whirlwind: all
Life death does end and each day dies with sleep.

[Carrion Comfort]

Not, I'll not, carrion comfort, Despair, not feast on thee;
Not untwist – slack they may be – these last strands of man
In me ór, most weary, cry *I can no more*. I can;
Can something, hope, wish day come, not choose not to be.
But ah, but O thou terrible, why wouldst thou rude on me
Thy wring-world right foot rock? lay a lionlimb against me? scan
With darksome devouring eyes my bruisèd bones? and fan,
O in turns of tempest, me heaped there; me frantic to avoid thee and flee?

Why? That my chaff might fly; my grain lie, sheer and clear.
Nay in all that toil, that coil, since (seems) I kissed the rod,
Hand rather, my heart lo! lapped strength, stole joy, would laugh, chéer.
Cheer whom though? the hero whose heaven-handling flung me, fóot tród

Me? or me that fought him? O which one? is it each one? That night, that
    year
Of now done darkness I wretch lay wrestling with (my God!) my God.

GEORGE HERBERT

Deniall

When my devotions could not pierce
Thy silent eares;
Then was my heart broken, as was my verse:
My breast was full of fears
And disorder:

My bent thoughts, like a brittle bow,
Did flie asunder:
Each took his way; some would to pleasures go,
Some to the warres and thunder
Of alarms

As good go any where, they say,
As to benumme
Both knees and heart, in crying night and day,
Come, come, my God, O come,
But no hearing.

O that thou shouldst give dust a tongue
To crie to thee,
And then not heare it crying! all day long
My heart was in my knee,
But no hearing.

Therefore my soul lay out of sight,
Untun'd, unstrung:
My feeble spirit, unable to look right,
Like a nipt blossome, hung
Discontented.

O cheer and tune my heartlesse breast,
Deferre no time;
That so thy favours granting my request,
They and my minde may chime,
And mend my ryme.

ELIZABETH JENNINGS

From *The Sonnets of Michelangelo*

LXXV

I wish, God, for some end I do not will.
Between the fire and heart a veil of ice
Puts out the fire. My pen will not move well,
So that the sheet on which I'm working lies.

I pay you mere lip-service, then I grieve;
Love does not reach my heart, I do not know
How to admit that grace which would relieve
My state and crush the arrogance I show.

Oh tear away that veil, God, break that wall
Which with its strength refuses to let in
The sun whose light has vanished from the world.

Send down the promised light to bless and hold
Your lovely bride. So may I seek for all
I need in you, both end there and begin.

SAMUEL TAYLOR COLERIDGE

Dejection: An Ode

Late, late yestreen I saw the new Moon,
With the old Moon in her arms;
And I fear, I fear, my Master dear!
We shall have a deadly storm.
Ballad of Sir Patrick Spence

I

Well! If the Bard was weather-wise, who made
The grand old ballad of Sir Patrick Spence,
This night, so tranquil now, will not go hence
Unroused by winds, that ply a busier trade
Than those which mould yon cloud in lazy flakes,
Or the dull sobbing draft, that moans and rakes
Upon the strings of this Æolian lute,
Which better far were mute.
For lo! the New-moon winter-bright!
And overspread with phantom light,
(With swimming phantom light o'erspread
But rimmed and circled by a silver thread)
I see the old Moon in her lap, foretelling
The coming-on of rain and squally blast.
And oh! that even now the gust were swelling,
And the slant night-shower driving loud and fast!
Those sounds which oft have raised me, whilst they awed,
And sent my soul abroad,
Might now perhaps their wonted impulse give,
Might startle this dull pain, and make it move and live!

II

A grief without a pang, void, dark, and drear,
A stifled, drowsy, unimpassioned grief,
Which finds no natural outlet, no relief,
In word, or sigh, or tear –
O Lady! in this wan and heartless mood,
To other thoughts by yonder throstle woo'd,
All this long eve, so balmy and serene,
Have I been gazing on the western sky,

And its peculiar tint of yellow green:
And still I gaze – and with how blank an eye!
And those thin clouds above, in flakes and bars,
That give away their motion to the stars;
Those stars, that glide behind them or between,
Now sparkling, now bedimmed, but always seen:
Yon crescent Moon, as fixed as if it grew
In its own cloudless, starless lake of blue;
I see them all so excellently fair,
I see, not feel, how beautiful they are!

III

My genial spirits fail;
And what can these avail
To lift the smothering weight from off my breast?
It were a vain endeavour,
Though I should gaze for ever
On that green light that lingers in the west:
I may not hope from outward forms to win
The passion and the life, whose fountains are within.

IV

O Lady! we receive but what we give,
And in our life alone does Nature live:
Ours is her wedding garment, ours her shroud!
And would we aught behold, of higher worth,
Than that inanimate cold world allowed
To the poor loveless ever-anxious crowd,
Ah! from the soul itself must issue forth
A light, a glory, a fair luminous cloud
Enveloping the Earth –
And from the soul itself must there be sent
A sweet and potent voice, of its own birth,
Of all sweet sounds the life and element!

V

O pure of heart! thou need'st not ask of me
What this strong music in the soul may be!
What, and wherein it doth exist,
This light, this glory, this fair luminous mist,
This beautiful and beauty-making power.

Joy, virtuous Lady! Joy that ne'er was given,
Save to the pure, and in their purest hour,
Life, and Life's effluence, cloud at once and shower,
Joy, Lady! is the spirit and the power,
Which wedding Nature to us gives in dower
A new Earth and new Heaven,
Undreamt of by the sensual and the proud –
Joy is the sweet voice, Joy the luminous cloud –
We in ourselves rejoice!
And thence flows all that charms or ear or sight,
All melodies the echoes of that voice,
All colours a suffusion from that light.

VI

There was a time when, though my path was rough,
This joy within me dallied with distress,
And all misfortunes were but as the stuff
Whence Fancy made me dreams of happiness:
For hope grew round me, like the twining vine,
And fruits, and foliage, not my own, seemed mine.
But now afflictions bow me down to earth:
Nor care I that they rob me of my mirth;
But oh! each visitation
Suspends what nature gave me at my birth,
My shaping spirit of Imagination.
For not to think of what I needs must feel,
But to be still and patient, all I can;
And haply by abstruse research to steal
From my own nature all the natural man –
This was my sole resource, my only plan:
Till that which suits a part infects the whole,
And now is almost grown the habit of my soul.

VII

Hence, viper thoughts, that coil around my mind,
Reality's dark dream!
I turn from you, and listen to the wind,
Which long has raved unnoticed. What a scream
Of agony by torture lengthened out
That lute sent forth! Thou Wind, that rav'st without,
Bare crag, or mountain-tairn, or blasted tree,
Or pine-grove whither woodman never clomb,

Or lonely house, long held the witches' home,
Methinks were fitter instruments for thee,
Mad Lutanist! who in this month of showers,
Of dark-brown gardens, and of peeping flowers,
Mak'st Devils' yule, with worse than wintry song,
The blossoms, buds, and timorous leaves among.
Thou Actor, perfect in all tragic sounds!
Thou mighty Poet, e'en to frenzy bold!
What tell'st thou now about?
'Tis of the rushing of an host in rout,
With groans, of trampled men, with smarting wounds –
At once they groan with pain, and shudder with the cold!
But hush! there is a pause of deepest silence!
And all that noise, as of a rushing crowd,
With groans, and tremulous shudderings – all is over –
It tells another tale, with sounds less deep and loud!
A tale of less affright,
And tempered with delight,
As Otway's self had framed the tender lay, –
'Tis of a little child
Upon a lonesome wild,
Not far from home, but she hath lost her way:
And now moans low in bitter grief and fear,
And now screams loud, and hopes to make her mother hear.

VIII

'Tis midnight, but small thoughts have I of sleep:
Full seldom may my friend such vigils keep!
Visit her, gentle Sleep! with wings of healing,
And may this storm be but a mountain-birth
May all the stars hang bright above her dwelling,
Silent as though they watched the sleeping Earth!
With light heart may she rise,
Gay fancy, cheerful eyes,
Joy lift her spirit, joy attune her voice;
To her may all things live, from pole to pole,
Their life the eddying of her living soul!
O simple spirit, guided from above,
Dear Lady! friend devoutest of my choice,
Thus mayest thou ever, evermore rejoice.

WILLIAM WORDSWORTH

From 'Ode: Intimations of Immortality from Recollections of Early Childhood'

I

There was a time when meadow, grove and stream,
The earth and every common sight,
To me did seem
Apparelled in celestial light,
The glory and the freshness of a dream.
It is not now as it hath been of yore; –
Turn wheresoe'er I may,
By night or day,
The things which I have seen I now can see no more.

II

The Rainbow comes and goes,
And lovely is the Rose,
The Moon doth with delight
Look round her when the heavens are bare,
Waters on a starry night
Are beautiful and fair;
The sunshine is a glorious birth;
But yet I know, where'er I go,
That there hath past away a glory from the earth.

III

Now, while the birds thus sing a joyous song,
And while the young lambs bound
As to the tabor's sound,
To me alone there came a thought of grief:
A timely utterance gave that thought relief,
And I again am strong:
The cataracts blow their trumpets from the steep;
No more shall grief of mine the season wrong;
I hear the Echoes through the mountains throng,
The Winds come to me from the fields of sleep,
And all the earth is gay
Land and sea

Give themselves up to jollity,
And with the heart of May
Doth every Beast keep holiday; –
Thou child of Joy,
Shout round me, let me hear thy shouts, thou happy Shepherd-boy!

IV

Ye blessèd Creatures, I have heard the call
Ye to each other make; I see
The heavens laugh with you in your jubilee;
My heart is at your festival,
My head hath its coronal,
The fulness of your bliss, I feel – I feel it all.
Oh evil day! if I were sullen
While Earth herself is adorning,
This sweet May-morning,
And the Children are culling
On every side,
In a thousand valleys far and wide,
Fresh flowers; while the sun shines warm,
And the Babe leaps up on his Mother's arm: –
I hear, I hear, with joy I hear!
– But there's a Tree, of many, one,
A single Field which I have looked upon,
Both of them speak of something that is gone:
The Pansy at my feet
Doth the same tale repeat:
Whither is fled the visionary gleam?
Where is it now, the glory and the dream?

V

Our birth is but a sleep and a forgetting:
The Soul that rises with us, our life's Star,
Hath had elsewhere its setting,
And cometh from afar:
Not in entire forgetfulness,
And not in utter nakedness,
But trailing clouds of glory do we come
From God, who is our home:
Heaven lies about us in our infancy!
Shades of the prison-house begin to close

Upon the growing Boy
But He beholds the light, and whence it flows,
He sees it in his joy;
The Youth, who daily farther from the east
Must travel, still is Nature's Priest,
And by the vision splendid
Is on his way attended;
At length the Man perceives it die away,
And fade into the light of common day.

VI

Earth fills her lap with pleasures of her own;
Yearnings she hath in her own natural kind,
And even with something of a Mother's mind,
And no unworthy aim,
The homely Nurse doth all she can
To make her Foster-child, her Inmate Man,
Forget the glories he hath known,
And that imperial palace whence he came.

VII

Behold the Child among his new-born blisses
A six years' Darling of a pigmy size!
See where 'mid work of his own hand he lies,
Fretted by sallies of his mother's kisses,
With light upon him from his father's eyes!
See, at his feet, some little plan or chart,
Some fragment from his dream of human life,
Shaped by himself with newly-learned art;
A wedding or a festival,
A mourning or a funeral;
And this hath now his heart,
And unto this he frames his song:
Then will he fit his tongue
To dialogues of business, love, or strife;
But it will not be long
Ere this be thrown aside,
And with new joy and pride
The little Actor cons another part;
Filling from time to time his 'humorous stage'
With all the Persons, down to palsied Age,

That Life brings with her in her equipage;
As if his whole vocation
Were endless imitation.

VIII

Thou whose exterior semblance doth belie
Thy Soul's immensity;
Thou best Philosopher, who yet dost keep
Thy heritage, thou Eye among the blind,
That, deaf and silent, read'st the eternal deep,
Haunted for ever by the eternal mind, –
Mighty Prophet! Seer blest!
On whom those truths do rest,
Which we are toiling all our lives to find,
In darkness lost, the darkness of the grave;
Thou, over whom thy Immortality
Broods like the Day, a Master o'er a Slave,
A Presence which is not to be put by;
[To whom the grave
Is but a lonely bed without the sense or sight
Of day or the warm light,
A place of thought where we in waiting lie;]
Thou little Child, yet glorious in the might
Of heaven-born freedom on thy being's height,
Why with such earnest pains dost thou provoke
The years to bring the inevitable yoke,
Thus blindly with thy blessedness at strife?
Full soon thy Soul shall have her earthly freight,
And custom lie upon thee with a weight,
Heavy as frost, and deep almost as life!

IX

O joy! that in our embers
Is something that doth live,
That nature yet remembers
What was so fugitive!
The thought of our past years in me doth breed
Perpetual benediction; not indeed
For that which is most worthy to be blest;
Delight and liberty, the simple creed
Of Childhood, whether busy or at rest,

With new-fledged hope still fluttering in his breast: –
Not for these I raise
The song of thanks and praise;
But for those obstinate questionings
Of sense and outward things,
Fallings from us, vanishings;
Blank misgivings of a Creature
Moving about in worlds not realised,
High instincts before which our mortal Nature
Did tremble like a guilty Thing surprised:
But for those first affections,
Those shadowy recollections,
Which, be they what they may,
Are yet the fountain-light of all our day,
Are yet a master-light of all our seeing;
Uphold us, cherish, and have power to make
Our noisy years seem moments in the being
Of the eternal Silence: truths that wake,
To perish never:
Which neither listlessness, nor mad endeavour,
Nor Man nor Boy,
Nor all that is at enmity with joy,
Can utterly abolish or destroy!
Hence in a season of calm weather
Though inland far we be,
Our Souls have sight of that immortal sea
Which brought us hither,
Can in a moment travel thither,
And see the Children sport upon the shore,
And hear the mighty waters rolling evermore.

x

Then sing, ye Birds, sing, sing a joyous song!
And let the young Lambs bound
As to the tabor's sound!
We in thought will join your throng,
Ye that pipe and ye that play,
Ye that through your hearts today
Feel the gladness of the May!
What though the radiance which was once so bright
Be now for ever taken from my sight,

Though nothing can bring back the hour
Of splendour in the grass, of glory in the flower;
We will grieve not, rather find
Strength in what remains behind;
In the primal sympathy
Which having been must ever be;
In the soothing thoughts that spring
Out of human suffering;
In the faith that looks through death
In years that bring the philosophic mind.

XI

And O, ye Fountains, Meadows, Hills, and Groves,
Forbode not any severing of our loves!
Yet in my heart of hearts I feel your might;
I only have relinquished one delight
To live beneath your more habitual sway.
I love the Brooks which down their channels fret,
Even more than when I tripped lightly as they;
The innocent brightness of a new-born Day
Is lovely yet;
The Clouds that gather round the setting sun
Do take a sober colouring from an eye
That hath kept watch o'er man's mortality;
Another race hath been, and other palms are won.
Thanks to the human heart by which we live,
Thanks to its tenderness, its joys, and fears,
To me the meanest flower that blows can give
Thoughts that do often lie too deep for tears.

JALÁLU'DDÍN RÚMÍ

(translated by E. H. Whinfield)

The song of the spheres in their revolutions
Is what men sing with lute and voice.
As we all are members of Adam,
We have heard these melodies in Paradise.
Though earth and water have cast their veil upon us,
We retain first reminiscences of these heavenly songs;

But while we are thus shrouded by gross earthly veils,
How can the tones of the dancing spheres reach us?

HENRY VAUGHAN

The Retreat

Happy those early days! when I
Shined in my Angel-infancy.
Before I understood this place
Appointed for my second race,
Or taught my soul to fancy aught
But a white, celestial thought,
When yet I had not walked above
A mile, or two, from my first love,
And looking back (at that short space,)
Could see the glimpse of his bright-face;
When on some *gilded cloud*, or *flower*
My gazing soul would dwell an hour,
And in those weaker glories spy
Some shadows of eternity;
Before I taught my tongue to wound
My conscience with a sinful sound,
Or had the black art to dispense
A several sin to every sense,
But felt through all this fleshly dress
Bright *shoots* of everlastingness.
    O how I long to travel back
And tread again that ancient track!
That I might once more reach that plain,
Where first I left my glorious train,
From whence the enlightened spirit sees
That shady city of palm trees;
But (ah!) my soul with too much stay
Is drunk and staggers in the way.
Some men a forward motion love,
But I by backward steps would move,
And when this dust falls to the urn
In that state I came return.

THOMAS TRAHERNE

Wonder

How like an angel came I down!
How bright are all things here!
When first among his works I did appear,
Oh, how their Glory me did crown!
The world resembled his Eternity,
In which my soul did walk;
And every thing that I did see
Did with me talk.

The skies in their magnificence,
The lively, lovely air;
Oh, how divine, how soft, how sweet, how fair!
The stars did entertain my sense,
And all the works of God so bright and pure,
So rich and great did seem
As if they ever must endure
In my esteem.

A native health and innocence
Within my bones did grow,
And while my God did all his glories show,
I felt a vigour in my sense
That was all spirit. I within did flow
With seas of life, like wine;
I nothing in the world did know,
But 'twas divine.

Harsh, ragged objects were concealed,
Oppressions, tears, and cries,
Sins, griefs, complaints, dissentions, weeping eyes,
Were hid: and only things revealed
Which heavenly spirits and the angels prize.
The State of Innocence
And Bliss, not trades and poverties,
Did fill my sense.

The streets were paved with golden stones,
The boys and girls were mine;
Oh, how did all their lovely faces shine!
The Sons of Men were Holy Ones,
Joy, Beauty, Welfare did appear to me,
And every thing which here I found,
While like an angel I did see,
Adorned the ground.

Rich diamond, and pearl, and gold
In every place was seen;
Rare splendours, yellow, blue, red, white, and green,
Mine eyes did everywhere behold;
Great Wonders clothed with Glory did appear,
Amazement was my Bliss.
That and my wealth was everywhere:
No Joy to this . . .

WILLIAM WORDSWORTH

From 'Lines'

Composed a few miles above Tintern Abbey, on Revisiting the Banks of the Wye during a tour. July 13, 1798

These beauteous forms,
Through a long absence, have not been to me
As is a landscape to a blind man's eye:
But oft, in lonely rooms, and 'mid the din
Of towns and cities, I have owed to them,
In hours of weariness, sensations sweet,
Felt in the blood, and felt along the heart;
And passing even into my purer mind,
With tranquil restoration: – feelings too
Of unremembered pleasure: such, perhaps,
As have no slight or trivial influence
On that best portion of a good man's life,
His little, nameless, unremembered acts
Of kindness and of love. Nor less, I trust,
To them I may have owed another gift,

Of aspect more sublime; that blessed mood,
In which the burthen of the mystery,
In which the heavy and the weary weight
Of all this unintelligible world,
Is lightened: – that serene and blessed mood,
In which the affections gently lead us on, –
Until, the breath of this corporeal frame
And even the motion of our human blood
Almost suspended, we are laid asleep
In body, and become a living soul:
While with an eye made quiet by the power
Of harmony, and the deep power of joy,
We see into the life of things.

. . .

For I have learned
To look on nature, not as in the hour
Of thoughtless youth; but hearing oftentimes
The still, sad music of humanity,
Nor harsh nor grating, though of ample power
To chasten and subdue. And I have felt
A presence that disturbs me with the joy
Of elevated thoughts; a sense sublime
Of something far more deeply interfused,
Whose dwelling is the light of setting suns,
And the round ocean and the living air,
And the blue sky, and in the mind of man:
A motion and a spirit, that impels
All thinking things, all objects of all thought,
And rolls through all things. Therefore am I still
A lover of the meadows and the woods,
And mountains; and of all that we behold
From this green earth; of all the mighty world
Of eye and ear, – both what they half create,
And what perceive.

JOHN OF THE CROSS

More Stanzas Applied to Spiritual Things

(translated by K. Kavanaugh and O. Rodrigues)

I went out seeking love,
And with unfaltering hope
I flew so high, so high,
That I overtook the prey.

That I might take the prey
Of this adventuring in God
I had to fly so high
That I was lost from sight;
And though in this adventure
I faltered in my flight,
Yet love had already flown so high
That I took the prey.

When I ascended higher
My vision was dazzled,
And the most difficult conquest
Was achieved in darkness;
But since I was seeking love
The leap I made was blind and dark
And I rose so high, so high,
That I took the prey.

The higher I ascended
In this so lofty seeking
The lower and more subdued
And abased I became.
I said: No one can overtake it,
And sank, ah, so low,
That I was so high, so high,
That I took the prey.

In a wonderful way
My one flight surpassed a thousand,
For the hope of heaven

Attains as much as it hopes for;
This seeking is my only hope
And I have not been disappointed,
Because I flew so high, so high,
That I took the prey.

HENRY VAUGHAN

The Morning-Watch

O joys! Infinite sweetness! with what flowers,
And shoots of glory, my soul breaks, and buds!
        All the long hours
        Of night, and rest
        Through the still shrouds
        Of sleep, and clouds,
    This dew fell on my breast;
        O how it *bloods*,
And *spirits* all my earth! hark! In what rings,
And *hymning circulations* the quick world
        Awakes, and sings;
        The rising winds,
        And falling springs,
        Birds, beasts, all things
    Adore him in their kinds.
        Thus all is hurled
In sacred *hymns*, and *order*, the great *chime*
And *symphony* of nature. Prayer is
        The world in tune,
        A spirit voice,
        And vocal joys
    Whose *echo is* heaven's bliss.
        O let me climb
When I lie down! The pious soul by night
Is like a clouded star, whose beams though said
        To shed their light
        Under some cloud
        Yet are above,

And shine, and move
Beyond that misty shroud.
So in my bed
That curtained grave, though sleep, like ashes, hide
My lamp, and life, both shall in thee abide.

From the *Bhagavad-Gita*

Book XVIII (the 'Mokshasanyāsayōg')
(translated by Sir Edwin Arnold)

[Krishna addresses Arjuna, son of Kunti]

Learn from me, Son of Kunti! also this,
How one, attaining perfect peace, attains
BRAHMA, the supreme, the highest height of all!

Devoted – with a heart grown pure, restrained
In lordly self-control, forgoing wiles
Of song and senses, freed from love and hate,
Dwelling 'mid solitudes, in diet spare,
With body, speech, and will tamed to obey,
Ever to holy meditation vowed,
From passions liberate, quit of the Self.
Of arrogance, impatience, anger, pride;
Freed from surroundings, quiet, lacking nought –
Such an one grows to oneness with the BRAHM;
Such an one, growing with BRAHM, serene,
Sorrows no more, desires no more; his soul,
Equally loving all that lives, loves well
Me, Who have made them, and attains to Me.
By this same love and worship doth he know
Me as I am, how high and wonderful,
And knowing, straightway enters into Me,
And whatsoever deeds he doeth – fixed
In Me, as in his refuge – he hath won
For ever and for ever by My grace
Th' Eternal Rest.

AL-JUNAID

(translated by A. J. Arberry)

Now I have known, O Lord,
What lies within my heart;
In secret, from the world apart,
My tongue hath talked with my Adored.

So in a manner we
United are, and One;
Yet otherwise disunion
Is our estate eternally.

Though from my gaze profound
Deep awe hath hid Thy Face,
In wondrous and ecstatic Grace
I feel Thee touch my inmost ground.

ELIZABETH JENNINGS

Teresa of Avila

Spain. The wild dust, the whipped corn, earth easy for
footsteps, shallow to starving seeds. High sky at night
like walls. Silences surrounding Avila.

She, teased by questions, aching for reassurance. Calm
in confession before incredulous priests. Then back – to
the pure illumination, the profound personal prayer,
the four waters.

Water from the well first, drawn up painfully. Clinking
of pails. Dry lips at the well-head. Parched grass bending.
And the dry heart too – waiting for prayer.

Then the water-wheel, turning smoothly. Somebody
helping unseen. A keen hand put out, gently sliding
the wheel. Then water and the aghast spirit refreshed
and quenched.

Not this only. Other waters also, clear from a spring or a
pool. Pouring from a fountain like child's play – but the
child is elsewhere. And she, kneeling, cooling her
spirit at the water, comes nearer, nearer.

Then the entire cleansing, utterly from nowhere. No
wind ruffled it, no shadows slid across it. Her mind
met it, her will approved. And all beyonds, backwaters,
dry words of old prayers were lost in it. The water
was only itself.

And she knelt there, waited for shadows to cross the
light which the water made, waited for familiar
childhood illuminations (the lamp by the bed, the
candle in church, sun beckoned by horizons) – but this
light was none of these, was only how the water looked,
how the will turned and was still. Even the image of
light itself withdrew, and the dry dust on the winds of
Spain outside her halted. Moments spread not into
hours but stood still. No dove brought the tokens of
peace. She was the peace that her prayer had promised.
And the silences suffered no shadows.

ROBERT BROWNING

Abt Vogler

(After he has been extemporising upon the musical instrument of his invention)

Would that the structure brave, the manifold music I build,
Bidding my organ obey, calling its keys to their work,
Claiming each slave of the sound, at a touch, as when Solomon willed
Armies of angels that soar, legions of demons that lurk,
Man, brute, reptile, fly, – alien of end and of aim,
Adverse, each from the other heaven-high, hell-deep removed, –

Should rush into sight at once as he named the ineffable Name,
And pile him a palace straight, to pleasure the princess he loved!

Would it might tarry like his, the beautiful building of mine,
This which my keys in a crowd pressed and importuned to raise!
Ah, one and all, how they helped, would dispart now and now combine,
Zealous to hasten the work, heighten their master his praise!
And one would bury his brow with a blind plunge down to hell,
Burrow awhile and build, broad on the root of things,
Then up again swim into sight, having based me my palace well,
Founded it, fearless of flame, flat on the nether springs.

And another would mount and march, like the excellent minion he was,
Ay, another and yet another, one crowd but with many a crest,
Raising my rampired walls of gold as transparent as glass,
Eager to do and die, yield each his place to the rest:
For higher still and higher (as a runner tips with fire,
When a great illumination surprises a festal night –
Outlining round and round Rome's dome from space to spire)
Up, the pinnacled glory reached, and the pride of my soul was in sight.

In sight? Not half! for it seemed, it was certain, to match man's birth,
Nature in turn conceived, obeying an impulse as I;
And the emulous heaven yearned down, made effort to reach the earth,
As the earth had done her best, in my passion, to scale the sky:
Novel splendours burst forth, grew familiar and dwelt with mine,
Not a point nor peak but found and fixed its wandering star;
Meteor-moons, balls of blaze: and they did not pale nor pine,
For earth had attained to heaven, there was no more near nor far.

Nay more; for there wanted not who walked in the glare and glow,
Presences plain in the place; or, fresh from the Protoplast,
Furnished for ages to come, when a kindlier wind should blow,
Lured now to begin and live, in a house to their liking at last;
Or else the wonderful Dead who have passed through the body and gone,
But were back once more to breathe in an old world worth their new:
What never had been, was now; what was, as it shall be anon;
And what is, – shall I say, matched both? for I was made perfect too.

All through my keys that gave their sounds to a wish of my soul,
All through my soul that praised as its wish flowed visibly forth,

All through music and me! For think, had I painted the whole,
 Why, there it had stood, to see, nor the process so wonder-worth:
Had I written the same, made verse – still, effect proceeds from cause,
 Ye know why the forms are fair, ye hear how the tale is told;
It is all triumphant art, but art in obedience to laws,
 Painter and poet are proud in the artist-list enrolled: –

But here is the finger of God, a flash of the will that can,
 Existent behind all laws, that made them and, lo, they are!
And I know not if, save in this, such gift be allowed to man,
 That out of three sounds he frame, not a fourth sound, but a star.
Consider it well: each tone of our scale in itself is nought;
 It is everywhere in the world – loud, soft, and all is said:
Give it to me to use! I mix it with two in my thought:
 And, there! Ye have heard and seen: consider and bow the head!

Well, it is gone at last, the palace of music I reared;
 Gone! and the good tears start, the praises that come too slow;
For one is assured at first, one scarce can say that he feared,
 That he even gave it a thought, the gone thing was to go
Never to be again! But many more of the kind
 As good, nay, better perchance: is this your comfort to me?
To me, who must be saved because I cling with my mind
 To the same, same self, same love, same God: ay, what was, shall be.

Therefore to whom turn I but to thee, the ineffable Name?
 Builder and maker, thou, of houses not made with hands!
What, have fear of change from thee who art ever the same?
 Doubt that thy power can fill the heart that thy power expands?
There shall never be one lost good! What was, shall live as before:
 The evil is null, is nought, is silence implying sound;
What was good shall be good, with, for evil, so much good more;
 On the earth the broken arcs; in the heaven, a perfect round.

All we have willed or hoped or dreamed of good shall exist;
 Not its semblance, but itself; no beauty, nor good, nor power
Whose voice has gone forth, but each survives for the melodist
 When eternity affirms the conception of an hour.
The high that proved too high, the heroic for earth too hard,
 The passion that left the ground to lose itself in the sky,

Are music sent up to God by the lover and the bard;
    Enough that he heard it once: we shall hear it by-and-by.

And what is our failure here but a triumph's evidence
    For the fulness of the days? Have we withered or agonized?
Why else was the pause prolonged but that singing might issue thence?
    Why rushed the discords in but that harmony should be prized?
Sorrow is hard to bear, and doubt is slow to clear,
    Each sufferer says his say, his scheme of the weal and woe:
But God has a few of us whom he whispers in the ear;
    The rest may reason and welcome: 'tis we musicians know.

Well, it is earth with me; silence resumes her reign:
    I will be patient and proud, and soberly acquiesce.
Give me the keys. I feel for the common chord again,
    Sliding by semitones, till I sink to the minor, – yes,
And I blunt it into a ninth, and I stand on alien ground,
    Surveying awhile the heights I rolled from into the deep;
Which, hark, I have dared and done, for my resting-place is found,
    The C Major of this life: so, now I will try to sleep.

SEAMUS HEANEY

From *Station Island* Part II, xii

Like a convalescent, I took the hand
stretched down from the jetty, sensed again
an alien comfort as I stepped on ground

to find the helping hand still gripping mine,
fish-cold and bony, but whether to guide
or to be guided I could not be certain

for the tall man in step at my side
seemed blind, though he walked straight as a rush
upon his ash plant, his eyes fixed straight ahead.

Then I knew him in the flesh
out there on the tarmac among the cars,
wintered hard and sharp as a blackthorn bush.

His voice eddying with the vowels of all rivers
came back to me, though he did not speak yet,
a voice like a prosecutor's or a singer's,

cunning, narcotic, mimic, definite
as a steel nib's downstroke, quick and clean,
and suddenly he hit a litter basket

with his stick, saying, 'Your obligation
is not discharged by any common rite.
What you must do must be done on your own

so get back in harness. The main thing is to write
for the joy of it. Cultivate a work-lust
that imagines its haven like your hands at night

dreaming the sun in the sunspot of a breast.
You are fasted now, light-headed, dangerous.
Take off from here. And don't be so earnest,

let others wear the sackcloth and the ashes.
Let go, let fly, forget.
You've listened long enough. Now strike your note.'

It was as if I had stepped free into space
alone with nothing that I had not known
already. Raindrops blew in my face

as I came to. 'Old father, mother's son,
there is a moment in Stephen's diary
for April the thirteenth,* a revelation

set among my stars – that one entry
has been a sort of password in my ears,
the collect of a new epiphany,

* See the end of James Joyce's *Portrait of the Artist as a Young Man* (S. H.).

the Feast of Holy Tundish.' 'Who cares,'
he jeered, 'any more? The English language
belongs to us. You are raking at dead fires,

a waste of time for somebody your age.
That subject people stuff is a cod's game,
infantile, like your peasant pilgrimage.

You lose more of yourself than you redeem
doing the decent thing. Keep at a tangent.
When they make the circle wide, it's time to swim

out on your own and fill the element
with signatures on your own frequency,
echo soundings, searches, probes, allurements,

elver-gleams in the dark of the whole sea.'
The shower broke in a cloudburst, the tarmac
fumed and sizzled. As he moved off quickly

the downpour loosed its screens round his straight walk.

10.
LANGUAGE AND SILENCE

This section is about silence, so the introduction must be very short. It is enough to say that it is here perhaps that the mystic and the poet part company. It is of the essence of the poetic gift that it must express itself in words. As Swinburne said, any of us might have the 'vision divine', but unless we can put it into words there is no poetic gift. The mystic is concerned with the silence of his experience, though many mystics actually did want to write about it afterwards in poems and in learned treatises. Yet the poet is very well aware that he is trying to say something that nobody else has ever said before, and that what he is trying to say is often ineffable. He often chooses to express the unsayable nature of what he is telling us in cryptic or difficult language precisely to preserve the ineffability of his vision.

The first part of the section consists of poems in which the poets struggle with this apparent conflict between language and silence, particularly in the writing of religious poetry, because religion is about silence not speech. Yet in the second part of the section, when poets write about incidents in the Bible or doctrines of the Church, it is clear – even from this short selection – how they preserve mystical values. They turn away from rationality, from historical proof. They stress the importance of Love not Thought, just as the mystic does; they are content to remain in 'doubts and uncertainties instead of irritably reaching after facts and reason', and express the paradox of belief simply, without feeling any need to explain. They see that religion is not a matter of outward, verifiable events, but an inward creation in the 'mind of man'. Finally, they dwell on the need for the self to disappear for miracles to happen in this world, and know that religion is a matter of silence and of the dark night of the mystics.

R. S. THOMAS

In a Country Church

To one kneeling down no word came,
Only the wind's song, saddening the lips
Of the grave saints, rigid in glass;
Or the dry whisper of unseen wings,
Bats not angels, in the high roof.

Was he balked by silence? He kneeled long,
And saw love in a dark crown
Of thorns blazing, and a winter tree
Golden with fruit of a man's body.

GEORGE HERBERT
The Forerunners

The harbingers are come. See, see their mark;
White is their colour, and behold my head.
But must they have my brain? must they dispark
Those sparkling notions, which therein were bred?
    Must dulnesse turn me to a clod?
Yet have they left me, *Thou art still my God.*

Good men ye be, to leave me my best room,
Ev'n all my heart, and what is lodged there:
I passe not, I, what of the rest become,
So *Thou art still my God*, be out of fear.
    He will be pleased with that dittie;
And if I please him, I write fine and wittie.

Farewell sweet phrases, lovely metaphors.
But will ye leave me thus? when ye before
Of stews and brothels onely knew the doores,
Then did I wash you with my tears, and more,
    Brought you to Church well drest and clad:
My God must have my best, ev'n all I had.

Lovely enchanting language, sugar-cane,
Hony of roses, whither wilt thou flie?
Hath some fond love tic'd thee to thy bane?
And wilt thou leave the Church, and love a stie?
    Fie, thou wilt soil thy broider'd coat,
And hurt thy self, and him that sings the note.

Let foolish lovers, if they will love dung,
With canvas, not with arras, clothe their shame:
Let follie speak in her own native tongue.
True beautie dwells on high: ours is a flame
    But borrow'd thence to light us thither.
Beautie and beauteous words should go together.

Yet if you go. I passe not; take your way:
For, *Thou art still my God*, is all that ye
Perhaps with more embellishment can say.

Go birds of spring: let winter have his fee;
    Let a bleak palenesse chalk the doore,
So all within be livelier then before.

ALFRED, LORD TENNYSON

From *In Memoriam A. H. H.*

v

I sometimes hold it half a sin
    To put in words the grief I feel;
    For words, like Nature, half reveal
And half conceal the Soul within.

But, for the unquiet heart and brain,
    A use in measured language lies;
    The sad mechanic exercise,
Like dull narcotics, numbing pain.

In words, like weeds, I'll wrap me o'er,
    Like coarsest clothes against the cold:
    But that large grief which these enfold
Is given in outline and no more.

PETER LEVI

Tree of roses. The water crashed headlong
tearing the darkness out of the stone face.
A god of war might be a god of song.
The sign of faith is a physical grace:
thinness colour and smell like Asian clover,
the informal appearance of a lover.
Water is religion, it has no voice,
but drowns the silence of God in its noise.
There is no life to be had in the pure air,

and passion for goodness not having it
is rank swan-music and water-spirit.
Ice and a hundred moving points of fire:
the monks in the illuminated cave
only love what cannot love and will save.

In England morning colours like fruit-skin,
it darkens again with a whisp of light:
apple-trees to work at, grass to play in,
the blossom in the deepest woods is white.
That sun is cultivated, the sky even:
the god of song can love nothing but heaven.
He is exploding stars, the piston-rod
in the sky's dying engine, true and good.
His sudden, light drumming in a back street:
what passes is love, it is not belief,
love's religion is destructive of life
it is the heavy seed in the pale wheat.
Death shakes out the last words, what they release
is the old god of nature and of peace.

Living in the religion of peace
where God is outward, the world ingrowing,
I break my life to pieces in my voice,
to be like God in his imagining:
the origin of goodness was a fable
piety cast off made it available:
passion for goodness is love in the end,
it is broken language nothing can mend.
The throaty agitation of the trees,
snowinfected, colourstained by the air,
expresses green nature like a despair:
whatever lives has inward boundaries.
God has none, he is natured like a stone
frosteaten and sunbitten and alone.

ANONYMOUS

Adam lay ibounden,
Bounden in a bond;
Foure thousand winter
Thought he not too long;
And all was for an appel,
An appel that he tok,
As clerkës finden
Wreten in here book.

Ne hadde the appel takë ben,
The appel take ben,
Ne haddë never our Lady
A ben Hevene Quen.
Blissèd be the time
That appel takë was!
Therfore we moun singen,
'Deo gracias!'

GERARD MANLEY HOPKINS

Spring and Fall

to a young child

Márgarét, áre you gríeving
Over Goldengrove unleaving?
Léaves, líke the things of man, you
With your fresh thoughts care for, can you?
Áh! ás the heart grows older
It will come to such sights colder
By and by, nor spare a sigh
Though worlds of wanwood leafmeal lie;
And yet you wíll weep and know why.
Now no matter, child, the name:
Sórrow's spríngs áre the same.

Nor mouth had, no nor mind, expressed
What heart heard of, ghost guessed:
It ís the blight man was born for,
It is Margaret you mourn for.

CHARLES CAUSLEY

At Kfar Kana

The bus halts its long brawl
With rock and tar and sun.
The pilgrims trudge to where
The miracle was done:
Each altar the exact
Authenticated site
Of a far, famous act
Which if performed at all
May well have been not here.

I turn away and walk
And watch the pale sun slide,
The furry shadows bloom
Along the hills' rough hide.
Beneath a leafy span
In fast and falling light
Arabs take coffee, scan
The traveller, smoke, talk
As in a dim, blue room.

The distant lake is flame.
Beside the fig's green bell
I lean on a parched bay
Where steps lead to a well.
Two children smile, come up
With water, sharp and bright,
Drawn in a paper cup.
'This place, what is its name?'
'Kfar Kana,' they say,

Gravely resuming free
Pure rituals of play
As pilgrims from each shrine
Come down the dusty way
With ocean-coloured glass,
Embroidered cloths, nun-white,
And sunless bits of brass –
Where children changed for me
Well-water into wine.

Bible Story

In August, when the air of love was peeled,
I saw a burning boy upon the bed,
Shut a green shade against the harvest field
And held one shaking hand behind his head.

Stripped of his skin of breath, his heart untied,
I searched his threaded throat of serpentine,
And lying on the pallet at his side
I drew his beaten breast of milk to mine.

In this stone shell I poured such seas of prayer
His sailing soul was driven down from heaven,
His prodigal parents on the ringing stair
Heard, as the sun struck six, the boy sneeze seven,

And as he wandered, innocent, from my prison
Cried, *Hail, Elisha, for our son is risen!*

ANONYMOUS

I sing of a maiden
    That is makèless:
King of all kingès
    To her son she ches.

He came all so stillè
    There his mother was,
As dew in Aprìllè
    That falleth on the grass.

He came all so stillè
    To his mother's bower,
As dew in Aprìllè
    That falleth on the flower.

He came all so stillè
    There his mother lay,
As dew in Aprìllè
    That falleth on the spray.

Mother and maiden
    Was never none but she;
Well may such a lady
    Goddès mother be.

ALFRED, LORD TENNYSON

From *In Memoriam A. H. H.*

XXXI

When Lazarus left his charnel-cave,
    And home to Mary's house return'd,
    Was this demanded – if he yearn'd
To hear her weeping by his grave?

'Where wert thou, brother, those four days?'
There lives no record of reply,
Which telling what it is to die
Had surely added praise to praise.

From every house the neighbours met,
The streets were fill'd with joyful sound,
A solemn gladness even crown'd
The purple brows of Olivet.

Behold a man raised up by Christ!
The rest remaineth unreveal'd;
He told it not; or something seal'd
The lips of that Evangelist.

XXXII

Her eyes are homes of silent prayer,
Nor other thought her mind admits
But, he was dead, and there he sits,
And he that brought him back is there.

Then one deep love doth supersede
All other, when her ardent gaze
Roves from the living brother's face,
And rests upon the Life indeed.

All subtle thought, all curious fears,
Borne down by gladness so complete,
She bows, she bathes the Saviour's feet
With costly spikenard and with tears.

Thrice blest whose lives are faithful prayers,
Whose loves in higher love endure;
What souls possess themselves so pure,
Or is there blessedness like theirs?

HENRY VAUGHAN

The Night

(John 2:3)

Through that pure *Virgin-shrine*,
That sacred vail drawn o'r thy glorious noon
That men might look and live as Glo-worms shine,
And face the Moon:
Wise *Nicodemus* saw such light
As made him know his God by night.

Most blest believer he!
Who in that land of darkness and blinde eyes
Thy long expected healing wings could see,
When thou didst rise,
And what can never more be done,
Did at mid-night speak with the Sun!

O who will tell me, where
He found thee at that dead and silent hour!
What hallow'd solitary ground did bear
So rare a flower,
Within whose sacred leafs did lie
The fulness of the Deity.

No mercy-seat of gold,
No dead and dusty *Cherub*, nor carv'd stone,
But his own living works did my Lord hold
And lodge alone;
Where *trees* and *herbs* did watch and peep
And wonder, while the *Jews* did sleep.

Dear night! this worlds defeat;
The stop to busie fools; cares check and curb;
The day of Spirits; my souls calm retreat
Which none disturb!
Christs progress, and his prayer time;
The hours to which high Heaven doth chime.

Gods silent, searching flight:
When my Lords head is fill'd with dew, and all
His locks are wet with the clear drops of night;
His still, soft call;
His knocking time; The souls dumb watch,
When Spirits their fair kinred catch.

Were all my loud, evil days
Calm and unhaunted as is thy dark Tent,
Whose peace but by some *Angels* wing or voice
Is seldom rent;
Then I in Heaven all the long year
Would keep, and never wander here.

But living where the Sun
Doth all things wake, and where all mix and tyre
Themselves and others, I consent and run
To ev'ry myre,
And by this world's ill-guiding light,
Erre more than I can do by night.

There is in God (some say)
A deep, but dazling darkness; As men here
Say it is late and dusky, because they
See not all clear;
O for that night! where I in him
Might live invisible and dim.

SELECT BIBLIOGRAPHY

ARBERRY, A. J., *Sufism: An Account of the Mystics of Islam*, London, 1950.

BERGER, PETER L. (ed.), *The Other Side of God: A Polarity in World Religions*, New York, 1981.

JACOBS, LOUIS, *Jewish Ethics, Philosophy and Mysticism*, New York, 1969.
Hasidic Thought, New York, 1976.

JAMES, WILLIAM, *The Varieties of Religious Experience: A Study in Human Nature*, New York, 1902.

JOHNSTON, WILLIAM, *Silent Music: The Science of Meditation*, London, 1974.

KATZ, STEVEN T. (ed.), *Mysticism and Religious Traditions*, Oxford, 1983.

KOLAKOWSKI, LESZEK, *Religion*, London 1982.

LASKI, MARGHANITA, *Ecstasy: A Study of Some Secular and Religious Experiences*, London, 1961.

NICHOLSON, R. A., *The Mystics of Islam*, London, 1914.
Eastern Poetry and Prose, Cambridge, 1922.

SANGHARAKSHITA, THE VENERABLE (DENIS LINGWOOD), *A Survey of Buddhism*, London, 1957.
The Three Jewels: An Introduction to Buddhism, London, 1977.
Human Enlightenment, London, 1980.

SMART, NINIAN, *The Religious Experience of Mankind*, London, 1969.

SNOW, C. P., *The New Men*, London, 1954.

SUBHUTI, DHAMACHARI (ALEX KENNEDY), *Buddhism for Today*, Salisbury, 1983.

THOMAS, J. E. (transl.), *Early Buddhist Scriptures*, London, 1935.

TOYNBEE, ARNOLD, *A Study of History*, Oxford, 1954.

WOLTERS, CLIFTON (transl.), *The Cloud of Unknowing and Other Works*, London, 1961.

WOODS, RICHARD (ed.), *Understanding Mysticism*, London, 1981.

ACKNOWLEDGEMENTS

For YEHUDA AMICHAI: to Penguin Books Ltd for 'On the Day of Atonement' from *The Penguin Book of Hebrew Verse*, edited and translated by T. Carmi (Penguin Poets, 1981), Copyright © T. Carmi, 1981.

For W. H. AUDEN: 'The More Loving One' from *Collected Poems*, reprinted by permission of Faber & Faber Ltd and Random House, Inc.

For BÁBÁ KÚHÍ OF SHÍRÁZ: to Cambridge University Press for 'In the market, in the cloister – only God I saw' from *Eastern Poetry and Prose*, translated by Reynold A. Nicholson.

For JOHN BETJEMAN: to John Murray (Publishers) Ltd for 'In Westminster Abbey' from *Collected Poems*.

For ELIZABETH BISHOP: 'Sandpiper' from *The Complete Poems 1927–1979* by Elizabeth Bishop, Copyright © 1962, 1969 by Elizabeth Bishop. Reprinted by permission of Farrar, Straus & Giroux, Inc.

For JOHN BROUGH: to Penguin Books Ltd for 'When he saw her' from *Poems from the Sanskrit*, translated by John Brough (Penguin Classics, 1968), Copyright © John Brough, 1968 (originally from *The Paddhati of Śārṅgadhara: A Sanskrit Anthology*, edited by Peter Peterson, 1888).

For CHARLES CAUSLEY: to David Higham Associates Ltd for 'King's College Chapel', 'I am the Great Sun', 'Legend', 'At Kfar Kana' and 'Bible Story' from *Collected Poems*.

For DANTE ALIGHIERI: to David Higham Associates Ltd for *The Divine Comedy: 3*, translated by Dorothy L. Sayers and Barbara Reynolds (Penguin Classics, 1962), Copyright © Anthony Fleming, 1962.

For DHU 'L-NÚN: to George Allen & Unwin Ltd for 'I die, and yet not dies in me' from *Sufism*, translated by A. J. Arberry.

For EMILY DICKINSON: 'I heard a Fly buzz – when I died –', 'The Wind – tapped like a tired man –', 'Through the strait pass of suffering –' and 'There's a certain Slant of light' reprinted from *The Collected Poems of Emily Dickinson*, edited by Thomas H. Johnson, Cambridge, Mass.: The Beiknap Press of Harvard University Press, Copyright 1951, © 1955, 1979, 1983 by the President and Fellows of Harvard College.

For T. S. ELIOT: 'Marina' from *Collected Poems 1909–1962*, reprinted by permission of Faber & Faber Ltd and Harcourt Brace Jovanovich, Inc.

For FARÍDU'DDÍN 'AṬṬÁR: to Penguin Books Ltd for *The Conference of the Birds*, translated by Afkham Darbandi and Dick Davis (Penguin Classics, 1984). Copyright © Afkham Darbandi and Dick Davis, 1984.

For ROBERT FROST: 'Stopping by Woods on a Snowy Evening' and 'The Most of It' from *The Poetry of Robert Frost*, edited by Edward Connery Lathem, Copyright 1923, © 1969 by Holt, Rinehart & Winston Publishers, Copyright © 1970 by Lesley Frost Ballantine. Reprinted by permission of Holt, Rinehart & Winston Publishers and Jonathan Cape Ltd.

For ḤAFÍẒ: to Cambridge University Press for 'My soul is the veil of his love', 'Love's hidden pearl is shining yet' and 'Mortal never won to view thee' from *Eastern Poetry and Prose*, translated by Reynold A. Nicholson.

For SEAMUS HEANEY: 'On the Road' and 'Like a convalescent, I took the hand' from *Station Island*, reprinted by permission of Faber & Faber Ltd and Farrar, Straus & Giroux, Inc.

For GEOFFREY HILL: to Andre Deutsch Ltd for 'Genesis' from *For the Unfallen*.

For IBNU 'L-'ARABÍ: to Cambridge University Press for 'My heart is capable of every form' from *Eastern Poetry and Prose* (1921), translated by Reynold A. Nicholson.

For IBNU 'L-FÁRIḌ: to Cambridge University Press for 'Let passion's swelling tide my senses drown!' from *Eastern Poetry and Prose* (1921), translated by Reynold A. Nicholson.

For ELIZABETH JENNINGS: to David Higham Associates Ltd for 'To a Friend with a Religious Vocation', 'The Counterpart' and 'Teresa of Avila' from *Selected Poems*.

For JOHN OF THE CROSS: to I C S Publications (Institute of Carmelite Studies) for 'Song of the Soul that Rejoices in Knowing God through Faith', 'Stanzas of the Soul that Suffers with Longing to See God', 'Commentary Applied to Spiritual Things' ('Without support and with support'), 'Commentary Applied to Spiritual Things' ('Not for all of beauty') and 'More Stanzas Applied to Spiritual Things' from *Collected Works of St John of the Cross*, translated by Kieran Kavanaugh and Otilio Rodrigues, Copyright © Washington Province of Discalced Carmelites, Inc.

For JOSEPH IBN ABITHUR: to David Higham Associates Ltd for 'Sanctification' from *Jewish Poets of Spain*, translated by David Goldstein (Penguin Classics, Revised edition, 1971), Copyright © David Goldstein, 1965.

For JUDAH HA-LEVI: to David Higham Associates Ltd for 'Heal me, my God' and 'Jerusalem' from *Jewish Poets of Spain*, translated by David Goldstein (Penguin Classics, Revised edition, 1971), Copyright © David Goldstein, 1965.

For ABBA KOVNER: to Penguin Books Ltd for 'My Sister' from *The Penguin Book of Hebrew Verse*, edited and translated by T. Carmi (Penguin Poets, 1981), Copyright © T. Carmi, 1981.

For PHILIP LARKIN: 'Days' from *The Whitsun Weddings*, reprinted by permission of Faber & Faber Ltd.

For D. H. LAWRENCE: 'The Man of Tyre' and 'Maximus' from *The Complete Poems of D. H. Lawrence*, reprinted by permission of Laurence Pollinger Ltd and the Estate of Mrs Frieda Lawrence Ravagli, and Viking Penguin, Inc.

For PETER LEVI: to the Anvil Press for 'In stone settlements when the moon is stone' from *Five Ages* (1978) and 'When does it end? When does a new poem', 'I imagine where God has never been' and 'Tree of roses. The water crashed headlong' from *Collected Poems 1955–1975* (1984), Copyright © Peter Levi; to Penguin Books for 'Zeus, whoever Zeus may be, if he' (Aeschylus; translated by Peter Levi) from *A History of Greek Literature* (Penguin Books, 1985), Copyright © 1985.

For CZESLAW MILOSZ: to the Ecco Press for 'Proof' from *Bells in Winter*; 'To Raja Rao' from *Selected Poems*; and '*Esse*' from *The Separate Notebooks*.

For MOSES IBN EZRA: to David Higham Associates Ltd for 'The Garden of Song' and 'The Sources of my Being' from *Jewish Poets of Spain*, translated by David Goldstein (Penguin Classics, Revised edition, 1971), Copyright © David Goldstein, 1965.

For RÁBI'A: to George Allen & Unwin for 'Two ways I love Thee: selfishly' from *Sufism*, translated by A. J. Arberry.

For CRAIG RAINE: 'Plain Song' from *Rich*, reprinted by permission of Faber & Faber Ltd.

For RAINER MARIA RILKE: 'Sonnet I' from *Sonnets to Orpheus* from *Selected Works II*, translated by J. B. Leishman, Copyright © 1960 by the Hogarth Press Ltd. Reprinted by permission of New Directions Publishing Corporation, The Hogarth Press Ltd and St John's College, Oxford.

For JALÁLU'DDÍN RÚMÍ: to Cambridge University Press for 'I died as mineral and became a plant', 'If there be any lover in the world, O Moslems, 'tis I' and 'Lo, for I to myself am unknown. . .' from *Eastern Poetry and Prose*, translated by Reynold A. Nicholson; to Bell & Hyman Ltd for 'The song of the spheres in their revolutions' from *Mystics of Islam*, translated by Reynold A. Nicholson (Routledge & Kegan Paul Ltd, 1975).

For SAMUEL HA-NAGID: to David Higham Associates Ltd for 'I Look Up to the Sky' from *Jewish Poets of Spain*, translated by David Goldstein (Penguin Classics, Revised edition, 1971), Copyright © David Goldstein, 1965.

For ANNE SEXTON: 'With Mercy for the Greedy' from *Selected Poems*, reprinted by permission of A. D. Peters & Co. Ltd and The Sterling Lord Agency, Inc.

For SOLOMON IBN GABIROL: to David Higham Associates Ltd for 'Separation from the Torah', 'Before I was Born', 'His Illness', and 'In the Morning I Look for You' from *Jewish Poets of Spain*, translated by David Goldstein (Penguin Classics, Revised edition, 1971), Copyright © David Goldstein, 1965.

For WALLACE STEVENS: 'The Irish Cliffs of Moher' from *The Collected Poems of Wallace Stevens*, reprinted by permission of Faber & Faber Ltd and Alfred A. Knopf, Inc.

For TERESA OF AVILA: to Sheed & Ward Ltd and Sheed & Ward, Inc. for 'I gave myself to Love Divine', 'Soul, thou must seek thyself in Me' and 'I Die because I Do Not Die' from the *Complete Works of St Teresa* (1946), translated by E. Allison Peers.

For D. M. THOMAS: to Secker & Warburg Ltd and Viking Press, Inc. for 'The Puberty Tree' from *Selected Poems*.

For DYLAN THOMAS: to David Higham Associates Ltd for 'Do Not Go Gently into That Good Night' and 'Over Sir John's Hill' from *Collected Poems*.

For R. S. THOMAS: to Granada Publishing Ltd for 'A Person from Porlock', 'Coleridge' and 'In a Country Church' from *Song at the Year's Turning*.

For TODROS BEN JUDAH ABULAFIA: to David Higham Associates Ltd for 'From Prison' from *Jewish Poets of Spain*, translated by David Goldstein (Penguin Classics, Revised edition, 1971), Copyright © David Goldstein, 1965.

For DEREK WALCOTT: 'Rest Christ! from tireless war' from *Midsummer*, reprinted by permission of Faber & Faber Ltd and Farrar, Straus & Giroux, Inc.

For ALEKSANDER WAT: to Ardis Publishers for 'Japanese Archery', translated by Richard Lourie, from *Mediterranean Poems*, edited by Czeslaw Milosz.

For W. B. YEATS: 'Sailing to Byzantium', 'Cuchulain Comforted' and 'Crazy Jane Talks with the Bishop' from the *Collected Poems of W. B. Yeats*, reprinted by permission of Michael B. Yeats and Macmillan London Ltd.

Every effort has been made to trace copyright holders. The publishers would be interested to hear from any copyright holders not here acknowledged.

INDEX OF AUTHORS

INDEX OF FIRST LINES